Build Apps Without Code

Describe an App and Ship It — v0, Bolt.new, Lovable, and Replit Agent

Ken Tannenbaum

2026

Finnoybu Press

Build Apps Without Code

2026 Edition

Describe an App and Ship It — v0, Bolt.new, Lovable, and Replit Agent

---

Published by Finnoybu Press

For permissions and inquiries: press@finnoybu.org

First Edition: 2026

About the Author

Ken Tannenbaum is a technologist, entrepreneur, and AI governance researcher. He is the founder of Finnoybu Press and the founder/steward of the AEGIS Initiative, an open framework for AI safety and accountability. Learn more at aegis-initiative.com.

When he's not building governance standards for artificial intelligence, he's helping everyday people understand and use it.

Dedication

For everyone with an app in their head and no idea where to start — and for the skeptics who said you'd still need a developer. You both have a point.

The AI for Everyone Series

This book is part of the **AI for Everyone** series by Finnoybu Press, designed to help real people use AI tools effectively. Visit **press.finnoybu.org** for the latest titles and updates.

Collection One: Product Deep Dives

- *ChatGPT: The Definitive Guide (2026 Edition)*
- *ChatGPT: The Power User Guide (2026 Edition)*
- *Claude: The Definitive Guide (2026 Edition)*
- *Claude Code: The Power User Guide (2026 Edition)*
- *Gemini: The Complete Guide (2026 Edition)*
- *Gemini: The Advanced Guide (2026 Edition)*
- *Copilot: The Workplace AI Guide (2026 Edition)*
- *Copilot: The Advanced Workplace Guide (2026 Edition)*
- *Perplexity: The Research Playbook (2026 Edition)*
- *Perplexity: The Advanced Research Playbook (2026 Edition)*

Collection Two: Product Guides

- *NotebookLM: From Sources to Audio Overviews (2026 Edition)*
- *DeepSeek: Code, Math, and Reasoning (2026 Edition)*
- *Cursor: The AI Code Editor (2026 Edition)*
- *OpenClaw: Agentic AI for Everyday Work (2026 Edition)*

Collection Three: Cross-Platform Skills

- *AI Systems Playbook (2026 Edition)*
- *AI Prompt Engineering (2026 Edition)*
- *AI for Developers (2026 Edition)*
- *AI for Business (2026 Edition)*
- *AI for Students (2026 Edition)*
- *AI Governance for Practitioners (2026 Edition)*
- *Securing Agentic AI (2026 Edition)*

The Extended Series — Product Guides, Volume II

- *Codex: The Cloud Coding Agent (2026 Edition)*
- *Grok: Real-Time AI from xAI (2026 Edition)*
- *Mistral: Vibe and the Open European AI (2026 Edition)*
- *DeepL: Translation, Writing, and Voice (2026 Edition)*

The Extended Series — The Capability Set

- *Automate Your Work with AI (2026 Edition)*
- *Build Apps Without Code (2026 Edition)*
- *AI Literacy for the Workplace (2026 Edition)*

Table of Contents

Introduction

For most of the history of software, there was a wall, and you were either on the side that could build apps or the side that could only wish for them. The wall was code. If you could write it, the gap between an idea and a working application was a matter of effort. If you could not, that gap was uncrossable, and your idea stayed an idea — or waited in a queue for a developer who never had time, or died for want of a budget you did not have.

I wrote this book because that wall now has a door in it. A new generation of AI-powered tools — v0, Bolt, Lovable, and Replit, the four at the center of this book — lets you build real, working software by describing what you want in plain language and refining it through conversation. Not a mockup, not a configured template, but an actual app with a real interface, a real database, and real behavior, deployed to a real URL that other people can use. People who have never written a line of code are building tools they need in an afternoon. The popular name for it is *vibe coding*: you describe the vibe, the AI writes the code, and you steer by reacting to what it makes.

This is genuinely one of the most exciting shifts in software in a generation, and this book is enthusiastic about it. It is also honest about it, which the enthusiastic version of the story often is not. Because the same tools that build you a polished app in an hour can build you a polished app that quietly mishandles your users' data, exposes secrets it should have hidden, or works in the demo and breaks on the tenth real user. Making software got radically easier. The judgment about whether the software is actually good, safe, and ready — that did not get easier, and as the building gets easy, the judgment is the whole job. This book teaches both halves: how to build fast, and how to know what you have actually built.

Why Now, and Not Five Years Ago

It is worth pausing on why this door opened when it did, because the answer shapes how much you should trust what comes through it. No-code tools are not new. For more than a decade you could assemble a website, a form, or a simple workflow by dragging blocks around on a screen — tools like Bubble, Webflow, and a long line of others let non-programmers ship real things. But those tools worked by giving you a fixed set of pre-built pieces and letting you arrange them.

You were limited to whatever the block library could express, and the moment your idea reached past the edge of that library, you hit a wall inside the wall.

What changed is that large language models got good enough at writing code that the building block stopped being a draggable widget and became *the code itself.* Instead of arranging components someone else designed, you describe what you want and the model writes the same kind of code a human developer would write — and then it can write anything that code can express, which is to say almost anything. That is the difference in kind, not degree, between the old no-code and the new AI builders. The old tools hit a ceiling because their vocabulary was finite. The new ones have, in principle, no ceiling at all, because their vocabulary is the full language of software.

That power is exactly why the honesty in this book matters. A tool with no ceiling can build you things you have no way to evaluate. The old no-code tools were safe partly because they were limited — you could not accidentally write an insecure authentication system if the tool would not let you write authentication at all. The new tools will happily write you authentication, payments, a database schema, and a deployment pipeline, all from a sentence, all looking finished, and some of it quietly wrong. The ceiling moved up. The responsibility moved with it, onto you.

What This Book Covers, Briefly

This is a practical guide to the AI app builders, across the four leading tools. **v0** (by Vercel) is the one most known for polished, production-grade interfaces tightly tied to fast deployment. **Bolt** (by StackBlitz) builds full-stack apps in a real development environment inside your browser, with the most portable output. **Lovable** gives non-coders a complete product with a working backend out of the box. **Replit** builds inside a real cloud development environment with hosting and a database included — closest to "describe it and get a deployed, running app."

You will learn what these tools are and how they work; what you can and genuinely cannot build with them; how to choose among the four and build your first app in each; how to add the real-world parts — data, accounts, outside services, design polish; how to ship to a live URL with a custom domain; and then the part the hype skips: the honest limits — security and your users' data, scaling and lock-in, when you still need a developer, and the all-important line between a prototype and something safe to put into production.

A word on what this book is *not*. It is not a reference manual for any single tool — those go stale in weeks, and the vendors' own documentation will always be more current than anything printed. It is not a coding tutorial; you will finish it no closer to being a programmer than when you started, and that is on purpose. And it is not a sales pitch for any of the four builders. I have no stake in which one you choose. What I am trying to give you is the durable layer underneath all of them: the mental model of how these tools work, the judgment to tell a good idea for them from a bad one, and the discipline to ship something you will not regret. Those things outlast any particular tool, and they are what the rest of the field rarely bothers to teach.

Who This Book Is For

- **Non-technical people with a specific need** — the small-business owner, the teacher, the operations lead who needs a tool and has no developer to build it.
- **Founders and product people** who want to prototype an idea into something real and testable in an afternoon, before committing to full engineering.
- **Developers** who want to move faster on the tedious parts, or spin up quick internal tools without a full project — and who want a clear-eyed read on where the generated code falls short.

You do not need to be technical to build with these tools — that is their entire point. But you are making software, and this book treats you as someone capable of understanding what that responsibility involves. The more technical material is signposted so you can lean in or route around it.

Let me say a little more about each of those three readers, because the same book serves them in three different ways, and knowing which one you are will tell you where to lean.

If you are the **non-technical person with a need**, you are the reader I picture most often, and the one this book most wants to protect. Your danger is not that you will fail to build something — you will be astonished how quickly you build something. Your danger is the opposite: that you will build something that looks finished, put it in front of real people, and not realize until later that it was leaking data the whole time, because nothing on the screen told you. For you, Part VI is not optional background reading. It is the part that keeps your weekend project from becoming a weekend you wish you could undo.

If you are the **founder or product person**, your danger is mistaking a convincing prototype for a real product. These tools make it so easy to produce something clickable and impressive that it is genuinely tempting to skip the engineering and ship the prototype itself. Sometimes that even works. Often it works just well enough to get you a hundred users and then collapse under the hundred-and-first, at the worst possible moment. The chapter on prototype versus production exists almost entirely for you.

If you are the **developer**, you are the reader least likely to be hurt by these tools and most likely to be impatient with the cautions written for the other two. Skim where you must. But do read the chapters on lock-in and on the catches each tool carries, because the failure modes that bite experienced people are not the obvious ones — they are the subtle architectural decisions a builder makes on your behalf, silently, while you are admiring how fast it went.

How to Read This Book

The book is in seven parts, plus reference.

Part I: The Vibe-Coding Moment explains what these tools really are, how they work under the hood, and the honest map of what they can and cannot build.

Part II: Meet the Builders introduces v0, Bolt, Lovable, and Replit on their own terms, then helps you choose the right one for your project.

Part III: Building Your First App is hands-on — how to describe an app well, then a first build in each of the four, and how to iterate when the first result isn't right.

Part IV: Making It Real covers the parts that turn a toy into a tool — data and backends, accounts and login, outside services, and design.

Part V: Shipping takes you live — deployment, custom domains, and understanding what it costs to run.

Part VI: The Honest Limits is the part to read before you ship anything real — security and your users' data, scaling and lock-in, and when you still need a developer.

Part VII: Judgment is the close — the line between a prototype and production, and how to tell which one you've actually built.

Reference wraps with a builder comparison, a project checklist, a glossary, and resources.

Read straight through, or jump. New to all of this: Part I, then build something from Part III. Choosing a tool: Part II. About to put an app in front of real users or real data: Part VI, end to end, before you do — this is not optional reading.

One practical suggestion, whichever path you take: do not read this book without a real idea in mind. The tools reward a concrete goal in a way no amount of abstract reading can substitute for. If you have a tool you have always wished existed — a tracker, a form, a small internal app, a clickable version of an idea — hold it in your head as you read, and run each chapter against it. By the time you reach Part III you will not be learning to build *an* app; you will be ready to build *yours*, which is a far better way to learn and a far more honest test of whether your idea sits inside the envelope these tools can handle.

The Shift This Book Is Really About

Underneath all the practical material — the tool comparisons, the prompting tips, the deployment steps — this book is about a single shift in what skill *is*, and it is worth naming directly before you start, because everything else makes more sense in its light.

For the whole history of software, the scarce and valuable skill was *production*: the ability to translate an idea into working code. That skill took years to acquire, it gated who could build, and once you had it, the rest — knowing what to build, judging whether it was any good — was almost a secondary concern, something you got to after the hard part was done. The AI builders invert that completely. Production is no longer scarce; you can produce a working app from a sentence. What is scarce now is everything that production used to overshadow: knowing what is worth building, judging whether the result actually works, recognizing when something is unsafe, and deciding what is ready to put in front of real people. Those were always part of making good software. They were just hidden behind the wall of code, available only to people who had already climbed it.

That is the deep reason this book spends as much time on judgment as on building. It is not that judgment is more important than it used to be in some abstract moral sense. It is that judgment is now the *binding constraint* — the thing that actually determines whether what you make is good or dangerous, useful or a liability. When producing the code was the bottleneck, you could be a mediocre judge and still ship something safe, because the code was the hard part and you sweated over it. When producing the code is trivial, your judgment is no longer backstopped by the difficulty of building. The tool will build whatever you ask, instantly, confidently, including the things you should not have asked for. Nothing stands between your judgment and the result anymore. That is the freedom and the danger in the same sentence, and it is the through-line of everything ahead.

A Realistic Picture of What This Costs

One more piece of expectation-setting before the chapters begin, because money surprises are the most common sour note in the otherwise happy story these tools tell, and a little forewarning prevents most of it.

These tools are not free to use seriously, and they are not free to run once you have built something. The *building* cost is usually a subscription, often metered by how much you ask the tool to do — credits, tokens, or messages, depending on the tool. For exploring and prototyping, this tends to be modest, in the range of a streaming-service subscription, and some tools have free tiers generous enough to build a real first project in. The surprise, when it comes, is rarely the subscription. It is the second and third costs that the subscription does not cover.

The *running* cost is what it takes to keep a live app serving real people — hosting, a database, a custom domain — and it is separate from what you paid to build. For a small app or one only you use, this can be nearly nothing. For a successful app with real users putting real data in, it grows with that success, and it lands on a different bill than your builder subscription, which is exactly why it catches people. Then there is the cost of any *outside service* your app leans on — a payment processor taking its cut, an email-sending service charging per message — which scales with use and is easy to forget you signed up for.

None of this should scare you off; the numbers for most personal and small-team projects are genuinely reasonable, and a great many useful apps cost very little to build and almost nothing to run. The point is only that "I pay one monthly subscription" is an incomplete picture the moment your app becomes real and used, and the people who get an unwelcome surprise are almost always the ones who never separated the cost of *building* from the cost of *running* in their heads. Chapter 21 lays out the full picture tool by tool. For now, just carry the shape of it: there is more than one meter, and the second one starts running when you succeed.

A Note About Accuracy

This is the fastest-moving corner of an already fast-moving field. These tools ship major changes monthly; prices, plan names, credit systems, the underlying AI models they run on, and their exact capabilities will all have drifted by the time you read this — one of them rebuilt itself substantially while this book was being written. This book is accurate as of mid-2026, and where a detail is the kind that changes fast — pricing and model names above all — I flag it and point you at the vendor's current page rather than pretending it's fixed.

Let me be concrete about what drifts and what does not, so you know how to read every claim in the chapters ahead. The things that change on a scale of *weeks to months*: the dollar amount of any plan, the name of any plan, the number of credits or tokens or messages a tier includes, which AI model powers a given tool, and the exact list of features any single builder offers. When you see a price or a model name in this book, read it as a snapshot — a rough sense of the shape, not a number to plan a budget around. Always check the vendor's current pricing page before you commit money.

The things that change on a scale of *years, if at all*: how to describe an app so the tool builds the right thing; how to iterate when the first result is wrong; how to tell a prototype from something production-ready; how to recognize when generated software is unsafe to ship; and the basic trade-offs — polish versus portability, convenience versus control, speed versus correctness — that distinguish one tool from another. Those are the bones of this book, and they will still be true when the model names have all changed twice. When in doubt about whether to trust a detail, ask which category it falls into. The numbers will move. The judgment will not.

A Note About Security, Up Front

I am going to repeat one warning often enough that it may annoy you, and I am going to make no apology for it: an app that looks finished is not the same as an app that is safe. These tools can produce software that appears polished while mishandling data, exposing secrets, or leaving the door open to anyone who knows where to push. This is not a rare edge case — it is a well-documented, common failure mode of vibe-coded apps, and it has already exposed real users' real data in the wild. Part VI explains exactly what to check and how. If you are going to put an app in front of other people, that part is the price of admission, and this introduction is your first notice that you'll be asked to pay it.

The reason this warning has to come this early, before you have built anything, is that the failure mode is invisible by design. When a bridge is unsafe, it looks unsafe — there are cracks, it sways, something is visibly wrong. When a vibe-coded app is unsafe, it looks exactly like a safe one. The login screen still appears. The data still saves. The page still loads in under a second. Nothing on the surface tells you that the database is readable by anyone who asks it nicely, or that an API key worth real money is sitting in plain view in the page's source. The whole problem is that the signal you would normally trust — "it works, it looks done" — is precisely the signal that fails you here. So you cannot wait until something goes wrong to start caring about security, because by the time something visibly goes wrong, the data is already gone. You have to bring the suspicion with you from the first build. That is why this is in the introduction and not buried in an appendix.

Let's Get Started

The door in the wall is real, and walking through it is genuinely thrilling — there is nothing quite like describing a tool you need and watching it come to life in front of you. This book wants you to feel that, and to build boldly. It also wants you to ship responsibly, because you are making real software now, and real software touches real people. Hold both, and these tools will do for you what they did for the teacher with her booking page: turn an idea you could not build into a thing you actually use. Let's start with what they really are.

Part I: The Vibe-Coding Moment

Audience: everyone.

"For decades the only way through the wall was to learn its language. Now there is a door, and the password is a plain sentence describing what you want on the other side."

— A working principle

Chapter 1: What "Build Apps Without Code" Really Means

A friend of mine — a teacher, not a technologist, who has never written a line of code in her life — needed a small tool. Her school ran a tutoring program, and the sign-up was a mess of spreadsheets and email threads that she spent her Sunday evenings untangling. She wanted a simple web page where students could see open slots and book one, and where she could see the bookings. A real developer would have built it in a couple of days. She did not have a developer, or a budget, or two days. What she had was an afternoon and a willingness to try.

She opened one of the tools in this book, typed a description of what she wanted in plain English — "a booking page for tutoring sessions, students pick an open time slot, I can see who booked what" — and watched it build her a working app. Not a mockup. A real page, with a real database behind it, that she refined over the next hour by describing the changes she wanted the same way she had described the app: "make the available slots green," "send me an email when someone books," "let me cancel a booking." By dinner she had a tool she used for the rest of the year. She did not learn to code. She learned to *describe*, and the machine did the coding.

That afternoon is the whole subject of this book, and it is genuinely new. For the entire history of software until very recently, the gap between "I have an idea for an app" and "I have a working app" could only be crossed by someone who could write code. That gap was a wall, and most people lived on the wrong side of it. These tools put a door in the wall. This chapter is about what that door actually is, what it does and does not open onto, and why "describe an app and get one" turned out to be both more powerful and more limited than the breathless version of the story suggests.

The One-Sentence Definition

Building apps without code means using an AI-powered tool to create real, working software — a web app with a real interface, real data, and real behavior — by describing what you want in plain language and refining it through conversation, instead of writing the code yourself.

The popular name for this is *vibe coding* — you describe the vibe of what you want, the AI writes the actual code, and you steer by reacting to what it produces. A few parts of the definition deserve unpacking, because each corrects a common misreading.

"Real, working software." This is the line that separates these tools from what came before. Earlier no-code app builders gave you drag-and-drop blocks that assembled a limited, template-shaped result — useful, but bounded to what the block library allowed. The AI builders are different in kind: behind the conversation, an AI is writing genuine code — the same React, the same database queries, the same logic a developer would write — which means the ceiling is far higher and the output is a real application, not a configured template. There is actual code underneath, and in most of these tools you can see it, export it, and take it with you.

"By describing what you want." The input is language, not logic. You do not specify *how* to build the feature; you specify *what* you want it to do, and the AI works out the how. "Let users log in with their Google account" is a sentence; the authentication plumbing it implies is hundreds of lines you never see unless you go looking. This is the core move, and it relocates the hard part of building software from *writing* to *describing* — which is a skill far more people already have.

"Refining it through conversation." The first result is rarely the final one, and that is by design. You build by iterating — looking at what the AI made, saying what is wrong or missing, and watching it adjust. "The button should be on the right." "This is too slow." "Add a column for the date." Building an app this way feels less like engineering and more like directing — you are the one with the vision and the judgment, and the AI is the fast, tireless, occasionally wrong builder carrying it out.

What It Is Not

Four clarifications up front, because the hype around vibe coding has created as many misconceptions as the technology has created possibilities.

It is not learning to code. You will build working apps in this book without becoming a programmer, the way my friend the teacher did. But — and this matters — you are still *making software*, and software has irreducible realities (data, security, users, money) that do not disappear just because you did not type the code. Part of this book's honesty is insisting that not writing the code is not the same as not being responsible for it. The tool writes the code; the consequences are still yours.

It is not magic, and it is not finished when it looks finished. A vibe-coded app can look polished and professional within an hour, and that surface can hide real problems underneath — insecure handling of data, secrets exposed where they should not be, logic that works in the demo and breaks on the tenth real user. The gap between "looks done" and "is actually done" is the single most important theme in this book, and Part VI is devoted to it. The tools are genuinely powerful; they are also genuinely capable of producing something that *appears* to work and is not safe to ship.

It is not the same as building automations. This is the companion to *Automate Your Work with AI*, and the distinction is worth getting right. Automation connects tools you already have and shuttles work between them; it does not produce a new application people log into. These builders do the opposite: they create a new piece of software with its own interface and its own users. If you need your existing tools to talk to each other, that is the other book. If you need a *new app* that did not exist before, this is the one. Chapter 3 draws the boundary of what these tools can and cannot build.

It is not one tool. "AI app builder" names a category, and the four at the center of this book — v0, Bolt, Lovable, and Replit — take meaningfully different shapes, each best at something different. One excels at polished interfaces, another at full-stack apps in your browser, another at giving non-coders a complete product with a working backend, another at building inside a real development environment with hosting included. Part II introduces each. The skill of describing and steering transfers across all of them; the strengths and the buttons differ.

Why the Bottleneck Moved

The deepest thing to understand about this shift is what it changed and what it did *not* change. It changed who can produce code: the act of translating an idea into working software no longer requires years of training in a programming language. That is enormous, and it is why someone who has never coded can build a real tool in an afternoon.

But it did not change what *makes software good.* Knowing what to build, deciding what the app should do and for whom, judging whether the result actually works, recognizing when something is insecure or about to break, deciding what is worth shipping — none of that moved. If anything, it became *more* important, because it is now the scarce part. When producing the code was the bottleneck, judgment was a luxury you got to once the hard part was done. When producing the code is easy, judgment is the entire job. The builder can generate a feature in seconds; whether that feature should exist, whether it handles a real user's data safely, whether it will survive contact with the world — those are questions the tool cannot answer for you, and they are exactly the questions that separate a useful app from a liability.

That is the through-line of this entire book, and it is why the cheerful early chapters about building fast are bound to the sober later ones about limits and security. The tools genuinely democratize *making*. They do not democratize *judgment* — and as making gets easier, judgment is what's left to supply.

What These Tools Actually Do

Set the philosophy aside and look at the concrete surface. Given a description, these builders can:

Generate a complete interface. Real, styled, responsive web pages — forms, dashboards, layouts, navigation — from a sentence describing what you want to see.

Stand up a backend and a database. Not just the visible page but the machinery behind it: storing data, retrieving it, the logic that ties the interface to the information. Most of these tools now handle the full stack, not just the front of it.

Add the hard parts you'd dread building. User accounts and login, connections to outside services, payments, email — the features that take a developer real time, requested in plain language.

Let you refine by talking. Every part of the app is changeable the same way it was made: describe the change, see it happen, react again. The build is a conversation, not a one-shot generation.

Deploy to a real, live URL. The end of the road is not a file on your computer; it is an app on the internet that other people can actually use, with hosting handled for you.

What you get, across all of it, is real software — which is the promise and the catch in the same breath. It is real enough to use, and real enough to hurt you if you ship it carelessly.

Who's Building This Way

Three overlapping groups, and you are probably one of them.

Non-technical people with a specific need — the teacher, the small-business owner, the operations lead who needs an internal tool and has no developer to build it. For them these builders are the difference between having the tool and not having it, and a prototype-grade app is often exactly enough.

Founders and product people who want to prototype fast — to turn an idea into something clickable and testable in an afternoon, validate it with real users, and learn before committing real engineering. Here the builders are a thinking-and-testing tool, and "prototype, not production" is a feature, not a limit.

Developers, increasingly — who use these tools to skip the tedious first 80 percent of a build and spend their expertise on the hard 20 percent, or to throw together a quick internal tool that does not merit a full project. They know what the generated code is doing, which makes them both the fastest users and the most clear-eyed about where it falls short.

This book serves all three, and it is honest with each about where the tools shine and where they stop.

The Through-Line

If you carry one idea out of this chapter, let it be the teacher and her booking page: the wall between "I have an idea" and "I have a working app" now has a door in it, and you do not need to be a programmer to walk through. That is real, and it is worth being excited about. But walking through the door means you are now making software, with all the responsibility that carries — and the thing the tools cannot hand you, the judgment about what to build and whether it is actually safe to ship, is precisely the thing that matters most once the building is easy.

The teacher got her tool by describing it and steering well. Learning to do both — and learning to tell, before you start, whether your idea is one these tools can actually build — is what the rest of this book is for.

Chapter 2: How AI App Builders Work

The first time I watched one of these tools build something, I typed a single sentence — "a page where I can keep a list of books I want to read, with a checkbox for the ones I've finished" — and then sat there a little dumbstruck as text scrolled past in a side panel. It was writing files. Not loading a template, not assembling blocks. It named a file, filled it with lines of code, named another, filled that one too, and a few seconds later a working page appeared next to all that scrolling text: an input box, a list, checkboxes that actually checked. I added a book. It showed up. I checked it off. It stayed checked.

What I want you to take from that scene is the thing the side panel made visible: there was no magic substituting for the software. There was *actual software*, being written, in real time, by a machine that had read more code than any human ever could. The whole experience of building apps without code rests on one fact, and once you understand it the rest of the book stops feeling mysterious. The fact is this: an AI is writing real code, and everything else — the preview, the chat, the deploy button — is wrapped around that single act to make it usable by someone who never reads the code at all.

This chapter opens the hood. Not to turn you into a mechanic — you do not need to be one — but because you cannot judge what you are getting if you have no picture of how it is made. A driver who knows roughly what an engine does makes better decisions than one who thinks the car runs on hope. Same here.

The Thing in the Middle Is a Language Model

At the center of every tool in this book sits a large language model — the same kind of AI that powers the chat assistants you have probably used. If you have read others in this series, you have met these models as things that write emails and answer questions. Here they are doing a more specialized job: writing code. And it turns out that writing code is something these models are unusually, almost surprisingly good at, for a reason worth understanding.

Code is *text* — strict, structured, unforgiving text, but text. And there is an enormous amount of it in the world, public and readable: decades of open-source projects, tutorials, answered questions, documented patterns. A model trained on that corpus has, in a real sense, seen how millions of working applications were built. When you ask for "a login form," it is not inventing the idea from nothing; it is drawing on the vast number of login forms it has effectively read, and producing one in the same shape. This is why the output is genuinely competent so often, and also — file this away for the security chapters — why it sometimes reproduces the *bad* patterns it saw alongside the good ones, with no way to tell which was which.

Which specific model is doing the work varies by tool and changes constantly. Some builders run on Claude-family models, some on others, some on a blend, and several wrap the underlying model in their own branding so you never see the real name. Do not anchor on any of this; it churns month to month. What is durable is the shape: a frontier language model, very good at producing code, sitting at the heart of the machine.

From Your Sentence to Working Software

So you type "a booking page for tutoring sessions." What happens between your sentence and the page that appears? Roughly four moves, and they repeat in a loop for the life of your project.

It plans. Before writing anything, the better tools work out what your request actually requires — what pages exist, what data needs storing, what pieces connect to what. You asked for a booking page; that quietly implies a list of time slots, a place to store who booked which one, a way to show the open ones. The model unpacks the sentence into its real requirements, the way a developer would sketch on a napkin before typing. Some tools show you this plan; some keep it hidden. Either way it is happening.

It scaffolds. Then it generates the files — the structure of a real application. This is the part I watched scroll past: the interface code, the logic, the connections to a database, all written out as genuine source files. "Scaffolding" is the industry word for standing up the skeleton of a project, and it is exactly right. In seconds you get what would take a person hours: a complete, organized starting point, not a blank page.

It runs it for you. A pile of code is not an app until something executes it. Each builder solves this differently — and the differences are a major reason they feel so distinct, which is why Part II gives each its own chapter — but the result is the same: your code runs, and you see it running, without you installing or configuring anything. Bolt does something genuinely clever here, running a real development environment *inside your browser tab* so the code executes on your own machine with nothing to set up. Others run it on their servers in the cloud and show you the result. You do not need to care which; you need to know that "it just runs" is a service the tool is providing, not a thing that happens by itself.

It shows you a preview. And finally, the live result appears — usually right beside the chat — as a working app you can click, type into, and poke at. This preview is the heart of the experience, because it closes the loop between describing and seeing. You do not imagine what your sentence produced; you look at it.

The Loop Is the Whole Method

Here is the part that matters most, because it is how you will actually spend your time. Building an app this way is not one command that produces a finished thing. It is a *loop*: build, look, refine, look again, repeated until the app is what you want.

You describe. The AI builds. You look at the preview and react — "the button should be on the right," "this list is empty when it should show today's bookings," "make the header smaller." The AI changes the code and rebuilds. You look again. Around and around. I think of it less as engineering and more as directing: you are the one with the vision and the judgment about whether the result is right, and the AI is the quick, fallible hand executing it.

Two things about this loop are worth internalizing now, because they shape everything that follows.

The AI does not remember the way you do. Each time you ask for a change, the tool feeds the model some version of your project plus your new instruction, and the model works from *that*. It is not a colleague who has been living inside your project for a week and holds the whole thing in their head. This is why being specific helps so much, why the model sometimes "forgets" a decision you made earlier, and why occasionally it will fix one thing and quietly break another it was not thinking about. None of this is a malfunction. It is the nature of the loop, and Chapter 14, on iterating, is largely about working with it skillfully.

Bigger projects cost more to change. To make a change, the tool generally has to show the model your code — and the more code there is, the more there is to send, every single message. This has a direct consequence on your wallet that surprises people, so I will be blunt about it here and return to it in detail in Chapter 21: a small app is cheap to iterate on, and a large one can get expensive fast, because every refinement re-sends a growing project to the model. Bolt in particular is open about this trade-off. It is not a trick; it is physics of the architecture, and knowing it now will keep a later invoice from stinging.

What "Real Code" Actually Buys You

I keep insisting there is real code underneath, and you might fairly ask: so what? Why should a non-coder care, if the whole point is not to look at it?

Because it determines what you are getting, and three consequences flow straight from it.

The ceiling is high. Because the tool is writing genuine code rather than arranging pre-built blocks, it is not boxed into a template library the way older no-code tools were. If a real developer could build it, there is at least a chance one of these can too. That is why the things you can make are so much more varied than the drag-and-drop era allowed — and also why the *can't* in the next chapter is more about judgment and complexity than about a fixed menu of features.

You can usually take it with you. The code is a real artifact, which means in most of these tools you can export it — push it to GitHub, hand it to a developer, move it somewhere else. How cleanly you can do this varies enormously between tools, and it is one of the most important differences between them, which is why Chapter 23 is partly devoted to lock-in. But the principle holds: there is something real to take, not just a configuration trapped inside a vendor's website.

The flaws are real too. This is the honest other edge. Real code can have real security holes, real bugs, real ways of breaking under load — and because no human reviewed it, those flaws ship silently. The polished preview tells you nothing about what is wrong underneath. That gap between "looks done" and "is actually sound" is the spine of Part VI, and it exists precisely *because* what you are getting is real software rather than a safe, sandboxed toy.

Then It Goes Live

The last piece of the machine is deployment — taking the app that has been running in a preview and putting it on the actual internet, at a real address, where other people can use it. The builders fold this into a button. Behind that button is a genuinely involved process — packaging the app, putting it on a server somewhere, wiring up the address — that the tool handles so you never see it. Several of these tools have their own hosting built in; some push your app to an outside service; the experience, again, ranges from one click to a short series of steps. Part V walks the whole road from preview to live URL, and Chapter 19 covers deployment specifically.

I will flag one thing here so it does not ambush you later: the moment your app is live and a real person can reach it is the moment all the underneath-the-surface concerns — the security, the data handling, the question of what happens on the hundredth user instead of the first — stop being theoretical. A preview only you can see forgives a great deal. A public URL forgives nothing. The machine makes crossing that line as easy as a click, which is wonderful and is exactly why the judgment to know whether you *should* cross it is the thing no button can supply.

That is the whole engine: a language model that writes real code, a loop that lets you steer it by reacting, and a wrapper that runs, previews, and ships the result without ever asking you to read a line. Everything else in this book is detail hung on that frame. Knowing the frame is what lets you tell, from here on, the difference between what the tool is genuinely doing for you and what it is only making *look* easy.

Chapter 3: What You Can (and Can't) Build This Way

A small consulting firm I know had a problem that will sound familiar. Their projects lived in one place, their invoices in another, their notes in a third, and the only person who could see the whole picture was the founder, in her head, on a good day. They did not need enterprise software. They needed one internal page where a handful of staff could log in, see the active projects, mark tasks done, and pull up a client's history without three browser tabs and a phone call. No off-the-shelf product fit without bending their whole process around it. A developer quote came back at a number that made the founder wince.

She built it herself, in a weekend, with one of these tools. Not a toy — a real internal app her team used every day, with logins and a database and the actual workflow they cared about. It was, by any honest measure, a complete success.

The same founder, six months later, tried to build something else: a tool to optimize her consultants' schedules across constraints — availability, skills, client priority, travel time — the kind of thing that sounds like a feature and is secretly a hard mathematical problem. She fought with it for two weeks. The app looked done. It produced schedules. The schedules were quietly, subtly wrong in ways that took a real person to notice, and no amount of "make the scheduling smarter" fixed it. She eventually shelved it and hired someone.

Both stories are true, and the gap between them is the entire subject of this chapter. These tools have an *envelope* — a real and generous space of things they do beautifully, bounded by a real and important edge past which they struggle or fail. The single most valuable skill in this whole book is learning to feel where that edge is *before* you spend two weeks discovering it. So let me draw the map.

The Sweet Spot: What These Tools Are Genuinely Great At

There is a category of software that these builders handle so well it can feel like cheating. It is worth naming precisely, because if your idea lives here, you should proceed with real confidence.

Apps that store, show, and edit information. The plain truth is that a very large fraction of all useful software is, underneath, some version of the same thing: a place to record items, see a list of them, look at one in detail, change it, and remove it. Developers have a slightly unlovely name for this pattern — CRUD, for create, read, update, delete — and it is the bread and butter of these tools. The consulting firm's project tracker is CRUD. A booking page is CRUD. A customer list, an inventory log, a simple project board, a personal habit tracker — CRUD, CRUD, CRUD. If you can describe your idea as "a place where people can keep track of *things*," you are squarely in the sweet spot, and you will likely be astonished how far an afternoon takes you.

It helps to see how wide this pattern really is, because "CRUD" sounds narrower than it is. A wedding-guest manager — add guests, mark RSVPs, track meal choices, see the count — is CRUD. A small landlord's tool for tracking which tenant owes what and when the lease renews is CRUD. A volunteer coordinator for a community garden — who signed up for which shift, who watered on Tuesday — is CRUD. A teacher's reading log, a freelancer's client tracker, a hobbyist's collection catalog, a nonprofit's donor list: all the same underlying shape, dressed in different clothes. When you train yourself to look past the surface of an idea and ask "is this, at heart, a list of things I want to add to, look at, edit, and remove?", you start seeing that an enormous share of the software people genuinely need is exactly this. And exactly this is where the tools are strongest.

Dashboards and internal tools. Pages that pull information together and display it clearly — for you, your team, your operations — are a standout strength. These apps live behind a login, serve a known handful of people, and do not have to survive a hostile internet of strangers. That smaller, friendlier audience forgives a lot, which makes internal tools the safest and most rewarding place to start. If something you are doing today involves a spreadsheet you wish were a real app, that is very often a one-weekend build.

The reason internal tools are such a forgiving starting point deserves spelling out, because it is one of the most useful insights in this book. When ten people you work with use your app, the entire threat model changes. You know who they are. They are not trying to break in. A bug means someone walks over to your desk, not that your data ends up on a forum. The performance only has to be good enough for ten simultaneous users, not ten thousand. The polish only has to satisfy colleagues who are grateful the spreadsheet is gone, not strangers comparing you to a billion-dollar product. Almost every reason these tools struggle — scale, security against hostile users, the cost of being wrong — is dialed down to nearly zero in an internal tool. That is why I push people toward internal tools first so insistently: it is the one place where the gap between "looks done" and "is done" is small enough to be safe to learn in.

Prototypes and MVPs. If your goal is to make an idea *clickable* — to turn "imagine an app that does X" into something a real person can hold and react to — these tools are close to magic, and this is arguably their highest use. A founder can validate an idea with actual users in a day instead of a quarter, learning what is wrong before committing real money to engineering. Here the rough edges are not a flaw; "this is a prototype, not a finished product" is the entire point. Chapter 25, on prototype versus production, is built around exactly this distinction, because using these tools as thinking-and-testing instruments is one of the most genuinely powerful things they offer.

There is a subtle skill inside prototyping well, which is knowing what you are trying to *learn* and building only enough to learn it. If your real question is "will people pay for this?", you do not need a working payment system — you need a convincing "Buy" button that records who clicked it, and a conversation with the people who did. If your question is "is this workflow actually faster than what they do now?", you need the workflow clickable end to end and nothing else — no accounts, no settings page, no polish on the screens nobody is testing. The temptation these tools create is to build everything, because everything is so cheap to build. Resist it. A prototype that answers one question clearly is worth more than a half-finished product that answers none, and it costs a tenth as much to make. The discipline is not building less because you have to; it is building less because building only what teaches you something is the whole point of a prototype.

The standard hard parts you would otherwise dread. User accounts and login, sending email, taking a payment, connecting to a common outside service — the features that cost a developer real time are, for these tools, well-trodden ground. They have effectively seen these patterns thousands of times. Asking for "let users sign in with Google" is a sentence, and you get working authentication. This is real leverage, and it extends the sweet spot well past simple list-keeping into apps that feel genuinely full-featured.

The thing to understand about *why* these particular hard parts are easy for the tools is the same thing that explains where they get hard later. A Google login, a Stripe checkout, a "send a confirmation email" — these are solved problems that millions of developers have implemented in nearly identical ways, and the model has seen that nearly identical pattern over and over. It is not reasoning from first principles; it is reproducing a path well worn into the collective code it learned from. That is exactly why it is reliable here and exactly why it gets unreliable the moment your need stops matching a path many people have walked before. Hold that idea — *the tool is strongest where the world has done this thousands of times, and weakest where almost no one has* — because it is the single most predictive rule for where the edge will turn out to be.

The unifying thread: these tools shine when your app is a *familiar shape*, made of well-understood pieces, serving a manageable number of people. An enormous amount of valuable software is exactly that. Do not let the existence of an edge convince you the space inside it is small. It is not. It is most of what people actually need built.

Where the Edge Is: What These Tools Struggle With

Now the honest other half, and I am going to be specific, because vague warnings help no one. There are four kinds of difficulty, and they shade into each other.

Complex, novel, or correctness-critical logic. This is the founder's scheduling tool, and it is the most important boundary to understand. When the *hard part* of your app is not its interface or its data but its *thinking* — an intricate algorithm, a genuinely novel problem, logic that has to be exactly right or it is worthless — these tools get unreliable in a particularly treacherous way. Recall from the last chapter that the model produces code in the shape of code it has seen. For a login form, it has seen a million; for your specific, never-before-built optimization, it has seen nothing exactly like it, so it produces something *plausible*. And plausible-but-wrong is the worst failure mode there is, because it looks like it works. The app runs. It gives answers. The answers are subtly incorrect, and the tool will defend them with total confidence. If being right matters more than looking right — financial calculations, anything where a quiet error is expensive — treat these tools with deep suspicion and get a human who can verify the logic.

It is worth collecting a few concrete examples of correctness-critical logic, because the danger is precisely that these tasks do not announce themselves as hard. Calculating someone's tax withholding. Splitting a bill across people with different shares and a tip and tax. Computing payroll across overtime rules and state-specific deductions. Pricing an insurance quote. Working out the right dosage from a patient's weight. Reconciling two lists of transactions to find the one that does not match. Every one of these *sounds* like an ordinary feature, and every one of these is a place where "looks like it works" and "is correct" can diverge invisibly. The tell is this: ask yourself whether you, looking at the output, could spot a wrong answer just by reading it. For a list of customers, you can — a missing name is obvious. For a number that is the result of a calculation, you usually cannot; one wrong figure looks exactly like a right one. When you cannot eyeball correctness, you have left the safe zone, no matter how simple the feature sounded.

There is a related trap worth naming: the tool will sometimes produce logic that is right for the cases you happened to test and wrong for the cases you did not think to. The founder's scheduler probably worked fine for a normal week and fell apart on the week with a holiday, a sick consultant, and a rush client — the messy edge cases that are the entire reason the problem was hard in the first place. These tools are very good at the happy path and much weaker at the unhappy ones, partly because the happy path is what most example code demonstrates. So when correctness matters, the demo working is close to meaningless. What matters is whether it survives the inputs you did not design for, and discovering that requires either deliberate, adversarial testing or a person who can read the logic and see the gap. The tool will not volunteer that it only handled the easy cases.

Heavy scale. An app that works flawlessly for you, your team, and your first fifty users can behave very differently at fifty thousand. The generated code is rarely built for serious load, and the architecture these tools produce is tuned for getting something working fast, not for serving a crowd efficiently. This is not usually a reason to avoid building — most apps never need to scale, and you can cross that bridge if you reach it — but it is a reason to know that "it works in the demo" and "it works for a hundred thousand people" are different claims, and the tools deliver the first, not the second. Chapter 23 covers what scaling actually demands.

The reassuring half of the scale story, which I do not want to undersell, is that *most apps never reach the scale where this matters*, and the ones that do reach it have, by definition, succeeded enough to afford the help to fix it. If your internal tool serves your forty-person company, scale is simply not your problem and never will be. If your side project finds a thousand happy users, you are in a wonderful position to bring in someone who can shore up the architecture, funded by the very success that strained it. The mistake is not building on these tools because you fear scale; the mistake is *assuming* the thing that worked for your test group will hold for a crowd, and being surprised when it does not. Build for the users you have. Just do not promise yourself, or your investors, that the prototype's architecture will carry a hundred thousand people, because it almost certainly will not, and pretending otherwise is how a launch becomes an outage.

Specialized and regulated domains. If your app touches health records, financial accounts, children's data, or anything a government regulates, you have stepped into a space where the rules are strict, the penalties are real, and "I built it in a weekend" is not a defense any regulator recognizes. The tool does not know your legal obligations and will not warn you that you have them. These domains are not impossible to build for, but they demand expertise the tool cannot supply, and the cost of getting it wrong is measured in lawsuits and fines rather than annoyed users. Chapter 22 deals with the security half of this, and the same caution applies to the legal half: when the domain is regulated, the builder is a starting point, never the whole answer.

The hidden danger here is that regulated domains rarely look regulated from inside a simple app. A small fitness app that lets clients log their workouts feels harmless — until it stores notes about their injuries and conditions, at which point you may be handling health data with obligations attached. A tutoring booking page feels harmless — until you realize your users are minors and a whole category of children's-data rules now applies. A tool that lets a small business track customer payments feels harmless — until you are storing card details you were never permitted to store. The builder will let you do every one of these things without a murmur, because it has no idea what jurisdiction you are in or what your data represents. In Europe, frameworks like the EU AI Act and long-standing data-protection law impose real duties on systems most people would never think of as "regulated"; the AI Act's transparency obligations under Article 4 became applicable on 2 February 2025, with broader enforcement arriving 2 August 2026, and the proposed Digital Omnibus that might adjust some of this is not yet law as of this writing. None of that is something a code generator can track for you. The lesson is not to memorize regulations; it is to develop the reflex to *ask*, before you build, "could the data this app touches be the kind someone regulates?" — and if the answer is even maybe, to get advice from a human who knows, rather than from a tool that does not know it does not know.

Anything where you can't tell whether it's right. This is the quiet one that catches careful people. The tool will happily build things you are not equipped to evaluate — a security model, a payment flow, a data architecture — and present them looking finished. The danger is not that it always gets these wrong; it is that *you cannot tell* whether it did. The further your app gets from things you can verify by clicking around, the more you are trusting work you cannot check. This is precisely where the judgment that runs through this whole book becomes load-bearing, and where Chapter 24, on when you still need a developer, earns its place.

There is a way to think about this that makes it operational rather than just worrying. Everything the tool builds for you falls somewhere on a spectrum of *checkability*. At one end are things you can verify just by using the app: does the list show my items, does the button save the form, does the page look right on my phone. You are fully qualified to judge those, and you should judge them ruthlessly. At the other end are things whose correctness lives entirely under the hood, where no amount of clicking will reveal whether the work is sound: whether the database is locked down so strangers cannot read it, whether secrets are hidden from the page source, whether the payment flow can be tricked, whether the architecture will survive a real crowd. You are usually *not* qualified to judge those, and — this is the crucial part — the app behaving normally tells you nothing about them. The skill is to know which bucket each part of your app is in, to trust your own eyes for the first bucket, and to bring in someone who can check, or at least to slow down and verify deliberately, for the second. The mistake careful people make is letting the obvious correctness of the first bucket reassure them about the invisible correctness of the second. A login that looks perfect on screen can be wide open underneath, and the screen will never tell you.

How to Tell, Before You Start, Which One You Have

Here is a practical test you can run on your own idea in about a minute, before you sink a weekend into it.

Ask yourself: **where is the hard part?** If the hard part of your app is the *interface and the data* — showing things, storing things, letting people do ordinary operations on them — you are in the sweet spot, and you should build with confidence. If the hard part is the *thinking* — a tricky algorithm, a correctness-critical calculation, a genuinely new problem nobody has solved in a standard way — slow down, because that is exactly where these tools produce confident, plausible, possibly-wrong output.

Then ask: **who is it for, and what happens if it's wrong?** A tool for you and five colleagues, where a bug means a moment's annoyance, is a wonderful place to be bold. An app for ten thousand strangers, holding data whose exposure would genuinely hurt someone, is a place to be careful and to bring in help before you go live. Most ideas sit comfortably toward the bold end. The skill is recognizing the ones that do not.

Let me add a third question that catches the cases the first two miss: **can I tell whether the result is right just by using it?** Run your idea through that one honestly. If your app's job is to display and organize information, the answer is usually yes — you will see at a glance whether it is working. If your app's job is to *compute* something, *decide* something, or *protect* something, the answer is often no, and that no is the warning. The three questions work together. The first finds the apps whose hard part is logic the tool cannot reliably get right. The second finds the apps where being wrong is expensive enough to demand caution. The third finds the apps where you would not even *notice* the tool got it wrong — which is the most dangerous category of all, because there is no moment of discovery to save you. An idea that is data-shaped, low-stakes, and checkable is a green light. An idea that is logic-shaped, high-stakes, and unverifiable by clicking around is the one to approach with help and humility, or not at all.

And here is a fourth, almost a meta-question, for the borderline cases: **is most of my idea in the sweet spot, with one risky piece?** Many ideas are not wholly safe or wholly dangerous — they are a perfectly buildable app with one hard, dangerous feature bolted on, exactly like the consulting firm's tracker that later sprouted a scheduler. When that is the shape, the right move is often to build the safe ninety percent with these tools and treat the risky piece as a separate problem — done by hand, verified carefully, bought from a service that already solves it, or deferred until you can get help. You do not have to swallow your whole idea or abandon it. You can split it at the edge, take the part that lives in the sweet spot, and be deliberate about the part that does not. That decomposition — building the easy majority fast and handling the hard minority with care — is one of the most practically valuable habits a thoughtful builder can develop.

I want to be careful not to leave you over-cautioned, because the cautious half of this chapter is louder on the page than it should be in your head. The envelope these tools cover is *enormous* — it includes the great majority of the small, useful, real software that individuals and small teams actually need and have never been able to build for themselves. The consulting firm got a real tool that genuinely improved their days, and that is the typical outcome, not the lucky one. The edge exists, and knowing it is what keeps you from the two-week fight that ends in a shelved project. But inside the edge is a remarkable amount of room.

The thing the tools cannot do is tell you which side of that edge your idea is on. That judgment is yours, and it is the first real judgment this book asks of you — before the building, before the prompting, before any of the fun. Get it right, and almost everything that follows goes well. Get it wrong, and no amount of cleverness in the prompt will rescue you. So spend the minute. Ask where the hard part is. The answer is worth a weekend.

Part II: Meet the Builders

Audience: everyone.

"There is no best builder, only the one that is best at the thing you are trying to make. The skill that matters is knowing which is which before you start."

— A working principle

Chapter 4: v0 by Vercel

Type "a clean pricing page with three tiers, the middle one highlighted as most popular" into v0, and forty seconds later what comes back is not a sketch. It is a pricing page you would be happy to ship. The spacing is right. The typography is right. The highlighted tier has the subtle lift and the little "Most Popular" badge that a good designer would have added without being asked. Plenty of tools produce *something* from a prompt; v0 is the one that produces something you do not immediately want to fix. That gap — between output you have to rescue and output you can use — is the whole reason v0 is worth its own chapter.

v0 is made by Vercel, a company whose actual business is hosting and deploying web applications, and that parentage explains almost everything about what v0 is good at and where it pulls you. This chapter is about what v0 does, the thing it does better than anyone, the major change that turned it from a one-trick tool into a real builder, and the catch that comes attached — because there is always a catch, and with v0 it is a specific and predictable one.

What v0 Is

v0 is an AI app builder that turns a plain-language description into a working web interface built from a particular, modern, widely respected stack — React and Next.js for the structure, Tailwind for the styling, and a component library called shadcn/ui for the polished building blocks. You do not need to know what any of those words mean to use v0, and I am not going to make you learn them. What matters is the consequence: v0 produces front-end work that looks like a competent professional made it, because the ingredients it reaches for are the same ones competent professionals reach for.

It is worth one paragraph on why those particular ingredients matter, because it explains v0's character rather than just listing its tools. Tailwind and shadcn/ui are not obscure choices — they are, as of this writing, near the center of how a great deal of modern web interface gets built professionally. shadcn/ui in particular is a collection of pre-designed, well-behaved components — buttons, dialogs, dropdowns, cards — that already look good and already handle the fiddly details, like keyboard navigation and screen-reader labels, that amateurs forget and professionals sweat over. When v0 assembles your interface out of those, it is not inventing button styling from scratch each time and hoping it looks consistent; it is reaching into a coherent kit where everything was designed to fit together. That is a large part of why v0's output looks unified rather than patched-together, and why it tends to be accessible and responsive without your asking. The taste is partly the model's, but it is also baked into the ingredients.

If you have read Chapter 1, you know the move at the center of all these tools — you describe what you want, the AI writes the actual code, you steer by reacting. v0 does exactly that. What distinguishes it is *taste*. Ask four of these builders for "a dashboard," and you will get four working dashboards; v0's will, more often than not, be the one that looks like it belongs in a real product rather than a tutorial. That is not an accident. Vercel sits at the center of the modern web-design world, and v0 was trained to produce the kind of interface that world considers good.

The Thing It Does Best: Interfaces You Don't Have to Apologize For

Every tool in this book has a center of gravity — the job it is unmistakably best at — and for v0 that job is the look and feel of the thing.

This is the part that genuinely sets it apart. When the screen is what matters — a landing page, a marketing site, a clean dashboard, a polished form, the visible surface a user actually touches — v0 is, in my experience, the one to beat. It has an eye. It reaches for sensible spacing and hierarchy and restraint without being told, and it produces components that are accessible and responsive by default rather than as an afterthought. If you have ever built something functional that nonetheless looked *off* in a way you could not name, v0 is the tool most likely to hand you the version that looks right.

Let me make "the look matters" concrete with the kinds of jobs where v0 pulls clearly ahead. A founder's landing page that has to make a strong first impression on a stranger in three seconds — v0. A marketing site for a small business where the design *is* the credibility — v0. An internal dashboard that the boss will see and judge — v0, because the version that looks like a real product changes how the work is received. A form that needs to feel trustworthy enough that people will actually put their information into it — v0, because trust on the web is largely conveyed through polish. In every one of these, the hard part is not the data or the logic; it is that the thing has to *look* like someone who knew what they were doing made it. That is precisely the gap v0 was built to close, and it closes it more reliably than anything else in this book.

It is built to be iterated visually. You describe a change — "make the header sticky," "tighten the spacing between cards," "give this a dark mode" — and v0 adjusts, the same conversational refinement Chapter 1 described. Because the components come from a coherent, consistent library, the changes stay coherent too; you rarely get the patchwork, mismatched result that ad-hoc generation can produce.

This visual iteration is worth dwelling on, because it is where v0 feels most like working with a designer rather than wrestling with a generator. You can be vague in a productive way — "this feels a little cramped," "make it more elegant," "I want this to feel premium" — and v0 tends to know what you mean, because it has internalized what those words map to in real design. Contrast that with describing the same change in precise terms, which you would have to do if you were editing the code by hand. The conversational, taste-aware iteration is a genuine strength, and it is most powerful exactly on the visual layer where v0 is strongest. A useful habit: when you like most of a result but one thing is off, name the one thing and leave the rest alone, rather than re-describing the whole screen. v0 holds the parts you did not mention steady, and small targeted nudges compound into a polished result faster than wholesale rewrites.

And it hands you real, takeable code. This matters more than it sounds. The output is standard React and Next.js, and you can export it to GitHub and carry it into a normal development project. A designer or developer can pick it up and keep going. v0 is not a walled garden in the way some tools are — the front-end work it produces is yours, in a format the rest of the industry understands. Hold onto that point; we will complicate it shortly.

There is a particular workflow this enables that is worth naming, because it is one of v0's best uses and one Chapter 25 will return to: the non-coder front-end handoff. A founder or a product person with no engineering skill can use v0 to produce a real, polished interface — not a Figma mockup that a developer then has to rebuild, but actual working front-end code — and hand that to a developer as a *starting point* rather than a specification. The developer skips the tedious work of translating a design into code and goes straight to wiring up the real behavior behind it. That collapses a step that traditionally caused friction and miscommunication. It only works because the output is genuinely standard code a professional can take seriously, which is exactly what v0 produces and what flimsier tools do not.

The Rebuild That Changed What v0 Is

For most of its life, v0 had a clear and honest limitation: it built the front of the app beautifully and largely stopped there. It was a *front-end* tool. If you wanted a database, user logins, server-side logic — the machinery behind the pretty page — v0 was not really where that happened. That was a fair criticism and an accurate description.

That description is now out of date, and you should know why, because it changes how you should think about the tool. A major rebuild in early 2026 (as of this writing, dated to around February — but treat the timing loosely) turned v0 from a front-end generator into something much closer to a full builder. The rebuilt v0 added genuine Git integration, a proper editor experience that will feel familiar to anyone who has seen a developer's screen, the ability to connect a real database, more autonomous "agentic" workflows where the tool plans and executes multi-step changes rather than responding one prompt at a time, and — notably — the ability to import an existing project from GitHub and work on it.

Each of those additions deserves a plain-language note, because together they explain how much v0 changed. *Git integration* means your project now has proper version history — a record of changes you can look back through and, when something breaks, roll back to. That is the difference between a tool you experiment in nervously and one you can build on with confidence, because mistakes become reversible. *Connecting a real database* means v0 can now store and retrieve actual data, which is the thing that turns a pretty page into an app that remembers things between visits. The *agentic workflows* are the most consequential shift in feel: instead of you driving every single step — change this, now change that — the tool can take a larger goal, make a plan, and carry out several steps on its own, checking its work as it goes. That moves v0 from a fast assistant toward something closer to a junior builder you delegate to. And the import-from-GitHub capability, as I said, reopens the door from the other side.

That last capability is quietly the biggest. It means v0 is no longer only a place to *start* something from a sentence; it is a place you can bring code that already exists and continue it. The wall between "v0 made this" and "a developer made this" got a lot lower. For our purposes, the takeaway is simple: if you read somewhere that v0 "only does front-ends," that was true and is no longer the whole truth. It now reaches the database and the back end. Whether it is the tool *you* should reach for to do that is a different question — and the honest answer involves the catch.

A fair caveat, in the spirit of this book's honesty: a capability being *present* is not the same as that capability being a tool's *strength*. v0 can now do back-end work, but its center of gravity — the thing it does better than anyone — is still the interface. A tool like Lovable, in the next chapters, was built from the ground up to make the back end disappear for a non-coder, and it shows. So read the rebuild correctly: it removes v0's old disqualifying limitation, it does not crown v0 the best at everything. v0 became a real full builder that is still, at heart, the best-looking one. That is a meaningful and useful thing to be, and it is not the same as being the most complete back-end experience.

The Catch: Gravity Toward Vercel

Here is the thing to understand about v0 before you commit a real project to it, and I would rather tell you plainly than let you discover it later.

v0's parent company makes its money hosting applications, and v0 is, among other things, a beautifully effective way to guide you toward hosting yours with Vercel. This is not a scandal — it is a perfectly reasonable business, and the integration is genuinely smooth, smoother than wiring things together yourself. But it has a consequence you should walk in knowing: of the four builders in this book, v0 has the **tightest coupling to its own ecosystem**. The path of least resistance runs through Vercel's hosting, Vercel's deployment, Vercel's way of doing things. Everything is engineered to make staying inside that ecosystem feel effortless and stepping outside it feel like swimming upstream.

Let me describe how that gravity actually feels in practice, because "lock-in" is an abstract word and the experience of it is concrete. You build something in v0, and when it is time to put it on the internet, there is a button. The button deploys it to Vercel. It works the first time, it works in seconds, and it works beautifully — and that is precisely the point. The alternative, deploying somewhere else, is not forbidden; it is just *harder*. You would be doing manually what the button does automatically, and you would be doing it without the smooth integration that makes the Vercel path feel like no decision at all. Most people, most of the time, press the button — not because they evaluated their options and chose Vercel, but because pressing the button is the path of no resistance and everything else is friction. That is how gravity works. It does not trap you with walls; it tilts the floor so that the easy direction and the vendor's preferred direction are the same direction. Multiply that across hosting, deployment, the database, and a dozen smaller defaults, and over months your app quietly becomes woven into one company's platform — not because anyone forced you, but because every individual easy choice pointed the same way.

Now, the front-end code itself is portable — I said that above and I meant it; you can export your React to GitHub and leave. But the *full-stack* convenience, the part where everything just works together, is most convenient precisely when you stay where Vercel wants you. The more of the back end and the deployment you let v0 and Vercel handle for you, the more your app's life is woven into one company's platform. Chapter 23, on scaling and lock-in, takes this question up across all four tools and gives v0 its honest grade; for now, just file the shape of it: **the polish is real and the convenience is real, and the convenience has a direction.**

And to be fair to v0, gravity is not automatically a bad deal — it is only a bad deal if it pulls you somewhere you did not want to go. If Vercel's hosting is good (it is), and reasonably priced for your needs (often it is), and you have no particular reason to be anywhere else, then the gravity is doing you a favor: it is making the right choice the easy choice. The problem only bites when your needs and Vercel's preferences diverge — when you grow into pricing that does not suit you, or need a capability the platform does not offer, or simply want the freedom to move and discover the floor has been tilted away from the exit for so long that leaving is real work. The honest counsel is not "avoid the gravity" but "go in with your eyes open about which direction the floor is tilted, and make the staying-or-going decision deliberately rather than letting a year of easy buttons make it for you."

When v0 Is the Right Tool

Set the comparison with the other three for Chapter 8, where it belongs. On its own terms, reach for v0 when:

The interface is the point. A landing page, a marketing site, a product page, a dashboard, anything where how it *looks* carries real weight — this is v0's home court, and you will spend less time fighting the result toward "professional" than with any other tool here.

You or your team already live in this world. If you use Vercel, or you know you will, or you have a developer who works in React and Next.js, v0's gravity stops being a catch and becomes a feature. The integration that locks others in is exactly the integration you want.

You want front-end output a developer can take seriously. Because the code is standard and exportable, v0 is a strong way for a non-coder to produce a real starting point that a professional can then run with — the prototype-to-handoff path Chapter 25 cares about.

And reach for something else when the look is secondary to a complicated back end you want maximum freedom to move later, or when avoiding any single platform's gravity is itself a goal. Those are real reasons, and the next three chapters introduce the tools that serve them better.

A Word on Prices and Model Names

v0's pricing is metered — you spend credits or tokens as you build, which is the norm across these tools and gets a full treatment in Chapter 21. As of this writing the tiers run from a free plan up through team and business levels at roughly thirty and a hundred dollars per user per month, but I am flagging that number the way I flag all of them: it will have moved by the time you read this, possibly more than once, and the current pricing page is the only honest source.

The same caution applies to the model underneath. Vercel brands v0's intelligence in its own terms — you will see names suggesting smaller and larger variants — but what frontier model actually powers it is a Vercel decision that can change without much announcement. Do not anchor on a model name. Anchor on what the tool *does*, which is the durable thing: take a sentence, give you back an interface that looks like someone with taste built it. That has been true through every version, and it is the reason to know v0 at all.

Chapter 5: Bolt.new by StackBlitz

What earns Bolt its trust is a small, almost boring moment. You build a little inventory app, decide you want to keep working on it in your own setup, click the export, and a few seconds later you have a perfectly ordinary folder of code on your machine — the kind of folder any developer in the world would recognize, with nothing weird, nothing proprietary, nothing that ties it back to where it came from. You open it, you run it, and it runs. No magic, no lock, no platform breathing down your neck. After tools that quietly make their output hard to take elsewhere, that unremarkable folder feels like a small act of respect. Bolt's defining quality is that it gives you back something you can actually leave with.

Bolt.new is made by StackBlitz, and to understand what is unusual about it you have to understand one genuinely clever piece of technology underneath it. This chapter is about that technology, about the freedom it produces, and about the very specific way Bolt can cost you money — because Bolt's honest limitation is not vague or hidden, it is mechanical and predictable, and once you understand it you can work with it instead of being surprised by it.

What Bolt Is

Bolt.new is an AI app builder that creates full-stack applications — front end and back end together — inside a development environment that runs entirely in your browser. You describe what you want, the AI writes the code, and you watch the app come to life in a real, working dev setup that lives in a browser tab. The same describe-and-steer loop from Chapter 1 applies; what is distinctive is *where the building happens* and *what you can do with the result*.

The technology that makes this possible is called WebContainers, and it is worth one plain-language paragraph because it explains so much of Bolt's character. Normally, running the kind of code these apps are made of requires a real computer with real software installed — a server environment called Node.js, among other things. StackBlitz figured out how to run that entire environment *inside the browser itself*. When you use Bolt, you are not looking at a simulation or a preview piped in from some server far away; you are running a genuine development environment locally, in your tab. That is a real engineering achievement, and it has two consequences that matter to you: Bolt is fast and responsive in a way remote tools often are not, and the code it produces is *standard* code, because it is running in a standard environment rather than a proprietary one.

It helps to understand the contrast with how most of these tools work, because it explains why Bolt feels different to use. Most AI builders run your app on the company's servers, somewhere out on the internet, and show you a preview piped back to your screen. That works, but it means there is a network round-trip between you and your own app — a small lag in everything, and a dependence on their servers being up and responsive. Bolt's in-browser environment removes that middleman. Your app is running on *your* machine, in *your* browser, which is why it tends to feel snappier, and why you can keep tinkering even when the connection is flaky. More importantly for the long run, it means the environment Bolt builds in is the same kind of standard environment a developer would use on their own laptop — so the code that comes out of it is not shaped by any platform's quirks. It is just code, the ordinary kind, which is exactly why that exported folder runs anywhere. The clever technology is not a gimmick; it is the root cause of both Bolt's speed and Bolt's portability.

The Thing It Does Best: Output You Can Take Anywhere

If every builder has a center of gravity, Bolt's is portability. Of the four tools at the heart of this book, Bolt produces the **most portable output**, and I do not say that loosely.

This is the part worth choosing Bolt for. The code Bolt generates is ordinary, standard code with no special dependence on Bolt itself. You can export it to GitHub with a click. You can download it as a plain folder, the one I described at the top of this chapter. And you can deploy the finished app wherever you like — to Bolt's own hosting, to Netlify, to any number of other places, or to your own setup entirely. Bolt does not assume it owns the rest of your app's life. It builds the thing and hands it to you, and where it goes next is your decision, not the platform's.

Why should a non-coder care about portability at all, when leaving the platform sounds like a developer's concern? Because portability is really about *who holds the power in the relationship*, and that matters to everyone. When your work can leave, the platform has to keep earning you — through good features, fair pricing, reliable service — because you can walk if it stops. When your work cannot leave, the platform can raise prices, let quality slip, or change terms, and you are stuck, because the cost of moving is too high. Portability is leverage you may never use but are far better off having. Concretely, it protects you against three real futures: the platform that gets expensive as you grow, the platform that gets acquired and shuts down or changes beyond recognition, and the happy problem of an app successful enough that you want to bring in a developer — who will be far more willing and far cheaper to hire if the project is in a standard form they can simply open, rather than locked inside a tool they have to reverse-engineer. None of those futures requires you to be technical. All of them are easier to survive when your work is yours to take.

If you have read Chapter 4, you will hear the contrast immediately. v0's gravity pulls toward one ecosystem; Bolt's design actively resists that pull. Where v0 makes staying convenient, Bolt makes leaving easy. Neither is wrong — they are different philosophies — but if the ability to walk away with your work matters to you, Bolt is built around exactly that value. Chapter 23 grades all four on lock-in, and Bolt comes out the most portable; this is why.

It is genuinely full-stack from the start. Bolt does not stop at the visible page. It builds the back end alongside the front, stands up the logic and the data handling, and runs the whole thing in that in-browser environment so you can see it actually working — not a mockup of working, but working. For an app with real behavior and not just a pretty surface, that completeness matters.

The phrase "see it actually working" is doing more work than it looks like, and it is one of Bolt's quieter strengths. Some tools show you a static preview — a picture of what the app will look like — which is reassuring right up until you click a button and discover the button does not do anything yet. Bolt runs the real thing, so when you click the button, the real behavior happens, the real data saves, the real error appears if there is one. You are testing the actual app the whole time you build it, not a representation of it. For someone who cannot read the code to check whether it is correct, this is genuinely valuable: the running app *is* your check. If it works when you click around, it works, because what you are clicking is the real software and not a promise of it.

There is one honest qualification to attach to "the running app is your check," because this book would be doing you a disservice to oversell it. Clicking around verifies the things you *can* see — that the visible behavior is right, that the data saves and comes back, that the screens do what they should. It does not verify the things that live below the surface, the invisible-correctness territory Chapter 3 mapped: whether your data is protected from strangers, whether secrets are hidden, whether the app would survive a crowd. Bolt running the real thing is a wonderful check on visible correctness and no check at all on the kind that does not show up when you click. So take the strength for exactly what it is worth — a fast, honest test of the behavior you can observe — and remember that the part you cannot observe still needs the deliberate verification the later chapters insist on, no matter how convincingly the running app behaves on screen.

The Catch: Token Burn Scales With Your Project

Now the honest limitation, and I want to be precise about it because it is the single most important practical thing to know about Bolt, and it is the kind of thing that turns a cheerful afternoon into a surprising bill if no one tells you.

Bolt is metered by tokens — you consume tokens as you build, the general pattern Chapter 21 covers across all these tools. But Bolt has a specific quirk in *how* it consumes them, and it comes straight from that clever in-browser architecture. Here is the mechanism, in plain terms: each time you send the AI a message, Bolt sends the AI a picture of your project so it knows what it is working with. As your project grows — more files, more features, more code — that picture gets bigger. And a bigger picture costs more tokens to send. So the cost of each message you send tends to **rise as your project gets larger.**

It is worth understanding *why* this happens rather than just that it happens, because the why tells you how to manage it. An AI model has no memory of your project between messages; it does not "remember" what it built for you yesterday or even one message ago. Every single time you ask it for a change, it has to be re-told what the project currently is — the relevant files, the existing structure, the context it needs to make a sensible change. That re-telling is measured in tokens, and you pay for it on every message. When the project is tiny, the re-telling is cheap. When the project is large, the re-telling is expensive, and you pay that expense *again on every message*, even for a trivial change. The cost of a small edit is not the cost of the edit; it is mostly the cost of reminding the AI what your whole project is so it can make the edit safely. That is the mechanism, and it is not unique to Bolt in principle — it is how these models fundamentally work — but Bolt's architecture makes it especially direct and especially visible.

This is the part that catches people. Early on, when your app is small, Bolt feels cheap and fast and you build with abandon. Then, a few weeks in, with a substantial app full of files, you notice that the same kind of small change — "move this button" — is burning through far more of your budget than it did at the start. You did not do anything wrong. The tool is working as designed; it is just that the design means big projects get expensive to keep editing. This is not a hidden fee or a trick; it is a direct, understandable consequence of how WebContainers and the AI work together. But you should know it before you build something large in Bolt and not after.

The practical wisdom that follows from it: Bolt rewards being deliberate. The more clearly you describe what you want up front, the fewer expensive back-and-forth messages you spend on a large project. Chapter 9, on prompting an app well, is doubly worth reading if Bolt is your tool, because in Bolt good prompting is not just better results — it is real money saved. And for very large, long-lived projects that you will edit heavily over time, the rising cost is a genuine reason to weigh Bolt against the alternatives rather than assume it.

Let me turn that wisdom into concrete habits, because "be deliberate" is easy to say and easy to ignore. First, batch your changes. Instead of "make the button blue," then "now move it right," then "now make it bigger" — three messages, each paying the full cost of re-explaining your project — say "make the button blue, move it to the right, and make it bigger" in one. You pay the re-telling cost once instead of three times. Second, think before you type rather than steering in tiny increments; the conversational, react-to-each-step style that feels natural is exactly the style that runs up the bill on a large project, because each step is a fresh expensive message. Third, get the structure right early, while the project is small and messages are cheap, rather than discovering a fundamental flaw late and paying large-project prices to rework it. Fourth — and this is the strategic one — recognize when a project has grown to the point where the per-message cost is no longer worth it, and consider whether this is the moment to take Bolt's exportable code and continue elsewhere. Bolt's great virtue, portability, is also the escape hatch from its great catch: you are never trapped paying rising costs, because you can always leave with your work. Few tools let their limitation and their strength rescue each other quite so neatly.

What Bolt Is Less Suited For

In the spirit of this book's honesty, it is worth saying plainly where Bolt is *not* the obvious choice, because a tool's strengths are easier to trust when you also know its edges.

The first is the one this chapter has circled: the very large, long-lived project that you will edit heavily over many months. Bolt's token economics make that pattern progressively more expensive, and while the deliberate habits above soften the blow, they do not erase it. If you know going in that you are building something you will live in and revise endlessly, the rising per-message cost is a genuine factor to weigh, and a more flat-rate or back-end-handled tool may serve that pattern better over its lifetime.

The second is the reader who wants the back end to be entirely invisible. Bolt builds a real full-stack app, but its philosophy is to give you the real thing — the actual environment, the actual code, the actual machinery — rather than to hide the machinery so thoroughly you forget it exists. For a developer or a comfortable tinkerer, that transparency is a virtue. For a complete non-coder who finds the very mention of a back end discouraging, the next chapter's tool, which makes the back end disappear, is often the gentler door. Bolt respects you enough to hand you the real thing; whether you *want* the real thing handed to you is a question of temperament, and it is a fair one to ask yourself before choosing.

The third, more subtle, is that Bolt's portability is a benefit you have to actually use to capture. The exportable folder protects you against lock-in only if you would, in a pinch, know what to do with it — or know a developer who would. For a non-coder who will never touch the exported code and has no one who would, the portability is more of a comfort than a daily benefit, and the choice between Bolt and a friendlier tool comes down more to the building experience than to the freedom to leave. None of this is a mark against Bolt; it is just the honest shape of who it fits best, which is people who value having the real thing and keeping their options open, and who are willing to be deliberate about cost as the price of both.

A Note on Price and the Models

As of this writing, Bolt's paid plan sits somewhere in the low-twenties of dollars per month — and I have to flag, honestly, that even the sources reporting it do not entirely agree on the figure, which tells you how soft these numbers are. Treat any price you read, here or elsewhere, as a snapshot of a moving target, and check the current pricing page before you commit. The relevant durable fact is not the dollar amount; it is the *structure* — tokens, metered, scaling with project size — which is the part that shapes how you actually use the tool.

The AI underneath Bolt has, for some time, drawn on the Claude family of models, which are well regarded for code. But model versions drift on a scale of months, and the specific version powering Bolt when you read this may not be the one powering it as I write. As with every tool in this book, anchor on what Bolt *does* rather than on which model is doing it.

When Bolt Is the Right Tool

On its own terms, before the full comparison in Chapter 8, reach for Bolt when:

Portability matters to you. If keeping your options open — being able to take your app to any host, hand it to any developer, walk away from the platform without a fight — is something you value, Bolt is built for that value more deliberately than any other tool here.

You want a complete, working full-stack app and you want to see it run for real. The in-browser environment is genuinely live, which makes Bolt satisfying for building something with real behavior rather than just a surface.

Your project will stay reasonably contained, or you are willing to prompt deliberately. For small-to-moderate apps, the token economics are kind. For large ones, they are something to manage with care — and going in aware of that is the whole point of this chapter.

And weigh something else when you know your project will grow large and you will edit it endlessly, or when you would rather have the back end and database handled for you with less thought — which is precisely the strength of the tool in the next chapter. Bolt gives you freedom and asks you to manage the cost of using it. That trade is a good one for a great many projects, as long as you know you are making it.

Chapter 6: Lovable

Consider the nutritionist with no technical background, building a side business, who wants an app where her clients can log in, fill out an intake form, and see their meal plans. She tries one of the more developer-flavored tools and bounces off it; the moment it starts talking about databases and back ends and where her data will live, she feels the old familiar message that this is not for her. Then she tries Lovable, and what wins her over is what *doesn't* happen. She describes her app, the logins work, the data saves, and her clients' information has somewhere real to go — and at no point does she have to learn what a "back end" is or wire one up herself. It has been handled. For someone on the wrong side of the wall this whole book is about, that quiet handling is the difference between having the app and giving up.

That is Lovable's entire personality, and it is a deliberate one. Of the four builders here, Lovable is the one most single-mindedly aimed at people who are not developers and do not want to become them — and it backs that aim up with a specific choice about the hardest, scariest part of building an app: the back end. This chapter is about what Lovable is, where it came from, the one decision that defines it, and a cost that the sticker price quietly leaves out.

Where Lovable Came From

A small piece of history, because it tells you something about the tool's instincts. Lovable, based in Stockholm, did not start under that name. It began as a project called GPT Engineer, and it rebranded to Lovable around the turn of 2025. That origin matters less for the trivia than for the lineage: this is a tool that has been wrestling with the problem of "turn a description into a real, working application" for longer than the current wave, and the rename came with a sharpening of purpose — away from a developer-ish experiment and toward a polished product for ordinary people. The name itself is a thesis. They are not trying to build the most powerful tool or the most portable one. They are trying to build the one you *like* using, the one that does not make you feel stupid.

That last phrase is worth taking seriously rather than as a throwaway, because "the one that does not make you feel stupid" describes a real design discipline that most tools lack. The non-coder's experience of software tools is, very often, a steady drip of small humiliations: a screen full of words you do not know, a step that assumes knowledge you do not have, an error message written by an engineer for an engineer. Each of those is a tiny moment where the tool communicates, intentionally or not, *this is not for you*. Lovable's whole product philosophy is to remove those moments — to hide the jargon, to make the scary steps invisible, to never present the user with a decision they are not equipped to make. You can feel the GPT Engineer lineage in this: a tool that once spoke to developers learned, deliberately, to stop speaking that way. The result is not that Lovable is more *powerful* than its rivals; it is that Lovable is more *welcoming*, and for the reader this book most often pictures, welcoming is frequently the feature that decides whether the app gets built at all.

What Lovable Is

Lovable is an AI app builder that creates a complete product — both the front end you see and the back end behind it — from a plain-language description, aimed squarely at non-coders. The describe-and-steer loop from Chapter 1 is here, as it is everywhere in this book. What distinguishes Lovable is the word *complete*: it is not trying to hand you a beautiful interface and leave the hard machinery as your problem. It is trying to hand you a whole working thing.

And the way it does that is the one decision you most need to understand.

The Thing That Defines It: The Back End Is Included

Lovable's center of gravity is the back end — specifically, that you do not have to think about it.

Here is the move. The hardest part of building real software, for a non-technical person, is rarely the visible page; it is everything behind it — where the data lives, how users log in, how any of that gets set up and kept running. Most tools make you confront some version of that. Lovable's answer is something it calls Lovable Cloud, which bundles in a real, capable back end — built on a well-regarded platform called Supabase, which provides the database and the user-login machinery — natively, as part of the experience. You ask for users to be able to log in; the login works, with a real database storing real accounts, and you did not have to go set up an account somewhere else, copy keys around, or understand what any of it was. It came included.

To appreciate how much friction that removes, it helps to know what the alternative actually involves, because most non-coders have never seen it and so cannot value its absence. In a less integrated tool, "add user logins and save their data" can unfold like this: go to a separate service's website, create an account there, create a project inside it, find a settings page, copy two or three long strings of letters and numbers called keys, paste them into the right places in your builder without making a typo, understand which key is the secret one that must never be shown to users and which is safe, and configure a handful of options whose names mean nothing to you. Every one of those steps is a place to get lost, get something subtly wrong, or simply give up — and getting the secret-key part wrong is one of the classic ways a vibe-coded app ends up leaking data, a point Part VI will return to. Lovable's bundled back end collapses that entire gauntlet into "it just works when you ask for it." That is not a minor convenience. For the right person, it is the difference between an app that exists and an app that died at the keys-and-settings step.

This is the part that makes Lovable the right tool for the right person. For a non-coder who wants a *whole product* — not a front end they will later have to find someone to finish, but an app with working accounts and saved data, end to end — Lovable offers the smoothest path of the four. The thing that stops most people, the back end, is the thing Lovable most deliberately takes off your plate. If you have read Chapter 4, this is nearly the opposite emphasis from v0: where v0's genius is the surface, Lovable's is the machinery underneath, handled so you need not look at it.

There is, in fairness, a flip side to "handled so you need not look at it," and intellectual honesty requires naming it even in the section praising the tool. The convenience of not seeing the back end is also a loss of *visibility into* the back end. When something behind the scenes behaves oddly — data not saving the way you expected, a permission not working as you thought — the same abstraction that spared you the setup now stands between you and understanding the problem. A more hands-on tool would show you the machinery; Lovable, by design, mostly does not, because showing it would reintroduce the complexity it worked so hard to hide. For most users building most apps, that trade is overwhelmingly worth it. But it is a real trade, and it foreshadows a security point worth holding onto: a back end you cannot see is a back end you cannot easily check, and "I never had to think about how my users' data is protected" is a comfort right up until it becomes a liability. Lovable handles the setup well; it cannot handle your *judgment* about whether the result is safe for the data you are putting into it. That remains yours, as it does with every tool here.

And it does not trap your code. This is the reassuring counterweight, and it matters. Despite being so beginner-friendly, Lovable offers bidirectional sync with GitHub — meaning your code can flow both ways between Lovable and a standard code repository that the rest of the development world understands. Your work is not sealed inside the platform. If you later bring in a developer, or want to take the project elsewhere, the door is open. That puts Lovable in a genuinely good position on the lock-in question that Chapter 23 takes up: friendlier to beginners than the portable tools, more portable than the friendliest tools. It is a nice place to sit.

The word "bidirectional" in that sync is the part worth understanding, because it is rarer and more useful than it sounds. A one-way export — code flows out of the tool and that is it — is helpful but limited: the moment a developer edits the exported code, their version and your in-tool version drift apart, and you can no longer use the friendly builder without losing their changes. Bidirectional sync means changes flow *both* ways: a developer can work on the code in standard tools, and you can keep working in Lovable's friendly interface, and the two stay reconciled. That enables a genuinely valuable collaboration pattern — the non-coder founder keeps iterating on the parts they understand in the welcoming environment, while a developer handles the parts that need a professional, both working on the same living project rather than two diverging copies. Few beginner-aimed tools offer that, and it is a large part of why Lovable scores well on lock-in despite being the most hand-holding of the four. You get the friendliness without paying for it in trapped work.

The Catch: The Sticker Price Is Not the Real Price

Now the honest part, and it is a particular kind of catch — not a flaw in the tool, but a gap in the number, and one I would rather you understand now than discover on a billing statement.

Lovable's subscription, as of this writing, runs around twenty-five dollars a month for its main paid tier and roughly fifty for a business level, metered by messages — and as always, flag that figure, check the current pricing page, assume it has moved. But here is the thing that price does *not* include, and it is the part people miss: the back end that Lovable so helpfully bundles in is real infrastructure, and real infrastructure has its own costs once your app grows past the free starter limits. The underlying database platform has its own paid tier. A custom domain costs money. As your app gets real usage and real data, the convenient included back end may need to be upgraded — and that cost lands separately from your Lovable subscription.

The deeper reason this catch exists is the same convenience that makes Lovable wonderful, viewed from the cost side. By bundling the back end in and hiding it, Lovable makes it easy to forget the back end is a *running service that someone pays for*. With a more hands-on tool, you set up the database yourself, so you saw its pricing page and you know there is a meter running. With Lovable, the back end appeared as if by magic when you asked for logins, and things that appear by magic do not feel like things you pay for — until they are. The free starter tier of the underlying database is generous enough that a small app or a prototype may never cost a cent beyond the subscription, which is genuinely great and which also lulls people. The bill arrives when success arrives: real users, real data accumulating, real traffic, and at some point the free tier is no longer enough and the database platform's own paid tier kicks in. The structure is not deceptive — every piece of it is documented — but the abstraction that spares you from thinking about the back end also spares you from thinking about what it costs, and those are the same convenience wearing two faces.

This is the part that surprises people, so let me be plain. The number on Lovable's pricing page is the cost of *building*, not the full cost of *running* a real, growing app. The total cost of ownership includes the downstream infrastructure that sits underneath. This is not Lovable being sneaky; it is just the nature of real software — the machinery that makes your app work is a service, and services cost money to run at scale. But "I am paying twenty-five dollars a month" is an incomplete picture if your app has hundreds of active users putting real data into a database. Chapter 21 walks through the full cost picture for all these tools; for Lovable specifically, the lesson is to add the infrastructure underneath to the subscription on top when you imagine what a successful app will actually cost.

A useful way to keep this straight, and one Chapter 21 develops further, is to mentally separate three different meters before you ever launch something real. The first is the *building* cost — the Lovable subscription and its message limits, which you pay while you are creating and iterating. The second is the *running* cost — the database tier, any custom domain, and whatever else keeps the live app serving real users, which scales with how successful you are. The third, easy to forget entirely, is the cost of any *outside services* your app calls on — a payment processor's cut, an email-sending service, anything that charges per use, which Chapter 17 covers. None of these is hidden, but only the first appears on the page you looked at when you decided Lovable cost twenty-five dollars a month. A small app that stays small may genuinely cost only that first meter. A successful app pays all three, and the time to form a rough picture of the total is before you put it in front of a crowd, not when the second and third meters start arriving by email.

What the Build Actually Feels Like

It helps to picture the experience concretely, because Lovable's whole pitch is about how building *feels*, and feel is hard to convey in the abstract. Take the nutritionist's app from the start of the chapter and imagine the arc of an afternoon with it.

You begin with a sentence — something like "an app where my nutrition clients can create an account, fill out an intake form about their goals and dietary restrictions, and see the meal plans I assign them." Lovable does not respond by asking you to choose a database or configure a service. It builds a first version: a login screen, an intake form, a place for meal plans, all wired to a working back end you were never asked to set up. You log in as a test user and it works — the account is real, stored in a real database, and you did nothing to make that true.

Then you steer, the way Chapter 1 described. "The intake form should have a field for allergies." "Let me, as the nutritionist, see a list of all my clients." "Clients should only see their own meal plans, not anyone else's." Each of these is a sentence, and each one quietly involves back-end work — new data fields, a new permission rule, a query that filters by user — that you never have to name as back-end work. That last request, about clients seeing only their own plans, is a perfect small illustration of both Lovable's gift and its risk: it is a *permission* rule, exactly the kind of invisible, under-the-hood correctness that the previous chapters warned you cannot verify just by clicking around. Lovable will implement it from your plain-language request, and it will probably get it right — but "probably right" on a privacy rule protecting your clients' health information is precisely the moment to slow down and verify deliberately rather than trust the surface, because the cost of that rule being subtly wrong is a client seeing another client's private data. The convenience that built it for you in a sentence is not a substitute for the judgment about whether it is actually safe, and on a feature like that one, the judgment is the whole game.

By the end of the afternoon you have a working product. That is the experience Lovable is selling, and for the right person it delivers it more smoothly than anything else here. The thing to carry forward is that the smoothness is real *and* the smoothness is not the same as safety — the better the tool is at making the hard parts feel effortless, the more deliberately you have to choose to check the hard parts that matter, because nothing in the effortless flow will prompt you to.

What Lovable Is Less Suited For

In fairness, and to help you choose well, here is where Lovable is not the obvious pick.

If interface polish is the dominant need — a landing page or marketing site where the look carries the credibility — v0 has the clearer edge, as Chapter 4 laid out. Lovable produces perfectly respectable interfaces, but design taste is v0's center of gravity, not Lovable's, and when the screen *is* the product you will usually be happier starting where the taste lives.

If you want maximum control over and visibility into the back end — to understand exactly how your data is structured, to tune it, to see the machinery — Lovable's defining choice to hide that machinery works against you. The abstraction that frees a non-coder constrains a tinkerer who *wants* to look under the hood. Bolt's give-you-the-real-thing philosophy fits that temperament better.

And if your app's hard part is logic rather than a familiar product shape — the correctness-critical, novel-algorithm territory Chapter 3 warned about — no amount of back-end convenience helps, because the difficulty is in the thinking, and that is hard for every tool here, Lovable included. Lovable's strength is making a *familiar-shaped complete product* easy for a non-coder. Stretch the app past a familiar shape and into genuinely hard logic, and Lovable's particular gift stops being the thing that matters.

When Lovable Is the Right Tool

On its own terms, ahead of the full comparison in Chapter 8, reach for Lovable when:

You are a non-coder who wants a whole product, back end and all. This is the clearest case. If the part that scares you is everything behind the page, Lovable is the tool that most thoroughly takes that fear away. It is the strongest "complete product for a non-developer" experience of the four.

You want logins and saved data without learning how they work. The included Supabase-based back end means accounts and a real database are part of the deal rather than a separate project you have to go assemble.

You want a beginner-friendly path that still leaves you an exit. The GitHub sync means choosing Lovable for its friendliness does not lock you in — a genuinely good combination, and not one every tool offers.

And consider something else when interface polish is the dominant need, where v0 has the edge, or when you want maximum control over and visibility into the back end rather than having it handled for you. But for the reader this book most often pictures — the teacher, the nutritionist, the operations lead with an idea and no developer — Lovable is frequently the gentlest door through the wall. Just walk through it knowing that the room on the other side has a utility bill the brochure didn't mention.

Chapter 7: Replit Agent

I gave Replit's Agent a deliberately lazy instruction once, just to see what it would do: "build me a habit tracker where I can add habits, check them off each day, and see a streak." Then I sat back. What happened next was closer to watching someone work than using a tool. It wrote out a plan — these are the pieces, here is the order I will build them. It set up a database. It installed the things it needed. It wrote the app, ran it, hit an error, read the error, and fixed it without me saying a word. And then it deployed the thing to a live web address I could open on my phone. I had typed one sentence and gotten back a running app on the internet, with the database and the hosting already handled. Of everything in this book, that moment came the closest to the promise the breathless headlines make: describe it, and get a deployed, working app.

Replit is the most *autonomous* of the four builders, and it is also the one that asks the most of you in a specific way you will not feel until later. This chapter is about what Replit's Agent does, the unusual completeness of the environment it does it in, and the trade buried inside that completeness — because Replit gives you the most hands-off path to a running app and, in exchange, ties that app most tightly to itself.

What Replit Is

Replit is, at its foundation, a complete development environment that runs in the cloud — a real one, the kind a working programmer might use, except it lives in your browser and you do not have to install or configure anything. On top of that environment sits the Agent (Agent 3 as of this writing — the version number will climb), which is the AI that does the building. So when you use Replit, you are not using a stripped-down app maker; you are using a full, genuine coding environment, with an AI agent driving it on your behalf.

That distinction shapes everything. The describe-and-steer loop from Chapter 1 is here, but Replit's Agent leans hard toward the *autonomous* end of it. Rather than responding to one instruction at a time and waiting, the Agent plans a multi-step job, then carries it out — scaffolding the app, installing dependencies, writing the code, running it, catching its own errors and fixing them, and deploying the result.

It works in stretches, and you watch it work, stepping in to correct course rather than dictating every move.

To make that concrete, it helps to know what is actually on the screen, because Replit shows you more than the other three. There is a chat panel where you talk to the Agent. There is a file tree — the list of every file in your project, which on Replit is a real folder of real code, not an abstraction. There is an editor where those files open. There is a "console" or "shell" pane where the running program reports what it is doing, including its errors. And there is a preview pane, the live app itself, which updates as the Agent builds. A non-coder can ignore most of this and live entirely in the chat panel; the point is that the machinery is all present and all real, which is exactly why the Agent can do so much without handing anything back to you.

How the Agent Actually Plans

The single most distinctive thing about working in Replit is watching the Agent think out loud before it builds. With most tools you type a request and the answer simply starts appearing. Replit's Agent more often pauses to lay out a plan first: it restates what it understood you to want, breaks the job into a numbered sequence of steps, and frequently tells you which of those steps it is about to do. Only then does it start writing files.

This is not decoration, and it is worth slowing down to read every time. The plan is your single best early-warning system. When the Agent says, in effect, "I will build a slot list, then a booking form, then a database table to store bookings, then an owner view," you get a chance to notice — *before any code exists* — that it misunderstood something. Maybe you wanted students to be able to cancel a booking and the plan never mentions cancellation. The cheapest moment to catch that is right there, by replying "good plan, but also add the ability for a student to cancel their own booking." Correcting the plan costs one sentence. Correcting a finished app costs an hour and risks breaking three other things.

The Agent also reaches *checkpoints* as it works — natural stopping points where a chunk of the job is done and the app is in a runnable state. These checkpoints matter for two reasons. First, they are how Replit's pricing meters effort, which we will come back to. Second, they are points you can return to. If a later instruction sends the build off a cliff, you are not stranded; the platform keeps a history of these checkpoints, and you can roll back to the last good one rather than trying to manually undo a tangle of changes. For a non-coder, that safety net is genuinely valuable, because the failure mode that stops beginners cold elsewhere — "I asked for one thing, everything broke, and I have no idea how to get back to where it worked" — has a built-in escape hatch here.

The Thing It Does Best: From Sentence to Running App

Replit's center of gravity is end-to-end autonomy — the shortest distance from a description to a deployed, running application.

This is the part that makes Replit feel like the future. Because the environment includes everything — the editor, the ability to run code, a built-in PostgreSQL database, and hosting — the Agent can take a job all the way to the end without handing pieces off to you or to other services. It does not build a front end and leave the database as your problem (Chapter 4's older limitation), and it does not bundle a back end from an outside provider (Chapter 6's approach). It has its *own* database and its *own* hosting, right there, included. So "build it, store the data, and put it live" can all happen in one continuous motion, driven by the Agent. When people imagine what "AI builds your app" should mean, Replit is the tool that most literally delivers it.

It catches and fixes its own mistakes. This is more important than it sounds for a non-coder. With many tools, when something breaks, you are staring at an error you do not understand, trying to describe a problem you cannot diagnose. Replit's Agent will frequently see the error itself, understand it, and fix it before you have to get involved. It does not always succeed — nothing here is magic, and Chapter 14 on iterating and fixing exists precisely because these tools still get stuck — but the Agent's instinct to run, observe, and repair on its own removes a category of frustration that stops beginners cold elsewhere.

Here is what that self-correction loop actually looks like in practice, because seeing it once demystifies it. Suppose the Agent writes the booking form but makes a small mistake — it tries to save a booking to a database column that does not exist yet. With a tool that only shows you the surface, you would refresh, click "book," and get a blank screen or a cryptic message, and you would be stuck. In Replit, the running program throws the error into the console, the Agent reads that console output as part of its own loop, recognizes "ah, the column is missing," adds the column, re-runs, and confirms the booking now saves. You watch this happen as a few lines of narration. You did nothing. The reason it can do this is precisely that the environment is real and complete: the Agent has access to the actual error from the actual running program, so it can diagnose the way a developer would.

The whole thing is genuinely beginner-accessible despite being a real dev environment. That is a neat trick. You get the power of a true coding setup without having to set up, understand, or maintain it. For a non-coder who wants to *make something* and not manage infrastructure, that combination is genuinely valuable.

A Worked Walkthrough: The Habit Tracker, Step by Step

Let me slow the opening story down, because the play-by-play teaches more than the highlight reel. I typed: "build me a habit tracker where I can add habits, check them off each day, and see a streak."

The Agent's first move was the plan — it told me it would create a place to store habits, build a screen to add and list them, add a daily check-off mechanism, calculate streaks from the check-off history, and then deploy. Reading that plan, I could already tell it had understood "streak" correctly to mean consecutive days, which is the part I was most worried it would get wrong.

Then it built. The file tree filled in. The console scrolled as it installed what it needed and started the program. The preview pane showed a bare but working page where I could add a habit. It hit one error along the way — something about how it was storing dates — saw it in the console, and fixed it without comment. Within a few minutes I had a page that let me add "drink water" and "read," check each one off for the day, and see a running count.

Then I steered, one note at a time, exactly as Chapter 9 will preach. "Show the streak as a number next to each habit." Done. "If I miss a day, the streak should reset to zero." This one is a *rule*, a mechanism, and I stated it plainly because the Agent cannot infer the rule in my head. Done. "Make it usable on my phone." Done. And because Replit's deploy is part of the same environment, "put it live so I can open it on my phone" was not a separate, scary step — it was one more instruction, and the Agent handed me a URL.

What I want you to notice is the rhythm: a plan I could correct, a build I could watch, a self-repair I did nothing for, and a steering loop of small, single-purpose instructions. None of that required me to know what the code said. It required me to know what I wanted and to read the plan carefully enough to catch a misunderstanding early.

Where the Agent Gets Stuck

Honesty demands the other side of the self-correction story, because the Agent's autonomy has a specific failure mode you should recognize. When the Agent *can* read an error and fix it, the loop is magic. When it cannot — when the problem is not a clean error message but a behavior that is subtly wrong — the same autonomy can work against you.

The classic version is the Agent confidently declaring victory on something that does not actually work. It says "I've added the cancellation feature and everything is working," but when you click cancel, nothing happens. The Agent believed it was done because the code ran without throwing an error; the gap is between "ran without crashing" and "does the thing I meant." This is the single most important habit to carry into Replit: *test the behavior yourself, do not trust the Agent's report*. Click the button. Refresh the page. Try to book the same slot twice. The Agent is a fast, capable builder who occasionally mistakes "it compiled" for "it works," and you are the one with the judgment to tell the difference.

A second sticking point is the long, ambitious build that wanders. Because the Agent is autonomous and works in stretches, a sprawling request can send it down a path that drifts further from what you wanted with each step, and because it is moving fast, a lot of wrong work can pile up before you intervene. The defense is the same one this whole book teaches and that Chapter 9 makes its core lesson: keep the requests scoped, read the plan, and stop the Agent early when the plan is off, rather than letting it grind through fifteen steps you will have to unwind. The checkpoint-rollback safety net helps, but it is a recovery tool, not a substitute for steering well in the first place.

A third, quieter one: the Agent occasionally loops on a fix it cannot land. It tries something, it does not work, it tries a variation, that does not work either, and it can burn real effort — and, on effort-based pricing, real money — circling a problem. When you see this happening, the move is to interrupt and reframe. Stop it, restate the problem more concretely, or roll back to the last checkpoint and approach the feature from a different angle. Letting it spin is the expensive mistake.

The Catch: This App Wants to Live Here

Now the honest limitation, and it is the most important thing to understand about Replit before you build something you care about, because it is the exact reverse of Bolt's defining quality and you should choose with your eyes open.

Everything that makes Replit so smooth — the included database, the included hosting, the environment that handles all of it for you — comes from the app being deeply woven into Replit's own platform. Your app uses Replit's database. It runs on Replit's hosting. The convenience and the coupling are the *same fact* seen from two angles. And that means, of the four builders in this book, Replit produces the app with the **highest migration friction** — the one that is hardest to pick up and move somewhere else later.

It is worth being concrete about what "woven in" actually means, because "lock-in" can sound like a vague warning rather than a real cost. Your app's data lives in Replit's database, addressed in a way that assumes it is running on Replit. The app expects the environment Replit provides — the way it starts up, the way it finds its database, the way it is served to the internet. To move it, you would not just copy the files (though you *can* copy the files — the code is yours and exportable). You would have to stand up your own database somewhere else, move the data into it, reconfigure the app to find the new database, and arrange your own hosting and your own way of running the program — the very chores Replit did for you and hid. None of that is impossible, and a developer could do it, but it is real work that did not exist while you stayed put, and it is work you discover only at the moment you want to leave.

This is the trade, stated plainly. With Bolt (Chapter 5), the output is standard and you can walk away with it easily; that freedom is the whole point of the tool. With Replit, you get a far more autonomous, hands-off, all-included experience — and the price of that experience is that your app is comfortable *here* and would take real work to relocate. If you decided in a year to move off Replit, you would not just copy a folder; you would be untangling your app from the database and hosting it grew up inside. That is not a reason to avoid Replit. It is a reason to know what you are choosing. For a prototype, an internal tool, a personal project, or anything where staying on Replit is perfectly fine, the lock-in simply does not bite. For something you suspect will outgrow the platform and need to move to dedicated infrastructure, it is a cost to weigh now rather than discover later. Chapter 23 grades all four on exactly this question, and Replit sits at the high-friction end; this is why.

A Note on Pricing and the Agent's Version

Replit's pricing is structured differently from the simple monthly fee you might expect, and the difference is worth knowing. Rather than charging only a flat subscription, it meters by the *effort* the Agent expends — built around the work it does and checkpoints it reaches as it builds. As of this writing, the plans run from a core tier in the low-to-mid twenties of dollars a month up to a pro tier near a hundred, but flag all of that hard: the structure and the numbers both move, and the current pricing page is the only source worth trusting. The practical implication of effort-based pricing is that a big, ambitious build the Agent grinds away at can cost more than a simple one, in a way that is not always obvious up front — Chapter 21 unpacks the full cost picture.

The reason effort-based pricing deserves a closer look is that it interacts with the Agent's autonomy in a way the other tools' pricing does not. With a tool that does one step per message, your cost tracks roughly with how many messages you send — a metric you can feel. Replit's Agent, by contrast, can do a great deal of work off a single instruction, which is wonderful for productivity and slightly disorienting for budgeting, because one sentence can trigger a long stretch of effort. The two practical habits that follow: first, scope your requests, because a vague "build me a CRM" can send the Agent on an expensive expedition, while "build a page to list my five clients and their phone numbers" is a contained job. Second, watch for the looping-on-a-fix pattern described above and interrupt it, because circling a problem is effort spent for nothing, and on this pricing model effort spent is money spent. Set whatever spending controls the platform offers while you are still learning your own patterns, the same discipline this series recommends for every metered AI tool.

And the Agent itself is a moving target. Agent 3 is current as I write; there will be an Agent 4. The capabilities described here — plan, scaffold, build, run, self-correct, deploy — are the durable shape of the tool, and they have deepened with each version rather than changed character. Anchor on that shape, not the version number.

When Replit Is the Right Tool

On its own terms, before the comparison in Chapter 8, reach for Replit when:

You want maximum hands-off, and you want it deployed. If your ideal is to describe an app and get back a running thing on the internet with the least manual assembly, Replit is the closest of the four to that ideal. It does the most for you.

You value everything-included over keeping your options open. Database, hosting, environment — all there, all handled. If you would rather not think about any of it, Replit's coupling is exactly the convenience you want.

The project is one where living on Replit is fine. Prototypes, internal tools, personal projects, anything that does not need to escape to dedicated infrastructure — these are where Replit shines without the lock-in ever costing you.

You are building something with real moving parts and want a tool that can debug itself. Apps that genuinely *do* things — store data, calculate, handle multiple steps — play to the Agent's self-correction strength, because that strength shows up most where there is real logic to get wrong and real errors to read and fix.

And lean toward something else when portability is a real requirement, where Bolt is built for the value Replit trades away. The two tools sit at opposite ends of one spectrum — most autonomous and most coupled at one end, most portable and most hands-on at the other — and knowing which end your project belongs at is most of the decision. The chapter ahead lays that spectrum out in full.

Chapter 8: Choosing the Right Builder

The most common question I get, after someone has read about these four tools, is also the least useful one: "So which is the best?" I understand the impulse – you want a verdict, a winner, a single recommendation so you can stop deciding and start building. But the honest answer is that the question has no answer, because "best" is not a property these tools have. They are not four runners in the same race; they are four different vehicles, and the right one depends entirely on the trip. A pickup truck is not better than a sedan. It is better *for hauling lumber*, and worse for almost everything else. The four builders in this book are like that. This chapter is not about which one wins. It is about which one is right for *you*, this time, for this thing.

The good news, which I want to state before any of the caveats, is that the core skill transfers. As Chapter 1 promised, the act of describing an app and steering it works across all four; if you learn it in one, you can use it in another. So choosing the "wrong" tool is rarely a disaster – you will not have wasted the skill. But choosing the *right* one means less friction, less surprise, and a result that fits what you actually need. So let us make the choice well.

Start With the Question That Actually Decides It

People tend to choose a builder by reputation or by which one a friend mentioned. That is backwards. The thing that should drive the decision is the *shape of what you are building and what you need from it*. Four questions sort it almost completely. Ask yourself, honestly, which of these is the true center of your project – because each points to a different tool.

Is the interface the point? Some apps live or die by how they look – a landing page, a marketing site, a polished public-facing surface where "professional" is not optional. If the look is the thing, that points one direction.

Do you need to be able to take it anywhere later? Some projects carry a requirement to stay portable – to be movable to any host, handed to any developer, kept free of any single platform's grip. If keeping your options open is a real need rather than a vague preference, that points another direction.

Are you a non-coder who needs a whole working product, back end and all? Some builders need the entire thing — logins, saved data, the machinery underneath — without wanting to learn or assemble any of it. If the back end is the part that scares you and you just want it handled, that points a third direction.

Do you want the most hands-off, all-included, get-it-deployed experience? Some projects are best served by describing the app and letting an agent take it all the way to a running URL with the least manual work. If maximum autonomy is what you are after, that points a fourth.

Notice that these can pull against each other — the tool best at portability is not the most hands-off, the most polished is not the most back-end-complete. That tension is exactly why there is no single winner. You are not looking for the best tool. You are looking for the tool that matches your *most important* answer.

Finding Your Most Important Answer

That last phrase — *most important* answer — is where people get stuck, because most projects say yes to more than one question. Of course you would *like* a polished interface, *and* portability, *and* a handled back end, *and* maximum autonomy. Who wouldn't. The work of choosing is not collecting wants; it is ranking them, and then being willing to trade the others for the one at the top.

The way to find the top is to imagine the project failing for lack of each thing, and see which failure you cannot accept. If your app shipped on time, worked correctly, and was easy to move later, but looked amateurish — is that a failure? For a public marketing page, yes, fatally; the look *was* the product. For an internal tool only your five coworkers will ever see, the ugly version is completely fine, and "interface is the point" was never your real answer. Run the same test on portability: if you could never move this app off its original platform, does the project die? For a weekend prototype you will throw away after the demo, no — you will never move it, so the lock-in is free. For the core system you are betting a business on, maybe yes, and portability climbs to the top.

This imagined-failure test cuts through the wishful thinking, because it forces you to distinguish a *preference* (nice to have, would not kill the project) from a *requirement* (its absence is fatal). You usually have exactly one or two real requirements and a pile of preferences dressed up as requirements. Find the requirement. That is your most important answer, and it is the one that picks your tool.

One more honest note on how to weight the four questions: if you are a genuine non-coder and the back end is the part that frightens you, let that fear carry more weight than it might seem to deserve. The reason is that an unhandled back end does not merely make a project harder — it can stop it dead. A beautiful interface with no working data storage is a picture of an app, not an app. So "I need the whole thing handled" tends to be a true requirement for non-coders far more often than "it must be portable," which is frequently a preference borrowed from advice written for developers.

The Four, Matched to the Need

Here is each builder reduced to the job it is unmistakably best at — the one-line version of the four chapters you just read. Think of these as the labels on the four vehicles.

Reach for v0 (Chapter 4) when the interface carries the weight. Its gift is taste — front-end work that looks like a professional with an eye made it, from a sentence. The early-2026 rebuild made it genuinely full-stack, so it is no longer only a front-end tool, but the look remains its home court. Its cost is gravity: it pulls hardest toward its parent company's ecosystem, which is wonderful if you live there and a coupling to weigh if you do not.

Reach for Bolt (Chapter 5) when you need to take your work anywhere. Its gift is portability — standard code, easy export, deploy wherever you like, walk away whenever you want. It builds genuine full-stack apps in a real in-browser environment. Its cost is mechanical: token consumption rises as your project grows, so large, heavily edited apps get expensive to keep working on. Deliberate prompting (Chapter 9) is how you manage it.

Reach for Lovable (Chapter 6) when you are a non-coder who wants a complete product. Its gift is the included back end — logins and a real database handled for you through its bundled cloud, so the part that stops most people simply gets taken off your plate. And it syncs to GitHub, so the friendliness does not lock you in. Its cost is the one the sticker price hides: the infrastructure underneath has its own bill as your app grows, so the true cost of ownership is more than the subscription.

Reach for Replit (Chapter 7) when you want the most hands-off path to a deployed app. Its gift is end-to-end autonomy — an agent that plans, builds, runs, fixes its own errors, and deploys, inside a complete cloud environment with database and hosting included. Its cost is the mirror image of Bolt's gift: the app is woven tightly into Replit's platform, so it carries the highest friction if you ever want to move it.

If you read those four and one of them made you think "that's my project," trust that. The match is usually clearer than people expect once they are honest about what they actually need rather than what sounds most impressive.

Three Projects, Three Choices

Abstractions are easy to nod along to and hard to apply, so let me walk three concrete projects through the decision, because seeing the reasoning beats memorizing the rule.

A consultant needs a one-page site to pitch her services and capture leads. What is the center? The look — this page *is* her professional first impression, and an amateurish version actively costs her clients. The back end is trivial (a contact form). Portability is a non-issue; she will never "migrate" a marketing page, and if she rebuilds it in two years she will start fresh anyway. Run the imagined-failure test: an ugly version fails, a non-portable version does not. Her requirement is "interface is the point," and v0 is the obvious pick. Its gravity toward Vercel's ecosystem is, for her, not a cost at all — it just means the easiest possible path to putting the page live.

A small nonprofit wants an internal tool to track volunteer sign-ups, with logins so each coordinator sees their own events. What is the center? A whole working product, back end and all — logins and saved data are the entire substance of the thing, and nobody on staff writes code. The look needs to be clean but not dazzling; it is internal. Portability is a preference at best. The requirement is "non-coder who needs the whole thing handled," and Lovable's bundled back end is built for exactly this. The honest caveat from Chapter 6 applies — the infrastructure underneath carries its own growing bill — so they should watch the true cost of ownership as the volunteer base grows, but the match is clean.

A founder wants to test whether an idea has legs by getting something clickable in front of real users this week. What is the center? Speed to a deployed, working thing, with the least manual assembly — the goal is to *learn*, fast, not to build something permanent. The look matters only enough to not embarrass; portability is irrelevant because if the idea works he will rebuild it properly with a real team anyway. The requirement is "most hands-off, get-it-deployed," and Replit's autonomous Agent is the shortest road from sentence to live URL. The lock-in that worries other people is, for a throwaway validation prototype, completely free — he is never moving this app; he is going to delete it.

Notice what each example has in common: the choice fell out of one honestly identified requirement, and the supposed downside of each tool turned out to be irrelevant *for that project*. That is the whole method. The downsides are real, but they only bite when they collide with one of your actual requirements — and usually they do not.

The Trade-Off Nobody Escapes: Convenience Versus Freedom

There is one tension running underneath all four tools that deserves to be named on its own, because it will shape your experience more than any feature list, and because it is genuinely a *trade* rather than a problem to be solved.

The more a tool does for you — the more it includes, handles, and hides — the more your app tends to depend on that tool. The more a tool leaves in your hands and your standard, portable code, the more it asks you to manage yourself. Replit sits at one end: maximally convenient, maximally coupled. Bolt sits at the other: maximally portable, more hands-on. v0 and Lovable fall in between, each with its own flavor of the trade — v0 convenient-but-coupled toward one ecosystem, Lovable beginner-friendly but honest enough to leave a GitHub exit open.

Here is the thing to internalize: neither end is right or wrong. For a quick prototype, an internal tool, a personal project — anything where you are testing an idea or serving a small, contained need — convenience wins easily, and the coupling never costs you a thing, because you are never going to move the app anyway. For something you suspect will grow, outlast its first home, and need to relocate to real infrastructure someday, freedom is worth paying for in extra effort now. The mistake is not picking one end. The mistake is picking one without knowing you were choosing. Chapters 23 and 25 — on lock-in and on the prototype-versus-production line — go deeper here; for now, just hold the spectrum in your head as you choose, and ask which end *this particular project* belongs at.

The reason this trade is so easy to get wrong is that the cost of convenience is invisible at the moment you pay it and only shows up later, while the cost of freedom is visible immediately and the payoff comes later. When you start, the convenient tool feels like a gift and the portable one feels like more work — because that is literally true on day one. The asymmetry tempts everyone toward convenience, which is the right call far more often than not, *provided you chose it on purpose*. The regret stories I hear almost never come from people who knowingly traded portability for speed on a prototype. They come from people who picked the convenient tool without thinking, watched the project quietly become important, and discovered the coupling only when they tried to leave. The fix is not to fear convenience. It is to ask, once, honestly, at the start: is this a thing I might someday need to move? If the answer is a clear no, take the convenience and never look back. If it is a real maybe, weight freedom more heavily than it feels like it deserves on day one.

A Note on Cost, Since It Shapes the Choice Too

The four questions are about the shape of your project, but money is its own quiet decider, and it is worth a word here even though Chapter 21 handles it in full. The tools price differently, and the differences interact with how you build. v0 and Bolt meter by tokens or credits, so a small app is cheap and a large, heavily edited one costs more — and with Bolt specifically, the cost of each edit rises as the project grows, which is its defining economic quirk. Replit meters by the Agent's *effort*, so one ambitious instruction can trigger a long, billable stretch of work. Lovable's subscription hides a second bill: the bundled infrastructure underneath has its own costs as your app and its data grow.

The practical upshot for choosing is this. If your project is small and exploratory, none of these cost structures will bite, and you can safely ignore the whole topic and pick on project shape alone. If your project is genuinely going to be large or heavily used, fold cost into the decision: Bolt's edit-cost-grows-with-size quirk argues for keeping its projects focused, Replit's effort pricing rewards scoped requests, and Lovable's hidden infrastructure bill belongs in your true-cost-of-ownership math. As of mid-2026 the headline prices cluster in a similar range across the four — free tiers to start, paid tiers from the low twenties to around a hundred dollars a month — but the numbers move constantly, so treat any figure in this book as a snapshot and check the current pricing page before you commit.

The Mistakes That Send People to the Wrong Tool

Since the method is "find your one real requirement," it is worth naming the predictable ways people miss it, because the wrong choice almost always traces back to one of a handful of errors rather than to genuinely bad luck.

Choosing by the most impressive feature instead of the most relevant one. A tool's flashiest capability is rarely the one your project needs. Replit's self-correcting autonomy is genuinely dazzling in a demo, and people pick it for projects whose actual requirement was a polished public interface — for which the dazzle is irrelevant and v0 would have served better. The corrective is to ignore what impressed you and return to your imagined-failure test: the feature that matters is the one whose *absence* would sink the project, not the one that made the best video.

Borrowing a developer's priorities when you are not a developer. Much of the advice online about these tools is written by and for people who code, and for them portability and code quality loom large. A non-coder who absorbs that advice can end up ranking "must be portable" above "must have a working back end I don't have to build" — exactly backwards for their situation, where an unhandled back end is fatal and portability is a someday-maybe. Read advice for who wrote it. Your requirement is yours, not the author's.

Treating the first choice as permanent. People agonize over the decision as if picking wrong means months lost, which inflates every preference into a requirement and freezes them. As the close of this chapter insists, switching is usually an afternoon for a small project, and the core skill transfers intact. The stakes of choosing are real but small, and overestimating them produces worse choices, not better ones, because fear of a wrong pick drives people toward the tool that *sounds* safest rather than the one that fits.

Letting a friend's enthusiasm stand in for your requirement. "My colleague built something great in X" is a data point about your colleague's project, not yours. If their requirement matched the tool and yours does not, their success tells you nothing useful. Hear the recommendation, then run your own imagined-failure test before you let it decide anything.

Permission to Just Pick One

I will close with the advice I most often give in person, because the analysis above can paralyze as easily as it can clarify. If you have a clear answer to one of the four questions, pick the matching tool and start — the match is real, and you will feel it working. If you genuinely cannot tell which question is your center, that is itself useful information: it usually means your project is small or exploratory enough that *any* of them will do, in which case pick the one whose chapter you found most appealing and begin. You learn more from one afternoon of actually building than from a week of comparing.

And remember that this is rarely a marriage. You can try a tool, find it does not fit, and move — the skill comes with you, and for a small project the cost of switching is an afternoon, not a catastrophe. The point of these five chapters was never to lock you into a perfect first choice. It was to make sure that when you choose, you are choosing on the things that actually matter — the shape of your project and what you need from it — rather than on a headline or a hunch. With that, Part II is done. The next part stops talking about the tools and starts building with them, beginning with the single most important skill that works in all four: describing what you want well enough that the machine can build it.

Part III: Building Your First App

Audience: everyone.

"The distance between a sentence and a running app is now an afternoon. The distance between a running app and a good one is still entirely up to you."

— A working principle

Chapter 9: Describing What You Want: Prompting an App

Two people sit down with the same builder, on the same afternoon, to make roughly the same thing — a small page to collect feedback from event attendees. One types a single sentence: "build me a feedback app." The other types a short paragraph: who would use the page, what they would do on it, what one screen should show, and what should happen when someone hits submit. An hour later the first is frustrated and convinced the tool is hype; the app it gave her is a generic, pretty shell that does none of the things she actually needed, and every attempt to fix it breaks something else. The second has a working tool. Same software. Same skill level — both of them non-coders. The only difference was how they described what they wanted.

That difference is the most useful thing I can teach you in this whole book, and it is also the most undersold. The marketing for these tools leans hard on the idea that you just say what you want and magic happens. The truth is closer to this: the tool is a very fast, very literal builder who will cheerfully build *exactly* what you describe, including all the parts you forgot to mention. The quality of your app is, to a startling degree, the quality of your description. This chapter is about how to describe well — not as a coding skill, but as a thinking-and-communicating skill you mostly already have.

Scope Before You Type

The single most common mistake is asking for too much at once. "Build me a project management app like Asana" is not a prompt; it is a year of someone's job compressed into seven words. The AI will try, because it always tries, and it will hand you a sprawling, half-working approximation of an enormous product, with a hundred things subtly wrong and no clear place to start fixing them. You will be lost, and so will the tool.

Before you write a word, decide what the *smallest version* of your idea is — the one screen, the one job, the core thing the app must do for it to be worth anything at all. My friend the teacher in Chapter 1 did not ask for a school management system. She asked for a page where students could see open slots and book one.

That is a scoped idea: one user, one action, one screen. You can always grow it afterward, one request at a time, and you should. But the first thing you describe should be small enough that you could explain it to a stranger in a single breath.

The test is whether you can name the core action. "A page where someone *books a slot*." "A form where a customer *submits a request*." "A dashboard where I *see this week's orders*." If you cannot finish the sentence "the main thing a user does here is ___," your idea is not scoped yet, and no amount of prompting cleverness will rescue it.

A useful trick for finding the core action when an idea feels too big is to ask what the app would have to do to be worth opening *even once*. Strip away everything else. For the project-management dream, the answer might be "see a list of my tasks and check them off." That is the seed. Logins, projects, teammates, due dates, comments, file attachments — all of that is growth you add later, after the seed is alive and working. People resist this because the small version feels embarrassingly modest next to the vision in their head. But the small version *exists* by dinnertime, and the grand version exists only as a frustration. A working modest thing you can grow always beats a broken ambitious thing you cannot fix.

Why "Too Much at Once" Fails, Mechanically

It helps to understand *why* a giant first prompt reliably disappoints, because the reason is not that the tool is dumb — it is structural, and knowing it changes how you work. When you ask for fifteen features in one breath, you are asking the AI to make fifteen sets of decisions simultaneously, every one of which depends on assumptions about the others, and you have given it no chance to check any of them with you. It guesses on all fifteen at once. Some guesses are fine; several are wrong; and because they were all built together, the wrong ones are now tangled into the right ones. You cannot pull one bad thread without disturbing the rest.

Compare that to building the seed first. When the app does one thing and does it correctly, every later request lands on solid, understood ground. The tool has a small, working thing to reason about, not a sprawling half-built one. And *you* have a small, working thing to inspect, so when the next feature goes wrong you know it was the next feature — the problem is isolated, named, and cheap to fix. Scope is not just about not overwhelming the tool. It is about keeping the app in a state where every problem has exactly one suspect.

Be Specific About the Things That Matter

Once you have the scope, the next move is to be specific where specificity changes the outcome and vague where it does not. You do not need to describe colors and fonts in your first prompt — the tool has good default taste and you can steer the look later. What you *do* need to describe is the behavior: what data the app handles, who does what, and what happens at the moments that matter.

Vague: "Let people sign up." Specific: "Visitors enter their name and email and pick one of the available time slots; once a slot is booked, it should no longer be available to anyone else." That second version answers the questions the AI would otherwise guess at, usually wrong: does booking remove the slot? Can two people grab the same one? What information are we collecting? Every ambiguity you leave is a decision you are handing to a machine that does not know your situation and will resolve it in whatever way is easiest to build.

I think of it as the difference between describing a *picture* and describing a *mechanism*. The look is a picture, and you can react your way to it. The behavior is a mechanism, and mechanisms have to be specified, because the tool cannot infer the rule you have in your head. When something matters — money, access, who can see what — say it plainly and say it early.

The Questions a Builder Silently Answers For You

To make "be specific about what matters" practical, here is the move that has helped non-coders most: before you send a prompt, picture the AI as a literal-minded contractor who, for every detail you leave out, will make the cheapest reasonable choice and never mention it. Then ask yourself what choices you are silently delegating. There are four families of question worth checking every time.

Who can do what? The tool will assume the simplest answer unless you say otherwise — usually that anyone can do anything. If your booking page should let students book but only *you* see the full list of bookings, that is a rule you must state, because the cheap default is "everyone sees everything." Access is the single most common thing people forget to specify and the most expensive to get wrong, because it is exactly where data leaks and privacy mistakes live.

What happens at the edges? The happy path — the everything-goes-right case — is what the tool builds by default. The edges are what it skips: What happens when two people try to book the same slot at the same moment? When someone submits the form with the email field blank? When there are zero available slots to show? You do not have to anticipate every edge, but the ones that matter to your situation should be named, because the tool will otherwise either ignore them or handle them in some way you would not have chosen.

What exactly is the data? "Save the booking" is vague; the tool has to invent what a booking *is*. Tell it: "Each booking has a student name, an email, a date and time, and a status that's either confirmed or cancelled." Now there is no guessing about the shape of the thing you are storing, which prevents a whole class of "it saved, but not the field I needed" surprises.

What does success look like, concretely? "It should work" is not a finish line the tool can aim at. "After a student books, the slot disappears from the list and the student sees a confirmation with their booked time" is. The more concretely you can describe the state of the world *after* the action succeeds, the more accurately the tool can build toward it — and the more precisely you can later test whether it actually did.

You will not need to answer all four for every feature. But running through them takes ten seconds and reliably surfaces the one or two silent decisions that, left to the tool, would have produced the wrong app.

Build in Steps, Not in One Breath

Here is a habit that separates people who get good results from people who don't: they do not try to describe the whole app in one giant prompt. They describe the core, look at what they get, and then add to it in deliberate steps.

There are two reasons this works better. The first is that you can catch a wrong turn early, while it is cheap to fix, instead of discovering it buried inside a finished-looking app where every change risks toppling three others. The second is more subtle and more important: these tools genuinely lose the thread on very large, very complex single requests. Ask for fifteen features in one message and you will reliably get some of them wrong, some of them missing, and no clear way to tell the tool which. Ask for the core, confirm it works, then add the email notification, then add the cancel button — and each step is small enough that the tool gets it right and you can see plainly whether it did.

There is a sequencing instinct worth developing here too: build the foundation before the decoration, and build the thing other things depend on before the things that depend on it. For the booking page, the sensible order is: first the list of slots (the foundation), then booking a slot (the core action), then saving bookings so they persist, then the owner's view of bookings, then niceties like a confirmation message or an email notification. Notice that each step rests on the one before — you cannot meaningfully test "the owner sees bookings" until bookings actually save, and you cannot test booking until slots exist to book. Adding a feature whose foundation is not yet in place just gives the tool more to guess at. When you are unsure what to ask for next, ask: what does the next thing I want *depend on*, and is that already built and working?

This is the rhythm of the whole craft, and Chapter 14 is devoted to it: build a little, look, react, build a little more. Your first prompt should establish the foundation. Everything after is steering.

Give Examples Instead of Adjectives

When you want the app to look or behave a certain way, the most powerful thing you can hand the AI is not an adjective but an example. "Make it look professional" means almost nothing — professional to whom? "Make it look like a clean, minimal booking page, similar to how Calendly looks" gives the tool a concrete target it actually understands. The same goes for behavior and content: if you want the app to handle a particular case, describe that case. "When someone tries to book a slot that was just taken, show them a message saying it's no longer available and let them pick another" is worth more than "handle errors gracefully," because it tells the tool the specific thing you mean.

This extends to data. If your app works with information that has a particular shape — a customer record, an order, an appointment — describe a real example of it. "Each booking has a student name, a date and time, and a status that's either confirmed or cancelled." Concrete examples collapse a hundred guesses into one clear instruction, and they are something you can produce without knowing anything about code, because you are simply describing the thing you already understand.

The reason examples beat adjectives is that adjectives are *your* compression of something specific into something vague, and the tool has to decompress them back into specifics — guessing at exactly the detail you had in mind and threw away. “Professional,” “modern,” “clean,” “user-friendly,” “intuitive”: every one of these is a word that means something precise in your head and nothing reliable on the page. When you catch yourself reaching for one, stop and ask what concrete thing you actually mean. “Modern” might mean “lots of white space and a single accent color.” “User-friendly” might mean “the booking takes one click, not a multi-step form.” Say *that*. The discipline of converting your adjectives into examples and concrete states is, more than anything else, what separates a description the tool can build from a wish it can only approximate.

Steer, Don’t Dump

There is a temptation, when something is not working, to respond by writing an enormous prompt — a wall of every concern, correction, and new idea all at once, as if volume will force the tool to finally understand. It almost never helps. A long, unfocused dump gives the AI too many targets, and it will hit some and miss others, and you will not be able to tell which instruction caused which result.

Steering means the opposite: one clear change at a time, stated plainly, so that you can see its effect before you move on. “Move the submit button to the bottom of the form.” Look. “Now make the date field required.” Look. This feels slower, and over a whole build it is dramatically faster, because you are never untangling a knot of five changes to figure out which one broke things. You are a director giving one note at a time, not a client emailing a novel of feedback.

When the tool clearly misunderstood, restate — don’t pile on. If you asked for something and got the wrong thing, resist the urge to add three more requirements on top. Stop, and rephrase the original request more concretely. The misunderstanding will only compound if you bury it under new instructions.

There is a sharper failure mode worth naming, because it traps people for an hour at a time: the doom loop, where you ask for a fix, it does not work, you ask again slightly differently, that does not work either, and you keep going, each attempt leaving the app a little more tangled than before. When you notice you are on the third or fourth try at the same thing, stop pushing. The loop almost never breaks by trying once more. Instead, do one of three things. Back up to the last version that worked — every tool in this book keeps some form of history, and rolling back to known-good ground is faster than digging out of a hole. Or restate the goal from scratch, describing the *outcome you want* rather than the fix you have been requesting, because you may have been steering toward your own wrong diagnosis. Or break the stuck thing into smaller pieces and confirm each piece separately, since a fix that fails as one big request sometimes lands cleanly as three small ones. The skill is not getting the fix right the first time; it is recognizing the loop early and changing tactics instead of feeding it.

What This Is Not

A few honest cautions, because describing well is a skill with real limits.

Good prompting does not rescue a bad idea. If you have not thought through what the app should actually do — who uses it, what problem it solves, what the rules are — no prompting technique will supply that thinking for you. The tool builds what you describe; it cannot build what you have not decided. The hard part was always the deciding, and it still is.

Good prompting does not make the output safe. You can describe an app perfectly and still ship something that exposes your users' data, because the security failures live underneath the behavior you described, in code you are not reading. Describing well gets you a working app. It does not get you a safe one — that is the separate, non-negotiable work of Chapter 22, and no amount of careful prompting substitutes for it.

The tool will fill silence with assumptions. Anything you do not specify, it decides. Most of the time its decisions are reasonable. Occasionally one of them is exactly wrong for you — it assumes data is public when you needed it private, or that anyone can edit when only the owner should. The discipline is to notice what you have not said about the things that matter, and to say it.

Describing well does not mean describing in code. A surprising number of newcomers think good prompting means learning to talk like a programmer — sprinkling in technical words to sound precise. It does the opposite. The tool already speaks code; what it needs from you is the clear human description of intent that it *cannot* generate on its own. Plain, specific English about who does what and what should happen is exactly the right register. If you find yourself guessing at technical terms, you are doing the tool's job badly instead of doing your own job well.

None of this requires you to think like a programmer. It requires you to think like someone who can describe what they want clearly, in the right order, one piece at a time — which is to say, like a good manager of a fast and literal builder. That is the actual skill. The next four chapters put it to work, building one small app four different ways, so you can feel how the same clear description lands in each of the four tools.

Chapter 10: Your First Build in v0

The first time I built something real in v0, I was struck by how much it felt like watching a competent designer work over my shoulder rather than like talking to a machine. I typed a description, and within a few seconds a clean, properly laid-out interface assembled itself on the right half of the screen — not a wireframe, not a sketch, but a finished-looking page with sensible spacing, real buttons, and the kind of polish that usually takes a front-end developer a day to get right. That polish is v0's whole personality, and it shapes everything about how you should approach your first build here.

To make the next four chapters comparable, we are going to build the same small app in each tool — the booking page from Chapter 1, scoped down: a page that shows available tutoring slots, lets a student book one, and lets the owner see the bookings. It is small enough to finish, real enough to teach something, and it exercises the parts of each tool that actually differ. This chapter does it in v0. The details of v0's plans, model names, and buttons drift on a scale of months — what I describe here is mid-2026, and you should expect the screen to have moved a little by the time you read this — but the shape of the experience is durable.

Getting In and the First Prompt

v0 lives on its own website (run by Vercel, the company behind it), and you sign in and land in front of a single, inviting text box. There is a free tier that is genuinely enough to do everything in this chapter; the paid tiers — something like a Team plan around thirty dollars a user and a Business plan around a hundred, as of this writing, though you should check the current pricing page — raise your usage ceilings rather than unlock fundamentally different magic. v0 meters by tokens or credits, which is a way of saying every message you send and every build it does draws down a budget. For a small app you will not come close to a limit. For a big, sprawling one you might, which is a Chapter 21 conversation.

Following the lesson of Chapter 9, I do not ask for everything. I scope, and I type something like:

> Build a tutoring booking page. Students see a list of available time slots, each showing a date and time. A student can click a slot to book it,

> entering their name and email. Once booked, a slot is no longer available to others. On a separate view, the owner can see all the bookings.

I hit send, and vo thinks, narrates a little of what it is doing, and builds. What comes back, the first time, is usually a strong interface and a partial brain — the page looks right, the slots are there, the form is there, and the polish is real.

Notice what that prompt is doing, because it is Chapter 9 in miniature. It names the core action (a student books a slot). It specifies the mechanism that the tool would otherwise guess wrong (a booked slot becomes unavailable). It names the data the app handles (name, email, date, time). And it scopes hard — there is no mention of cancellation, reminders, payment, or accounts, because those are growth for later, not the seed. A prompt like "build me a booking app" would have produced something prettier than you expected and emptier than you needed; this one gives vo a target it can actually hit.

What to Expect: Beautiful Front, Newer Back

For most of its life, vo's reputation was "the one that makes gorgeous interfaces" — it produces React and Next.js with Tailwind and shadcn under the hood, which are simply the names of the modern tools professional front-end developers use, and it produces them tastefully. If all you needed were a good-looking page, vo was unbeatable and a little one-dimensional.

A major rebuild in early 2026 changed that. vo became genuinely full-stack: it gained a proper code editor (laid out like the professional tool VS Code), the ability to work with a real database, agentic workflows that carry out multi-step builds, version control through Git, and even the ability to import an existing project from GitHub. So the modern vo can stand up the *back* of our app — the part that actually remembers bookings — and not just the front. To do that it connects to an outside database service; as of this writing it works smoothly with providers like Supabase and Neon, which handle storing your data. When our app needs to remember which slots are booked, vo will prompt you to connect one, and once connected, the bookings persist instead of vanishing when you refresh.

It is worth pausing on what "connect a database" actually means here, because for a non-coder it sounds more intimidating than it is. A database is just the app's memory — the place where a booking is written down so it is still there tomorrow. By itself, the interface vo first builds has no memory; it is a beautiful page that forgets everything the moment you refresh, which is exactly why your first version will *look* like it works and not actually save anything. When vo prompts you to connect Supabase or Neon, you are giving the app a notebook to write in. Practically, this means making a free account with the database provider when prompted and letting vo wire the connection — it walks you through it, and you do not need to understand the plumbing, only that this step is the moment your pretty page gains a memory. Skip it or stall on it, and you will have a demo, not a tool.

This connection step is also the most likely place a vo build stalls for a beginner, so it is worth naming the snag in advance. You may have to leave vo briefly to create the database account, copy a key or a connection string back into vo, and confirm the link. None of it is hard, but it is the one moment in an otherwise frictionless build where vo hands you a small chore from the outside world. Expect it, do not be thrown by it, and once it is done the rest of the build returns to the smooth describe-and-steer rhythm.

Expect the visible part to outrun the working part. This is the vo pattern to internalize: the interface will look done before the app *is* done. A slot list can look perfect while not yet actually saving bookings anywhere. This is not a flaw so much as vo's center of gravity — it leads with the surface. Your job is to keep asking "does it actually *do* the thing, or does it just look like it does?" and to test the behavior, not trust the appearance. We are going to repeat that warning in different keys throughout the book, because it is the single most reliable way these tools mislead a non-coder.

Refining the Build

With the first version on screen, the work becomes the steering loop from Chapter 9. I look at what vo made, find what is wrong or missing, and say so, one change at a time:

> When a student books a slot, save the booking so it's still there after a refresh.
>
> On the owner's view, show each booking's student name, email, and the slot they took.

After someone books, show a confirmation message instead of leaving the form on screen.

Each request, v0 carries out and re-renders, and I check the result before moving on. This is also where v0's editor earns its keep: if you are curious, you can open the actual files and *see* the code it wrote. You do not have to — you can build the entire app without reading a line — but the option is there, and it is more present and more central in v0's post-rebuild interface than it used to be. For a non-coder, the value of seeing the code is mostly that it demystifies what is happening: there is no magic, just files, and they are yours.

The most important word in "I check the result before moving on" is *check*, and with v0 specifically it means doing more than glancing at the screen. After "save the booking so it's still there after a refresh," do not accept v0's word that it is done — book a slot, then actually refresh the page, and see whether the booking survived. After "the booked slot becomes unavailable," open the page, book a slot, and confirm that slot is genuinely gone from the list, not merely greyed out for show. v0's gift for polish makes this discipline more necessary here than almost anywhere, because a v0 interface is more than capable of *looking* exactly like a working app while the memory underneath is not yet wired. The test is always behavior, and behavior means clicking the buttons and refreshing the page yourself, not trusting how convincing the surface looks.

A Realistic Snag and How to Steer Out of It

Let me walk through a stumble, because the smooth-build story is only half the truth and you will meet the other half. Suppose, after connecting the database, you book a slot, refresh, and the booking *does* persist — but the booked slot is still showing as available, so a second student could book the same time. The interface looks fine; the rule is broken.

The wrong response is to pile on: "fix the booking and also add an email and also make the confirmation prettier." The right response is the single, concrete steering note from Chapter 9: "When a slot is booked, remove it from the list of available slots so no one else can book the same time. Right now a booked slot still appears as available." That tells v0 exactly the mechanism that is wrong and the state you expect instead. Then test it the same way: book a slot, refresh, confirm it is gone, and — the edge case worth one more click — try to book it a second time and confirm you cannot. If v0 fixes the visible list but you can still sneak a second booking through, you have learned something specific to say next, rather than a vague sense that "it's broken." That is the loop working as designed: narrow problem, narrow instruction, behavioral test, repeat.

Exporting and Deploying

Here is where v0's biggest strength and its biggest tradeoff sit in the same place. v0 is made by Vercel, and Vercel's core business is hosting and deploying web apps. So when your app is ready, putting it live is about as smooth as this gets: a deploy to Vercel is a click or two, you get a real public URL, and the app is on the internet for other people to use. Nothing in the four tools makes the *deploy* step feel more native than v0, because for v0 it is the home turf.

The flip side is coupling. v0 is the most tightly woven into its parent company's ecosystem of the four builders in this book. That is wonderful while you are inside it and a consideration the moment you think about leaving. The good news, and it is real, is that v0 does let you export your code to GitHub — your project becomes a normal repository of standard code that a developer could pick up and run elsewhere. So you are not trapped; the door out is genuine. But the path of least resistance, the whole design, gently keeps you in the Vercel world, and the further you build, the more that world's conveniences become assumptions. We deal with this honestly under the heading of lock-in in Chapter 23; for now, just know that v0's deploy experience is the easiest you will meet, and that ease has a direction to it.

One practical note before you click deploy, because it is the first moment your app stops being a private sketch and becomes something the world can reach. The polished, working-looking page you are about to put live is exactly the thing whose underneath you have not inspected — and if real people are going to put real names and emails into it, the gap between "looks done" and "is safe" stops being theoretical. For our booking page, deployed for a class you teach, the stakes are modest. But the instinct to build the discipline now: before you deploy anything that collects other people's information, the work of Chapter 22 is not optional, and the smoothness of v0's deploy button is precisely what can lull you into skipping it. Deploying is easy here on purpose. Deploying *responsibly* is the same amount of work it is everywhere.

When the Code Window Is Worth Opening

v0's post-rebuild editor sits there the whole time, and a non-coder's honest question is: should I ever open it, or is it just noise meant for developers? The truthful answer is that you can build and ship this entire booking page without opening it once — but there are two specific moments when a glance pays off, and knowing them spares you from either ignoring a useful tool or drowning in detail you do not need.

The first moment is when you are stuck in the doom loop from Chapter 9 — you have asked for the same fix three times and it is not landing. Opening the file v0 keeps changing and simply *reading the words*, even without understanding the code, sometimes reveals the problem in plain sight: a field named "email" in one place and "e-mail" in another, a slot list that is hard-coded with three example slots rather than drawing from saved data. You are not debugging; you are spotting an inconsistency a human eye catches even when the meaning is opaque. More than once that glance has handed me the concrete sentence I needed — "the slots are hard-coded, make them come from the database instead" — that the vague "it's not working" never would have.

The second moment is when you want to confirm that something you care about is real rather than cosmetic. If the app is supposed to keep a booked slot from being rebooked, and you want to be sure the rule is enforced and not just hidden in the display, the code is where the truth lives. You do not have to read it fluently; you can paste a section back into the chat and ask v0 plainly, "does this actually prevent two people booking the same slot, or does it just hide the slot in the list?" Using the tool to interpret its own output is a legitimate and underused move, and it converts the editor from a wall of intimidation into a second source you can cross-examine.

Outside those two moments, leave it closed. The value of v0 showing you the code is not that you must read it; it is that nothing is hidden from you when you need it. For a non-coder, that is the right relationship to have with the machinery: ignore it by default, consult it on purpose.

Growing the Seed: What the Page Still Lacks

The booking page we built is the seed from Chapter 9 — one screen, one core action — and it is worth being honest about everything it is *not* yet, because the gaps are where the next afternoon of work lives and because some of them are not obvious from the working surface.

It has no accounts. Anyone with the link can book, and the "owner's view" is owner-only by convention, not by enforcement — which is to say, right now nothing actually stops a student from opening the owner's view if they find it. For a page you share privately with your own students that may be perfectly fine; the moment it is not, "only the owner can see all bookings" stops being a layout choice and becomes a real access rule you have to state and v0 has to enforce, which is the territory of Chapter 16 on authentication. This is exactly the kind of silent assumption Chapter 9 warned about: the cheap default is "everyone can see everything," and a tidy-looking owner page can hide the fact that the lock on the door is painted on.

It has no notifications. Nobody gets an email when a booking comes in, so the owner has to remember to check the page. Adding "email me when someone books" is a natural next step, and it is also the point where the app reaches outside itself to an email service — the connecting-to-services work of Chapter 17 — which is a meaningfully different kind of feature from anything we have added so far.

It does not handle the awkward real-world cases. What happens when there are no slots left to show? When a student mistypes their email? When someone wants to cancel? None of these crashed our happy-path demo, which is precisely why they are easy to ship without noticing — they only surface when a real user does the thing you did not test. Each is a one-sentence addition to the steering loop, but each is also a decision you now get to make deliberately rather than discover later.

I list these not to diminish what an hour produced — a real, working, deployed booking page is a genuine accomplishment — but to locate it accurately. What you have is a sound seed, and the chapters of Part IV are the deliberate growth: real accounts, real data, real connections, real polish. The point of building the seed first was never that the seed is the whole tree. It was that a living seed you can grow beats a sprawling, broken sketch you cannot.

Where v0 Fits

By the end of an hour, the booking page exists, it works, and — this being v0 — it looks markedly nicer than you had any right to expect for an hour's effort. That is the right summary of the tool. If your project leans heavily on a polished, professional interface, if you are comfortable in or curious about the Vercel ecosystem, or if you want the smoothest possible road from idea to deployed page, v0 is a superb first stop. Its newfound full-stack ability means it is no longer only a pretty-front-end machine; it can build the whole thing.

What v0 will not do is protect you from the gap between looking finished and being finished — if anything, its gift for polish *widens* that gap, because the surface is so convincing. Hold onto the discipline of testing behavior over trusting appearance; it matters in every tool, and it matters most precisely where the surface is most convincing. The same app feels markedly different built in Bolt, where the machinery is right out in the open.

Chapter 11: Your First Build in Bolt

The thing that surprised me about building in Bolt was watching an actual terminal scroll past — the kind of black-and-text developer console you associate with people who know what they are doing — installing packages, starting a server, reporting errors and fixing them, all inside my browser tab. I had not installed anything. I had not set up a development environment, the famously miserable first step that has scared off generations of would-be programmers. And yet a real one was running, right there on a web page, doing the things a real one does. That is Bolt's signature trick, and once you understand it, you understand why Bolt feels different from v0 in a way that matters.

We are building the same app as last chapter — the tutoring booking page: students see available slots, book one with their name and email, a booked slot disappears for everyone else, and the owner can view the bookings. Building it in Bolt will surface a different set of strengths and a different honest limit. As always, the specifics here are mid-2026 and the prices and model names drift monthly; treat them as a snapshot, not a contract.

A Real Development Environment, In Your Browser

Bolt is made by StackBlitz, and its defining technology — WebContainers, introduced in Chapter 5 — is what you are watching at work here: a genuine Node.js development environment running entirely inside your browser, nothing installed, no server rented. When you build in Bolt, you are not looking at a simulation or a preview service. You are looking at real code, really running, on your own machine, in a tab.

Why should a non-coder care about a piece of plumbing? Because it changes what you can see and trust. In Bolt, the files are right there, the running app is right there, the errors are right there, and when the AI fixes something you can watch it happen in the actual environment rather than taking a remote service's word for it. There is a transparency to it. Where v0 leads with a polished surface, Bolt leads with the honest machinery — which, for some people, is reassuring, and for others is more than they wanted to see. Both reactions are valid.

It is worth getting comfortable with what that scrolling terminal is actually telling you, because beginners often find it alarming and it is mostly mundane. Most of what scrolls past is bookkeeping: Bolt downloading the standard building blocks the app needs (the "installing packages" step), then starting the program, then noting that the app is now running and reachable in the preview pane. You do not need to read it line by line. The one thing worth learning to spot is a line that turns red or says "error" — that is the app telling you something went wrong, and as we will see, it is usually the same line Bolt itself reads to fix the problem. You can treat the terminal the way you treat the engine noise in a car: you do not need to understand every sound, but a sudden bad one is worth noticing. The rest is the normal hum of a real environment doing real work.

The First Prompt and the In-Browser Feel

You reach Bolt at bolt.new, sign in, and meet a prompt box much like the others. There is a free tier to start, and a Pro plan in the rough neighborhood of twenty to twenty-five dollars a month as of this writing — sources disagree on the exact figure, so check the current pricing page rather than trust mine. I give it the same scoped description I gave v0:

> Build a tutoring booking page. Students see a list of available time slots with dates and times, and can click one to book it by entering their name and email. A booked slot becomes unavailable to others. On a separate view, the owner can see all bookings.

Bolt goes to work, and here the experience diverges from v0. You watch it create the project files, install the dependencies it needs, and boot up the app — all narrated in that scrolling environment. When it finishes, the live app appears in a preview pane, and crucially, it is a *full-stack* app from the start: Bolt is comfortable building both the interface and the working logic behind it in one go, rather than leading with the front and bolting on the back later.

That difference from v0 is worth dwelling on, because it changes the rhythm of the first ten minutes. With v0, you got a beautiful page that did not yet remember anything, and "give it a memory" was a distinct later step you had to initiate. With Bolt, the working logic tends to arrive *with* the interface — the first version is more likely to actually save a booking, because Bolt's instinct is to build the whole stack at once rather than lead with the surface. This does not exempt you from testing behavior; a first version can still be wrong in a dozen ways. But the failure mode is different. v0's classic first-version gap is "looks done, has no memory." Bolt's is more likely to be "the whole thing is roughly there but rough" — a working but unpolished app rather than a polished but hollow one. Knowing which gap your tool leans toward tells you what to check first.

The feel is "developer workshop," not "design studio." That is the cleanest way I can put the v0-versus-Bolt difference. v0 makes you feel like you are art-directing. Bolt makes you feel like you are standing in a workshop where a build is happening and you can see every tool on the bench. Neither is better in the abstract; they suit different temperaments and different projects.

The Honest Limit: Token Burn Scales With Your Project

Now the part I would be doing you a disservice to skip, because it is Bolt's most important practical limit and the one new users hit without warning.

Bolt, like the others, meters by tokens — every message you send and every change it makes draws down a budget you are paying for. The wrinkle Chapter 5 named is the one to feel here in practice: because of how its in-browser environment works, the whole growing filesystem gets synced to the model on every message, so the cost of each change rises with the size of your project. On a small app like our booking page, this is a non-issue — you will sail through. But on a large, sprawling app, the cost of each tiny change creeps upward, sometimes startlingly.

The mechanism is the one Chapter 5 laid out: the model has to be re-shown your whole project to make any change safely, and you pay for that re-showing on every message, so a forty-file app costs far more per edit than a three-file one. The counterintuitive consequence is the part that catches people here: the cost of an edit is not about the size of the edit but the size of the *project the edit lands in*, which means a trivial change to a big app can cost more than a substantial change to a small one. Small change does not mean small cost, and with Bolt's design that surprises people.

This is not a hidden gotcha so much as a structural tradeoff of the very transparency that makes Bolt feel honest. The same design that lets you see the real environment is the design that makes big projects expensive to keep editing. The practical advice: keep your Bolt projects focused, do not let them balloon into kitchen-sink monsters, and watch your token usage on anything substantial.

There is a habit that follows directly from the mechanism above: batch your thinking, not your prompts. Because each message carries the whole project's weight, sending ten half-formed tweaks costs you ten full round-trips, while thinking for a moment and sending one clear, complete instruction costs you one. This pulls in slight tension with Chapter 9's "one change at a time," and the resolution is judgment: keep each instruction focused on one outcome you can test, but do not fire off sloppy, half-considered messages you will immediately need to correct, because on Bolt every correction is another full-freight trip. We treat the economics of all four tools properly in Chapter 21; here I just want it on the record that with Bolt, *project size is a cost*, in a way it is not quite for the others.

Refining, and Watching It Fix Itself

The refine loop in Bolt has a particular pleasure to it, which is watching the tool catch and fix its own errors in real time. Because a real environment is running, when something breaks, Bolt often *sees* the error in the running app and corrects it without you having to do anything — the terminal throws a red message, Bolt reads it, adjusts the code, and the preview reloads working. It is the closest thing in these tools to watching a developer debug.

This is the moment that scrolling terminal pays off, and it is worth understanding the loop because it tells you when to trust the tool and when to step in. The loop is: the program runs, hits a problem, prints the problem to the terminal as an error, and Bolt reads that error as its own next input and writes a fix. It works beautifully when the problem announces itself as a clear error — a missing piece, a typo in the code, a step done out of order. Where it cannot help is the class of problem that does *not* throw an error: a feature that runs perfectly and does the wrong thing. If Bolt builds a booking form that saves to the wrong place but does not crash, no red line appears in the terminal, so the self-fix loop never triggers, and Bolt may cheerfully report success. That is precisely the gap your own testing fills. The terminal catches the errors that *are* errors; you catch the behavior that is wrong-but-not-broken. Between the two of you, most things get caught — but only if you do your half.

I steer the same way I did in v0, one change at a time:

> Save bookings so they persist after a refresh.

On the owner's view, list each booking with the student's name, email, and chosen slot.

Prevent two people from booking the same slot.

Each change happens in the live environment, and I test the behavior rather than trust the look — the same discipline from the last chapter, no less necessary here just because the machinery is visible. Take that third instruction as the worked example, because it is the one most likely to expose a wrong-but-not-broken bug. After Bolt reports it has prevented double-booking, the test is not to read its confirmation; it is to open the app, book a slot, and then deliberately try to book the same slot again — ideally noticing what happens if two bookings race for the last open time. If the second booking sails through, nothing crashed, no terminal error fired, and only your own test caught it. Then you have the specific next note: "I was able to book the same slot twice. Once a slot is booked, no one else should be able to select it." Narrow problem, narrow instruction, behavioral test — the loop from Chapter 9, running inside the workshop.

Exporting and Deploying: The Most Portable Output

Here is where Bolt has a genuine, durable advantage over every other tool in this book, and it is worth stating plainly: Bolt produces the most portable output of the four.

Because Bolt builds with standard code in a standard environment, what you end up with is an ordinary project that runs anywhere an ordinary project runs. You can export it to GitHub as a normal repository. You can deploy it to Bolt's own hosting, or to Netlify (a popular host Bolt integrates with directly), or honestly to almost anywhere that hosts web apps. Nothing about the output is locked to Bolt. If you handed the exported project to a developer and said "take this and run with it," they could, with no special unwinding of proprietary anything. The door out is not just open; there is barely a door, because Bolt never closed you in.

It is worth being precise about why this matters and when it does not, so you weigh it honestly rather than treating "portable" as automatically good. Portability is insurance, and like all insurance it has a cost — Bolt asks a little more of you up front and meters in a way that punishes sprawl — and a payoff you may never collect. If your booking page is for one class you teach and you will never move it, the portability is real but worthless *to you*, the way a flood policy is worthless to someone on a hilltop. Where it earns its keep is the project that quietly becomes important: the internal tool a whole department starts depending on, the prototype that attracts real users and needs to grow up onto serious infrastructure. For those, the day you want to hand the code to a developer or move it to a dedicated host, Bolt's standard output means that day is an ordinary afternoon rather than a rebuild. So the value of Bolt's portability is not "more is better"; it is "exactly as much as the odds that this project outgrows its first home." Chapter 8's imagined-failure test is the right way to estimate those odds before you choose.

This portability is the counterweight to the token-burn limit, and the two together describe Bolt's whole character honestly: it shows you the real machinery, which costs more to keep editing as you grow, but leaves you with code that is genuinely, unambiguously yours to take anywhere. We will lean on that fact in Chapter 23 when we compare the four tools on lock-in, where Bolt comes out at the friendly end and Replit, as we will see, at the sticky one.

The Same App, Two Tools: What Building Twice Teaches

Having now built the identical booking page in both v0 and Bolt, it is worth pausing on what the comparison reveals, because the differences are exactly the ones Chapter 8 promised and feeling them firsthand is more convincing than reading the labels.

The first version arrived differently. v0 led with a polished, hollow surface — a page that looked finished and remembered nothing until you connected a database as a separate step. Bolt led with rougher, working machinery — a full-stack app from the first prompt, more likely to actually save a booking out of the gate and less likely to dazzle while doing it. Same prompt, same app, two different first impressions, each a faithful expression of the tool's center of gravity. If you found v0's beautiful-but-empty first draft slightly unnerving, you probably preferred Bolt's working-but-plain one, and vice versa. That reaction is genuinely useful information about which tool suits your temperament.

The thing that stayed identical was the part that matters most: the steering loop. The same three follow-up instructions — persist bookings, show them on the owner's view, prevent double-booking — worked the same way in both tools, and the same discipline of testing behavior rather than trusting the report was no less necessary in either. This is Chapter 1's promise made concrete: the core skill of describing and steering transferred completely from one tool to the other. You did not relearn how to build; you relearned where the buttons were and adjusted to a different personality. That is the whole reason "choosing the wrong tool" is rarely a disaster — the expensive skill comes with you.

And the differences that did show up were the ones worth choosing on. v0's deploy felt more native and its surface more polished; Bolt's output is plainly more portable and its machinery more visible, at the cost of an edit price that climbs with project size. Neither did the job better in some absolute sense. They did it differently, in exactly the dimensions Chapter 8 said to weigh. If you build this same page a third and fourth time in Lovable and Replit, as the next two chapters do, the pattern holds: the skill is constant, the personality varies, and the variation is the decision.

Where Bolt Fits

By the end, our booking page works in Bolt much as it did in v0 — and the app you can carry away from Bolt is, if anything, freer. If you like seeing the actual machinery, if portability and not being locked in matter to you, if you want full-stack from the first prompt and a tool that can fix its own errors as it goes, Bolt is a strong choice. If your project is going to grow large and you will be editing it heavily, keep one eye on the meter, because that is exactly the case where Bolt's transparency turns into Bolt's expense.

Lovable, next, takes the opposite stance: instead of showing you the machinery, it hides it almost completely and tries to hand a non-coder a finished product, backend and all.

Chapter 12: Your First Build in Lovable

Build the booking page in Lovable and the telling moment comes when you ask it to let the owner log in to see the bookings. In v0 and Bolt, "let users log in" is a real request that triggers real, sometimes fiddly, plumbing — accounts, passwords, sessions, a database to hold it all. In Lovable, it just happens. The login appears, it works, the accounts are really stored somewhere real, and at no point are you asked to understand or set up any of the machinery underneath. That is the entire promise of Lovable distilled into one moment: it is built, more deliberately than any of the others, to give a non-coder a *complete product* — front and back — without ever making them feel like a developer.

We are building the same app one more time: the tutoring booking page, with available slots, a booking form, and an owner's view. Lovable will make a couple of things that were work in the other tools feel like nothing, and it will introduce a cost consideration that the sticker price hides. As always, the plan names and prices here are a mid-2026 snapshot and drift fast; check the current pricing before you rely on a number.

A Quick Word on Where Lovable Came From

Lovable is a Stockholm company, and it has a small piece of history worth knowing because you will still see the old name floating around. It launched as "GPT Engineer" and rebranded to Lovable around the turn of 2025. So if you stumble onto references to GPT Engineer while searching, that is the same lineage. The rebrand came with a sharpening of focus: where some tools aim at developers who want speed, Lovable aimed squarely at non-coders who want a finished thing, and that target audience explains nearly every design decision you will meet.

That focus is worth holding in mind as you build, because it tells you what the tool is optimizing for and, by implication, what it is willing to trade away. A tool aimed at developers will surface controls, expose the code prominently, and assume you want to tinker. Lovable assumes the opposite — that you want the result, not the workshop — and so it tucks the workshop out of sight. This is a real strength when your goal is a finished product. It becomes a thing to compensate for, deliberately, exactly when you need to look under the hood — usually around security — because the tool's whole personality is built to keep you from feeling like you need to. Knowing the design intent up front lets you enjoy the smoothness without mistaking it for the absence of machinery.

The First Prompt, and the Backend That Comes For Free

You reach Lovable on its website, sign in, and meet — by now you can predict it — a friendly prompt box. There is a free tier to try it, a Pro plan around twenty-five dollars a month, and a Business plan around fifty as of this writing, though you should verify against the current page. Lovable meters by message credits: roughly, each instruction you give costs a credit, so the budget you are managing is "how many things I ask it to do," which is an unusually intuitive way to meter and easy to reason about.

That credit model rewards a specific habit, and it is the same habit Chapter 14 will argue is the most valuable one in this whole craft: think before you type, and pack a clear, complete instruction into each message rather than firing off a scattershot of half-formed ones. A vague prompt that produces something wrong, followed by three corrective prompts to fix it, has cost you four credits to arrive where one well-aimed prompt would have landed. The metering is not punishing you; it is quietly teaching you to describe well, which is the skill the whole book turns on.

I give it the same scoped description as before:

> Build a tutoring booking page. Students see available time slots with dates and times, and book one by entering their name and email. A booked slot becomes unavailable to others. The owner can log in to see all the bookings.

Lovable builds, and here is the distinctive part. The thing that was a separate, deliberate step in v0 — connecting an outside database so the app can *remember* things — is, in Lovable, baked in. Under a feature Lovable calls its Cloud, it bundles a real backend (built on Supabase, the same well-regarded service v0 connects to, but here pre-wired and managed for you) that handles storing your data and managing user accounts natively. You did not connect anything. You did not sign up for a second service. The bookings persist, the login works, and the database exists, all without you ever leaving Lovable or seeing a configuration screen. For a non-coder, this is the single most valuable thing about the tool: the backend, the historically hard and invisible half of any app, is simply *included and working* from the start.

This is the "complete product" experience, and it is real. Where v0 leads with the interface and Bolt leads with the machinery, Lovable leads with the *whole thing assembled* — a working app with a working backend that a non-technical person can stand up without ever confronting the parts that usually require a developer. If your need is "I want a real, full app and I do not want to think about backends," this is the tool built for exactly you.

What "It Just Worked" Actually Did

It is worth slowing the booking-page build down and naming the work that happened invisibly, because understanding what Lovable did *for* you is the only way to know what is still *yours* to check later. When the login "just happened," several distinct things occurred that, in another tool or another era, would each have been a chore.

A `bookings` table was created in the bundled database, with columns for the student's name, their email, the slot they chose, and the time the booking was made. A `users` table — or its equivalent inside Supabase's authentication system — was created to hold the owner's account. The login screen was generated, wired to that account store, and connected so that signing in actually grants access rather than just looking like it does. And a rule was implied, if not yet enforced strictly, that the owner's view reads from the `bookings` table while a student's booking writes to it. Five or six separate pieces of plumbing, each one a real task, all of it done from a single sentence and none of it shown to you.

The reason to walk through this is not to make you a database administrator. It is to give you a mental map of the thing you now own. When Chapter 15 talks about CRUD — create, read, update, delete — you will recognize that your booking page *creates* a row when a student books, *reads* rows when the owner views the list, and would need *update* and *delete* if you later let the owner cancel a booking. When Chapter 16 talks about who is allowed to read what, you will know that "the owner can see all bookings, students cannot" is a rule that lives somewhere in that invisible backend, and that "somewhere" is a place you can ask about even though Lovable never made you look at it. The smoothness hides the machinery; it does not abolish it. Knowing roughly what is back there is the difference between confidence and a comforting fog.

Refining, the Same Loop

The refine loop is the familiar one from the last two chapters — describe a change, look, react — and Lovable's flavor of it is conversational and forgiving, tuned for someone who is steering by reaction rather than by knowing what is under the hood:

> After someone books, show them a confirmation with the date and time they booked.
>
> On the owner's view, show each booking's student name, email, and slot.
>
> Only let the owner see the bookings view, not students.

That last request is worth pausing on, because it is exactly the kind of thing — who is allowed to see what — where the security discipline of Chapter 22 lives. Lovable will happily build the rule. Whether it built it *correctly and safely*, so that a student cannot reach the bookings by poking at the address bar, is something you still have to verify rather than assume, no matter how smooth the building felt. The smoothness of Lovable is a genuine gift and also a particular trap: the easier a tool makes it to *not think about the machinery*, the more deliberately you have to think about the machinery anyway when it comes to security. Ease is not safety. I will keep saying it.

Two more refinements are worth showing because they reveal how Lovable handles the kinds of requests that come up on every real project, not just the tidy demo path.

> When all the slots for a day are booked, hide that day instead of showing an empty list.

This is a *display logic* change — a rule about what to show under what condition — and Lovable handles these gracefully because they live almost entirely in the front end. You will find that requests about appearance and conditional display are the most reliable to make by description, because they are the least entangled with the backend. When a refinement is purely about what the user sees and when, expect it to land cleanly on the first or second try.

> Send me an email when someone books a slot.

This one is a different animal, and it is a useful early lesson in the texture of these tools. Sending email is not something the app can do on its own; it requires reaching out to an outside service that sends mail. Lovable can wire this up, but it is the first request in our build that crosses the boundary from "everything Lovable already includes" into "connecting to something external" — the subject of Chapter 17. You may be asked to provide a key or connect an account. The point to absorb here is that there is a category line: things inside Lovable's bundled world (data, login, the interface) are friction-free, and things outside it (email, payments, third-party services) involve a connection step. Knowing which side of that line a feature falls on tells you in advance whether to expect "it just happened" or "it needs a setup step first."

Reading What Lovable Made, Even As a Non-Coder

You do not have to look at the code Lovable generates, and most of the time you will not want to. But it is worth knowing that you *can*, because the moment you most need to — when something is wrong in a way you cannot fix by description, or when you want to confirm a security rule is real — that ability stops being optional.

Lovable shows you the project's files if you ask for them. You will not understand most of what you see, and that is fine; you are not reading the code to edit it. You are reading it for two narrow, achievable purposes. The first is *orientation*: seeing that there is, in fact, a real project with real files reassures you that there is something solid underneath the conversation, not a house of cards. The second is *targeted questions*: you can point at a file and ask Lovable, in plain English, "what does this do?" or "does this check that the user is the owner before showing the bookings?" and get an answer you can evaluate. Treating the code as something you can interrogate, rather than something you must author, is the right relationship for a non-coder, and it is a relationship Lovable supports even though it does not push you toward it.

GitHub Sync: The Door Out

For all its hide-the-machinery friendliness, Lovable does not lock you in, and the mechanism by which it keeps the door open is worth understanding: bidirectional GitHub sync.

GitHub, in plain terms, is the standard place developers store and share code. Lovable can connect your project to a GitHub repository and keep the two in sync in *both* directions — changes you make in Lovable flow to GitHub, and changes made in GitHub can flow back. The practical meaning for you, the non-coder, is twofold. First, your code is genuinely yours and genuinely portable: it lives in a standard place in a standard form, and a developer could take it from there. Second, and more interesting, it means a developer could collaborate with you on the *same* project — you building by description in Lovable, them working in the code through GitHub — with the two staying in step. That bidirectional sync is a real strength, and it puts Lovable at the friendlier end of the lock-in spectrum, behind Bolt's near-total portability but comfortably ahead of the more tightly coupled tools.

There is a practical reason to turn this sync on *early*, before you have invested weeks of refinement, rather than treating it as something to set up if you ever need it. GitHub also functions as a history of every version of your project, which means it is a safety net. If a future refinement goes badly wrong — the kind of tangle Chapter 14 describes, where one change breaks three things — having your project synced to GitHub gives you a clean record of the last good state to fall back to, independent of Lovable's own history. Connecting it on day one costs you a few minutes; reaching for it on the day you need it, only to discover it was never set up, costs you a great deal more. Treat it as cheap insurance you buy before the fire, not after.

A note on what the sync does *not* do, so the door's openness is not oversold. GitHub holds your *code*. It does not, by itself, hold your *data* or your *running app*. If you walked away from Lovable tomorrow, a developer could take the code from GitHub and run with it — but they would also need to move the database (the actual bookings, the actual accounts) and arrange new hosting. The code is the portable part; the live, running, data-filled version of your app is still partly anchored to the services Lovable wired up for you. This is not a criticism — it is true of nearly every tool — but "my code is portable" and "my whole live app is trivially portable" are different claims, and only the first is fully true. Chapter 23 maps this honestly across all four tools.

The Cost Caveat the Sticker Price Hides

Now the honest money note, because it is specific to Lovable's "everything included" model and easy to miss. The monthly price you see — the twenty-five or fifty dollars — buys you Lovable. It does not, by itself, buy you everything your *live, real-world* app will eventually need.

The bundled backend is generous for getting started, but a real app with real users may outgrow the free tier of the underlying database service, at which point you are paying for Supabase Pro on top of Lovable. If you put the app on your own web address, that is a domain to buy. None of these are large, and none are hidden in a sinister way — but the mental model "I pay Lovable's monthly fee and I'm done" is not quite right, and people are surprised by it. The true cost of running a live app is Lovable *plus* the infrastructure underneath it as you grow. I am flagging it here so the surprise does not land on you; Chapter 21 lays out the full economics across all four tools, and this is the place Lovable's number is most incomplete on its own.

It is worth separating two kinds of cost so the picture is clear. There is the cost of *building*, which is the credits you spend asking Lovable to make and change things, and which you pay whether or not anyone ever uses the app. And there is the cost of *running*, which is the database, the hosting, the domain, the email service — the standing infrastructure a live app consumes simply by existing and serving real users. The building cost is the one Lovable's pricing page is about. The running cost is the one it is quietest about, precisely because Lovable's gift is making the infrastructure invisible, and invisible infrastructure is exactly the kind whose bill you forget to anticipate. A prototype that lives only in Lovable's preview, used by you alone, incurs almost no running cost. The same app opened up to a few hundred real users, with their data accumulating in the database day after day, eventually does. The surprise is rarely the size of the bill; it is the existence of a second bill at all.

Where Lovable Fits

By the end, the booking page is built, the backend works, the owner can log in, and at no point did building it require you to understand a database or wire up authentication by hand. That is Lovable's case in a sentence: it gives a non-coder the most *complete*, backend-included product with the least exposure to anything developer-shaped, and it keeps a real door open through GitHub sync so you are not trapped by that convenience.

What it asks of you in return is to remember that “I never had to think about the machinery” is not the same as “the machinery is safe and free.” The backend you didn’t have to set up still has to be secured; the price you didn’t see still has to be paid as you grow. Replit, next, takes the full-product idea even further — database and hosting all in one place — and pushes both the convenience and the coupling to their highest setting of the four.

Chapter 13: Your First Build in Replit

Of the four tools in this book, Replit comes closest to the bare promise of vibe coding: describe it, and get a deployed, running app. Building the booking page here is the one that feels most like describing a wish and getting a finished thing, with the least visible seam between the asking and the having. You type what you want, and Replit's agent does not just generate a page — it announces a plan, sets up the project, installs what it needs, builds the front and the back, stands up a database, wires the parts together, runs the app, hits an error, fixes the error, runs it again, and then offers to deploy it to a live address. All of that, one continuous motion, while you mostly watch.

We are building the same app a final time — the tutoring booking page with available slots, a booking form, and an owner's view — so you can feel the contrast directly. Replit will make the end-to-end build feel the most complete and automatic of the four, and it carries the heaviest version of the tradeoff that completeness implies. The plan names and prices here are a mid-2026 snapshot; verify before relying on them.

A Real Cloud Computer, Not Just a Builder

The first thing to understand about Replit is that it is older and broader than the AI-builder wave. Long before any of this, Replit was a full, online development environment — a real computer in the cloud, in your browser, where people wrote and ran code, with editing, a terminal, file storage, a database, and hosting all in one place. The AI builder, which Replit calls its Agent (Agent 3 as of this writing), is layered *on top of* that complete environment. So when Replit's agent builds your app, it is building inside a real, full-service workshop that already has everything an app needs to live: somewhere to store data, somewhere to run, somewhere to be hosted. Nothing has to be connected from outside, because it is all already here.

This is the deepest difference from the other three. v0 connects out to a database. Lovable bundles one in. Replit simply *is* the place the database, the code, and the hosting all already are. That integration is the source of both its greatest convenience and its stickiest limitation, and we will meet both in this chapter.

It is worth dwelling for a moment on why this lineage matters to you even though you have no intention of using Replit as a hand-coding environment. The fact that there is a real, complete computer underneath the agent changes what the agent is *able* to do. When Replit's agent needs to install a piece of software to make a feature work, it can actually run the installation, because there is a real machine to install it on. When it needs to test whether the app runs, it can actually run it, because there is a real place to run it. When it hits an error, it can read the error off a real running system and respond to it. In tools that are primarily builders with services attached, some of this happens in a more managed, more constrained way. In Replit, the agent has a genuine workshop with genuine tools, and that is why its builds feel less like generation and more like watching a capable contractor work — it has the run of a real space.

The Agentic Build: Describe It, Watch It Happen

You sign in at Replit's website, start a new project with the agent, and describe what you want. There is a free way to try it, a Core plan in the rough range of twenty to twenty-five dollars a month, and a Pro plan up around ninety-five to a hundred as of this writing — verify the current figures, which move. Replit's pricing is worth a moment because it is structured differently from the others: rather than metering raw tokens or counting messages, it is built around *effort* and *checkpoints* — roughly, you are charged for the units of work the agent does as it builds and the milestones it reaches. The practical effect is similar to the others (more building costs more), but the mental model is "I'm paying for the agent's labor" rather than "I'm paying per word."

This effort-based model has a practical consequence that is easy to miss until your usage report surprises you: a single instruction from you can trigger a *large* amount of agent labor. Because Replit's agent is autonomous — it plans, then executes many steps without checking back at each one — one sentence like "add user accounts" might set off a long sequence of work: creating tables, generating the login flow, testing it, fixing what breaks, testing again. In a per-message tool, that one message costs one message. In Replit's effort model, it costs whatever the whole sequence of work amounts to. This is not a trap; it is the honest reflection of the fact that the agent really did a lot on your behalf. But it means the relationship between "how much I typed" and "how much I spent" is looser in Replit than anywhere else, and the way to stay in control of cost is to be deliberate about the *scope* of what you ask for, not just the number of times you ask.

I give the agent the same scoped description:

> Build a tutoring booking page. Students see available time slots with dates and times and can book one with their name and email. A booked slot becomes unavailable to others. The owner can log in to see all the bookings.

And then the distinctive Replit experience unfolds. The agent lays out a *plan* — it tells you, in plain language, the steps it intends to take — and then executes them: scaffolding the project, installing dependencies, creating a database (Replit includes a real PostgreSQL database, a serious production-grade one, built right in), generating the interface and the logic, running the app, watching for errors, and fixing what breaks. You are not steering each step; you are watching an agent carry out a build the way a contractor carries out a renovation from a brief, checking back in with you at the milestones. When it is done, the app is not a preview on someone else's terms — it is running, in your own cloud environment, ready to deploy with the hosting already part of the package.

This is the closest the four come to "it just builds the whole thing." If your wish is to describe an app and have a running, hosted, database-backed version of it appear with the least hands-on involvement, Replit is engineered for precisely that wish. The agent's plan-and-execute style means it handles the connective work — the dependencies, the database setup, the running and fixing — that you would otherwise nudge along yourself in the other tools.

Reading the Plan Before You Let It Run

The plan the agent shows you before it starts is not decoration, and learning to read it is one of the highest-value habits you can form with Replit specifically. Because the agent is about to do a lot of autonomous work off a single instruction, the plan is your one clean chance to catch a misunderstanding *before* it has been built into the app, when correcting it costs a sentence rather than a teardown.

Read the plan the way you would read a contractor's written estimate before they pick up a hammer. You are checking for two things. First, did it understand the *what* — does the plan describe the app you actually asked for, or has it quietly added something you did not want or dropped something you did? If the plan for our booking page mentions building a payment system, the agent has over-read the brief, and one sentence now ("no payments, this is free booking") saves a pile of unwanted work. Second, does the plan reveal a *decision* the agent is making that you have an opinion about — a choice of how login works, say, or what happens to a booking when it is cancelled? The plan often surfaces these in plain language, and the moment to weigh in is before execution, not after.

Most of the time the plan will be fine and you will simply let it proceed. But the few times it is not fine are exactly the times this habit pays for itself many times over, because a misunderstanding caught in the plan costs nothing, and the same misunderstanding caught after the agent has spent an hour of autonomous effort building on top of it costs that hour plus the unwinding. Spend the thirty seconds. Read the plan.

Refining With a More Autonomous Partner

The refine loop in Replit has a slightly different texture, because the agent is more autonomous than the other tools' build steps. When I ask for a change:

> Add a confirmation message after booking, showing the date and time.
>
> On the owner's view, show each booking's student name, email, and slot.
>
> Make sure only the logged-in owner can see the bookings view.

the agent often does not just make the one edit — it considers what the change implies, makes the related adjustments, tests, and reports back. This is powerful and it is double-edged. Powerful, because it handles the surrounding work you might not have known to ask for. Double-edged, because a more autonomous agent making more decisions on your behalf means more places where it can decide something you did not intend, and you have to watch the result rather than trust the motion. That last request — restricting the bookings view to the owner — is, once again, exactly the kind of access-control rule whose *appearance* of working is not proof it is *actually* secure, and Chapter 22's discipline applies here with full force no matter how confidently the agent reports success.

The autonomy changes how you should test, not just how you should read the plan. In a tool that makes one small edit per instruction, you can usually reason about what changed: you asked for the button to move, the button moved, nothing else should be different. In Replit, where one instruction can ripple into several related edits, you cannot assume the change was surgical. The discipline Chapter 14 calls “look at the actual behavior, not the report” matters *more* here than anywhere, because the agent’s report tells you what it intended and the autonomy means it may have touched things its report does not dwell on. After a refinement, do not just confirm the thing you asked for now works — spend an extra moment confirming the things you did *not* ask about still work. The booking still saves. The confirmation still shows. The owner’s view still loads. Autonomy that fixes the surrounding work you forgot to ask for is a gift; autonomy that changes the surrounding work you did not want changed is a cost, and they wear the same face until you test.

A Note on Checkpoints

Replit’s checkpoint system deserves a paragraph of its own, because it is both the unit it bills against and your single most important safety tool. A checkpoint is a saved, working state of your project — a point you can return to. As the agent builds and as you refine, Replit records these milestones, and that record is precisely the “go back to a version that worked” lifeline that Chapter 14 will tell you to reach for without shame when a change goes wrong.

The practical wisdom is to treat your checkpoints as a deliberate trail of breadcrumbs rather than a passive log. When you reach a state where the app genuinely works — the booking saves, the owner can log in, everything you have built so far behaves — register that in your own mind as a known-good point to fall back to. Then, when an ambitious refinement turns into the tangle Chapter 14 describes, your instinct should be not “let me keep prompting until it untangles” but “let me return to the last point where this worked and try the change again, more carefully.” Get comfortable with how Replit’s restore-to-checkpoint feature works *before* you are in a hole, because finding the exit while panicking in the dark is much harder than knowing where the door is in advance.

Deployment Included, and the Catch

Replit deploys from inside itself with about as little friction as v0’s home-turf deploy, because hosting was never a separate concern here — it was part of the environment from the first second. A click or two, and your app is live at a real address, running on the same Replit infrastructure it was built in. For the experience of going from idea to a working public app with the fewest moving parts, this is hard to beat.

There is a distinction here that catches people out, and it is worth making explicit. While you are building, your app is running in a *development* environment — a workspace that is live only while you have it open and active. Deploying is the separate, deliberate act of putting a *published* version on a stable, always-on address that the public can reach whether or not you are sitting in front of Replit. The two are not the same, and the gap between them is the source of a common confusion: "my app worked while I was building it, but my friend couldn't reach the link." The development version is for you, building; the deployed version is for the world, using. Deployment is the step that crosses from one to the other, and on Replit it is genuinely a click or two — but it is a step you take on purpose, not something that has silently already happened just because the app ran in your workspace. Chapter 19 covers deployment across all four tools properly; the thing to internalize now is that "it runs while I build" and "it is live for others" are two different states.

And here is the catch, stated as plainly as I can, because it is Replit's most important honest limit: of the four tools in this book, Replit has the highest migration friction. The very thing that makes it so seamless — that the code, the database, and the hosting are all one integrated whole inside Replit — is the thing that makes it hardest to *leave*. Your app is coupled to Replit's built-in database and Replit's hosting in a way that a Bolt project simply is not. Moving it elsewhere is not impossible, but it is real work: you would have to migrate the database, re-host the app, and untangle the conveniences that were doing quiet work for you. Where Bolt hands you a project that runs anywhere and Lovable keeps a clean GitHub door open, Replit's integration is deep enough that getting out is a project of its own.

This is not a reason to avoid Replit. It is a reason to choose it *knowingly*. If your app is going to live happily inside Replit — an internal tool, a prototype, something you are content to run where it was born — the integration is pure upside, and you should enjoy it. If you can foresee a day when you will need to take the app somewhere else, factor the cost of that move in from the start, because it is the highest of the four. Chapter 23 puts all four tools on the lock-in spectrum explicitly, and Replit sits at the sticky end of it for exactly these reasons.

There is one concrete habit that softens the lock-in without giving up the convenience, and it is the same one I recommended for Lovable: connect your project to GitHub early, so that at minimum your *code* lives somewhere standard and portable from the start. This does not move the database or the hosting — those remain the coupled parts — but it means the most labor-intensive thing you have produced, the code itself, is never trapped, and a developer could pick it up from GitHub even if everything else stayed inside Replit. It is the cheap half of an exit strategy, available for a few minutes' setup, and there is no reason to skip it even if you fully intend for the app to live in Replit forever.

Where Replit Fits

By the end, our booking page is built, hosted, database-backed, and live, and it required less hands-on steering than any of the other three — the agent did the connective work and handed back a running app. That is Replit's case: it is the closest thing to describing an app and getting a deployed, working one, inside a single complete environment where nothing has to be wired together from outside.

The price of that completeness is coupling — the same integration that makes everything seamless makes leaving expensive — and the price of the agent's autonomy is that it decides more on your behalf, which you must watch rather than trust. Four tools, four temperaments: v0 the polished surface, Bolt the open workshop, Lovable the complete product for non-coders, Replit the all-in-one environment that builds and hosts in one breath. You have now built the same small app in all four and felt how differently they hold the same idea. What none of them did, in any of these four chapters, was get everything right on the first try — and learning to work the gap between the first try and the working version is a craft of its own.

Chapter 14: Iterating: Editing, Fixing, and Refining

There is a moment that happens to nearly everyone the first time they build an app this way, and it is worth describing because recognizing it will save you a bad afternoon. You have a working app. You ask for one more small change — move a button, add a field, nothing dramatic. The AI makes the change, and something *else* breaks. A thing that worked a minute ago now doesn't. So you ask it to fix that, and now a third thing breaks. You ask again, and the tool confidently announces it has fixed the problem, and it has not — the same break is still there. Twenty minutes later you are further from working than when you started, increasingly convinced the tool is broken or you are stupid, and neither is true. You have simply hit the part of vibe coding that the cheerful demos skip: the iteration loop, where most of the real time goes, and where judgment matters most.

The first four chapters of this part were about getting to a first version. This one is about everything after — the refine loop, which is not a footnote to building but the *majority* of building. Getting a rough first draft is fast and feels magical. Turning a rough draft into a thing that actually works, and keeping it working as you change it, is the craft. Here is what that craft is made of.

The Basic Loop, Done Well

At its core, iterating is the rhythm we met in Chapter 9: describe a change, look at the result, react. The whole skill is in doing each of those three things deliberately rather than sloppily.

Describe one change at a time. I know I said this in Chapter 9, and I am saying it again because it is the single highest-leverage habit and the one people abandon first under pressure. When you want five things changed, the urge is to list all five in one message. Resist it. Make one change, confirm it landed and broke nothing, then make the next. The reason is not tidiness; it is *diagnosis*. When you change one thing and something breaks, you know exactly what caused it. When you change five things and something breaks, you are now debugging a mystery you created, with no idea which of the five is the culprit.

There is a real exception worth naming, because "one change at a time" stated too rigidly becomes its own kind of mistake. Some changes are genuinely a single coherent thing even though they sound like several — "add a date column to the bookings table, show it in the owner's list, and let the owner sort by it" is really one feature with three faces, and asking for it as one request is fine because the three parts only make sense together. The rule is better stated as *one logical change at a time*, where "logical" means one thing that either works as a whole or doesn't. The failure mode the rule guards against is bundling *unrelated* changes — fixing the date bug and restyling the header and adding email notifications in one breath — because those have nothing to do with each other and bundling them only destroys your ability to tell which one broke something. Group what belongs together; never group what merely happens to be on your list at the same moment.

Look at the actual behavior, not the report. The AI will tell you it did the thing. Believe the app, not the announcement. Click the button. Submit the form. Book the slot. Try it as a real user would. The gap between "the tool says it's fixed" and "it is fixed" is where hours quietly disappear, and the only defense is to test the behavior yourself every time.

There is a more thorough version of this test that pays off as your app grows, and it has a name worth knowing even though you will never do it formally: *regression testing*. The plain-English version is simply this — after a change, do not only test the thing you changed; quickly re-test the handful of things that matter most, even the ones you did not touch. On the booking page, that is a thirty-second routine: book a slot, confirm it saves, confirm it disappears for the next person, confirm the owner can still see it. You run this same short loop after every meaningful change. The reason is that the tool, regenerating code, can break a part you did not ask it to touch, and the only way to catch that is to look. A short, repeatable "does the core still work?" pass after every change is the cheapest insurance in this entire craft, and skipping it is how people ship apps that were working an hour before they broke them and never noticed.

React specifically. "That's wrong" is a weak note. "The confirmation message shows the wrong date — it shows today instead of the slot's date" is a strong one. The more precisely you can describe what is wrong, the more reliably the tool fixes the actual problem instead of guessing at it.

The anatomy of a strong bug report is worth spelling out, because most people under-specify by habit and then wonder why the fix misses. A good report has three parts: what you did, what you expected, and what actually happened. "I booked the 3pm Tuesday slot, I expected the confirmation to say Tuesday 3pm, but it said today's date at 3pm." That single sentence gives the tool everything it needs — the action that triggers the bug, the correct behavior to aim for, and the precise way reality diverged from it. Compare that to "the date is wrong," which forces the tool to guess at all three. The discipline is not about politeness or completeness for its own sake; it is that a vague report makes the tool *guess*, and a guessing tool is exactly the thing that wanders off and breaks something adjacent. You reduce the tool's need to guess by removing the ambiguity yourself, and you are far better positioned to remove it than the tool is, because you are the one who saw what happened.

Fixing the AI's Mistakes

The tool will make mistakes. Not occasionally — routinely. This is not a defect you can prompt your way out of; it is the nature of the thing, and your real job is less to prevent mistakes than to be good at catching and correcting them. A few patterns come up again and again.

It fixes the symptom, not the cause. You report a bug; the AI patches the specific case you mentioned and leaves the underlying problem, so the bug pops up again in a slightly different place. When you see the same kind of error twice, stop asking for another patch and instead describe the *pattern*: "this keeps happening whenever a date is involved — what's the underlying issue?" Aiming the tool at the cause rather than the latest symptom often breaks the cycle.

A useful move when you suspect a symptom-fix is to ask the tool to *diagnose before it fixes*. Instead of "fix the date again," try "before you change anything, explain why the date keeps coming out wrong." This does two things. It often surfaces the real cause, because forcing the tool to articulate the problem tends to produce a better-aimed fix than letting it leap straight to patching. And it gives you, the human steering, something you can actually evaluate — even as a non-coder, you can often tell whether a plain-English explanation sounds like it is addressing the root or just the surface. Asking for the reasoning before the repair turns the tool from a slot machine you keep pulling into something closer to a collaborator you can interrogate.

It "fixes" something by quietly removing it. A genuinely maddening failure mode: you report that a feature is broken, and the AI makes the error go away by deleting or disabling the feature, then reports success. The error is gone because the thing that errored is gone. This is why you test behavior — a passing-looking app with a missing feature looks fine in the report and is not fine. When it happens, say so directly: "don't remove the booking feature, fix it so it works."

This pattern is most dangerous precisely when you are *not* doing the regression check above, because a quietly removed feature produces no error, no complaint, no red text — it simply is not there anymore, and the report cheerfully says the problem is solved. The only thing standing between you and shipping an app with a silently amputated feature is the habit of testing the core behaviors after every change. A feature that errors loudly is annoying; a feature that has been deleted to silence the error is a trap, because the app now *looks* healthier than the one that was at least honestly broken. Catching it requires you to go use the feature, find it gone, and push back specifically.

It reintroduces a bug you already fixed. Because the tool is regenerating code, a fix you made an hour ago can vanish when it rebuilds a nearby part. This is normal and not a betrayal. Just re-report it, and know that the more sweeping a change you ask for, the more likely older fixes get disturbed — another argument for small, contained steps.

It half-applies a change across the app. A subtler cousin of the symptom fix: you ask for something that ought to be consistent everywhere — "use the same date format throughout" — and the tool changes it in two places and misses a third. The app now has the right format on the booking confirmation and the wrong one on the owner's list, which is arguably worse than getting it wrong everywhere, because the inconsistency looks like a one-off bug rather than an incomplete change. The defense is to be explicit about scope when a change should be universal ("everywhere a date appears, in every view, use this format") and to check the *less obvious* places after, not just the screen you were looking at when you made the request.

When It Loops

The most important skill in this chapter is recognizing the loop and getting out of it, because the loop is where people lose whole afternoons and conclude the tools don't work.

The loop looks like this: you ask for a fix, it doesn't work, you ask again, it still doesn't work, the tool keeps confidently trying variations of the same wrong idea, and each attempt may break something new. The defining feature is that you are going in circles, not making progress, and the tool shows no sign of noticing. Here is what to do, roughly in order.

Before the steps, one piece of meta-advice: *set yourself a limit in advance.* Decide, before you are in the heat of it, that two failed attempts at the same fix is your signal to change tactics rather than try a third time. The loop is so seductive precisely because each next attempt feels like it might be the one, and "just one more try" repeated ten times is how the afternoon vanishes. A pre-committed rule — "after the second failure, I stop and do something different" — is the cheapest way to protect yourself from your own optimism. The steps below are what "something different" means.

Stop feeding the loop. The instinct is to keep replying "no, that's still wrong, try again," but repeating the same request into the same context usually produces more of the same. The tool is stuck in a groove. More tries in that groove deepen it.

Go back instead of forward. Every one of these tools keeps a history — versions, checkpoints, snapshots, by whatever name. When you are in a hole, the fastest way out is often not to dig differently but to climb back to the last version that worked and start the change again from there, fresh. This is the most underused move new builders have, and it is the most powerful. A working past state is a safety line; use it. Get comfortable with your tool's "go back to a previous version" feature *before* you need it, because you will need it.

It helps to understand *why* going back so often beats pushing forward, because the reason is not obvious and the instinct fights it. When you push forward, you are asking the tool to fix a broken state — and a broken state is full of the very confusion that broke it, so the tool is reasoning from a tangled starting point. When you go back to a working state and re-attempt the change, you are asking the tool to make one clean change to a healthy app, which is a fundamentally easier task. You are not losing the work you did between the good state and now; most of that work was the *attempts to fix the breakage*, which were worthless anyway. Going back discards the failed repairs, not the progress. Reframing it this way — "I am deleting twenty minutes of failed flailing, not twenty minutes of good work" — makes the button much easier to press.

Rephrase from scratch. If you do push forward, do not refine the failed request — replace it. Describe what you want in completely different words, with a concrete example, as if explaining it to someone who just walked in. A stuck tool often unsticks when the framing changes, because you have given it a new path to the answer instead of nudging it down the blocked one.

A concrete example beats an abstract description almost every time when you are unsticking a loop. Instead of "the sorting is wrong," give it the exact case: "when I have bookings for Monday, Wednesday, and Tuesday in that order, the list should show Monday, Tuesday, Wednesday — top to bottom, earliest first." The worked example does for the tool what it does for a confused human: it replaces a fuzzy goal with an unambiguous target you can both check against. Many loops are really the tool and you disagreeing, without realizing it, about what "right" means; a concrete example collapses that disagreement instantly.

Start a fresh conversation. Sometimes the context itself has gotten muddy — too much back-and-forth, too many half-attempts cluttering the tool's view of the problem. Beginning a new session, describing the current state and the one change you want cleanly, can clear a fog that no amount of in-place retrying would lift.

Break the change into smaller pieces. If the tool cannot do the change as asked, the change is probably too big for one step. Decompose it. Ask for the smallest possible piece, get that working, then the next piece. A change that loops as a whole often goes through fine in parts.

A Worked Example of Getting Unstuck

To make all of that concrete, here is the loop and the escape in a single sequence, the kind you will live through yourself. Suppose, on the booking page, you ask: "stop people from booking a slot that is in the past." The tool makes a change. You test, and now *no* slots are bookable, not just past ones. You report that; the tool tries again, and now past slots are bookable again but the confirmation message has broken. You report that; the tool fixes the confirmation but past slots are still bookable. You are now three attempts in, two things have been broken and unbroken, and the original feature still does not work. This is the loop, recognized.

The escape, applied in order: first, you stop — that pre-committed two-strikes rule has tripped. Second, you go back to the checkpoint from before any of this, the last state where the app fully worked, accepting the loss of three attempts that produced nothing. Third, you re-attempt, but this time you rephrase from scratch and lead with a concrete example: "Each slot has a date and time. When I load the page, any slot whose date and time is earlier than right now should be hidden from the list entirely — for instance, if it is Tuesday afternoon, a Tuesday-morning slot should not appear, but a Wednesday slot should." Fourth, if even that loops, you break it down: first just get the slots to *display* a flag for past-or-future, confirm the tool can tell them apart at all, and only then ask it to hide the past ones. Somewhere in that sequence, the change goes through — and the total time is far less than the eleventh attempt at "no, still wrong, try again" would have cost. The skill on display is not magic prompting. It is recognizing the loop, refusing to feed it, and reaching for the structured exits instead of pushing harder on the door that will not open.

When to Stop and Edit by Hand (or Get a Hand)

There is a threshold, and part of doing this well is knowing it exists. Sometimes a problem is genuinely small in code and genuinely impossible to get the AI to do by description — a single value that needs changing, a one-line tweak the tool keeps misunderstanding. If you have some comfort with it, opening the code and changing that one line yourself can be faster than a tenth round of prompting. You do not have to; this whole book is premised on not having to. But the option exists, and in the tools with a visible editor it is right there.

If you do venture in, do it with a net. Make sure you are on a saved, working version first, so that if your hand-edit makes things worse you can return to where you were. And keep the edit as narrow as the problem: you are changing one specific value the tool kept fumbling, not redesigning anything. The point of the hand-edit is not to become a coder; it is to make one surgical correction that has proven faster by hand than by a dozen rounds of description, and then hand the wheel back to the tool. A focused one-line change you can see the effect of is a reasonable thing for a non-coder to attempt with care; treating the code as a place to start improvising is not.

And there is a higher threshold past which the honest move is to bring in a person. If you have looped repeatedly, gone back to working versions, rephrased, started fresh, and the thing still will not come together, that is real information: you may have hit a problem that genuinely needs someone who can read the code. This is not failure. It is the same judgment that tells you when a home repair has exceeded your tools. Chapter 24 is about exactly when you still need a developer, and "I have iterated honestly and thoroughly and I am still stuck" is one of the clearest signs that you are there.

The Mindset That Makes It Work

If I could install one attitude, it would be this: the first version is a draft, and drafting is the easy part. The iteration is the work, and the iteration is *supposed* to be bumpy. You are not failing when the tool makes a mistake; you are doing the normal thing, which is steering a fast and fallible builder toward something that actually works. The people who succeed with these tools are not the ones who write magic prompts that never need fixing. They are the ones who stay calm in the loop, test what they're told, keep their changes small, and reach for the "go back" button without shame. The building was always going to be quick. Getting it *right* is the part that takes judgment, and the judgment was always going to be yours.

Part IV: Making It Real

Audience: everyone.

"A demo impresses you once. A tool earns its keep on the tenth real user, with their real data, on a Tuesday — and that is the harder thing to build."

— A working principle

Chapter 15: Data and Backends

The first app I ever built this way was a little reading log — a page where I could type in a book I'd finished, give it a star rating, and see the list grow. It worked beautifully in the demo. I added three books, they showed up in a tidy list, I felt like a wizard. Then I closed the tab, reopened it the next morning, and the list was empty. The books were gone. Not deleted, exactly — they had never been *saved* anywhere. They had lived only in the page, in the browser's memory, and when the page went away so did they.

That empty list is the best possible introduction to what this chapter is about, because it shows you the difference between a thing that *looks* like an app and a thing that *is* one. The interface — the form, the list, the stars — is only half of an application. The other half is the part you cannot see: the place where the data actually lives so that it survives you closing the tab, so that it is still there when you come back, so that it is the same data whether you open the app on your laptop or your phone. That invisible half is the backend, and a database is its heart. If you skip understanding it, you will build apps that demo well and forget everything the moment a real person walks away.

What a Backend Actually Is

Strip away the jargon and a backend is just *the part of your app that runs somewhere other than the user's screen*. The screen — the page in the browser, the buttons, the layout — is the front end. It is what the user sees and touches, and it lives, for the moment they are using it, on their device. The backend is everything that happens out of sight: storing information so it persists, fetching it back when someone asks, running the logic that decides who can see what, talking to other services. It lives on a server — a computer somewhere on the internet that is always on, that every user shares, and that no single user controls.

The reason this matters to you, specifically, is that the difference between front end and back end is not a technical nicety. It is a *security boundary*, and it is the exact boundary that the most dangerous failure in this whole book runs across. Anything on the front end is, by definition, handed to the user — they have it, they can read all of it. Anything on the back end stays private. We will hit that wall hard in Chapter 22 (Security and Your Users' Data); for now, just plant the flag: *front end is public, back end is private,* and a great deal depends on knowing which is which.

It is worth making the "front end is public" claim less abstract, because people nod at it without feeling its force. When a page loads in someone's browser, *everything that page is made of* is now on their computer — the layout, the logic, and crucially anything the page was given to work with. A curious user can open their browser's developer tools, a built-in panel that exists in every browser, and read it all. This is not hacking; it is a menu item. So if your app, trying to be clever, tucks a secret password or a private key into the page where the front end can reach it, you have not hidden that secret — you have published it, to every user, in a form any of them can read in about four clicks. This single fact is the root of a whole family of disasters covered later, and the reason "put it on the backend" is not bureaucratic caution but the literal difference between a secret that is secret and one that is not.

A **database**, then, is the specific piece of the backend whose job is remembering. It is, at its plainest, a set of tables — think of a spreadsheet, because that is genuinely close to the truth. A table called `books` has a column for the title, a column for the rating, a column for the date you added it, and one row per book. When my reading-log app finally worked, it worked because every book I typed in became a new row in a real table on a real server, and the list on screen was just the app reading those rows back and showing them to me. Close the tab, reopen it, the rows are still there. That is the whole trick.

Tables, Rows, and Why the Shape Matters

The spreadsheet picture is worth pushing a little further, because the few concepts it makes visible are the ones that come up every time you describe data to a builder. A table is a kind of thing you are storing — books, bookings, users, orders. A column is one fact you keep about each of those things — a book's title, its rating, the date added. A row is one actual instance — one specific book, with its specific title and rating filling in the columns. When you tell a builder "store books with a title and a star rating," you are, without using the words, defining a table with two columns, and every book you add becomes a row.

Two ideas make this more powerful than a single spreadsheet, and both come up naturally on real apps. The first is that every row quietly gets a unique identifier — an ID — even if you never asked for one and never see it. This is how the app tells one row from another when two of them look similar. Two students named Alex Smith can both book a slot; the app does not confuse them because each booking is a distinct row with its own ID, regardless of matching names. You will meet these IDs again, sometimes uncomfortably, when Chapter 16 explains how a careless app lets a user change the ID in their address bar to peek at someone else's row. For now, just know they are there, doing the quiet work of keeping rows distinct.

The second idea is that tables often *relate* to each other, and recognizing this changes how you describe an app. In the tutoring app from Chapter 1, there is naturally a table of bookings and, once you add accounts, a table of users — and a booking *belongs to* a student. That relationship ("this booking was made by this user") is something databases handle well and something you will describe in plain English without thinking of it as a relationship at all: "show each owner only their own students' bookings." Underneath, that sentence is asking the app to follow the link between the bookings table and the users table. You do not need the vocabulary. But noticing that your app has *several kinds of thing that connect to each other* — orders that belong to customers, comments that belong to posts, tasks that belong to projects — helps you describe it clearly, because you can name each kind of thing and how it connects, and a clear description is the entire game.

Where Your Data Actually Lives: Supabase and Its Cousins

When one of these tools sets up a database for you, it is almost never building one from scratch. It is connecting your app to a hosted database service — a company whose entire business is running databases reliably so you don't have to. The one you will run into most is **Supabase**, and it is worth knowing its name because it shows up everywhere in this world.

Supabase is a hosted backend built around a standard, well-understood database (PostgreSQL, if you want the proper noun — you will not need to). It gives your app a place to store data, a way to handle user accounts (which is the next chapter), file storage, and more, all bundled together. The reason the builders love it is that it handles the genuinely hard, genuinely boring parts of a backend so the AI can wire your app to it in a few steps.

How you meet Supabase depends on which builder you're using, and the differences are real:

Lovable bundles it in, under its own name. Lovable's "Lovable Cloud" is Supabase underneath, presented so smoothly that as a non-coder you may never see the seams — you ask for data that persists, and it appears, backend and all. This is the most hands-off experience of the four, and for someone who has never thought about a database in their life, that is a genuine kindness. (Verify the exact branding as you read; these names get rebranded.)

vo and Bolt connect to it, but ask you to bring it. With vo (Vercel's builder) you typically point your app at a Supabase or Neon database you've set up, and the connection is a deliberate step. Bolt similarly integrates with Supabase. Slightly more setup, but the upside is you own the database account directly, which matters later if you ever want to leave the builder.

Replit includes its own. Replit gives you a built-in database and hosting inside its environment, so for a Replit app the backend is often right there, no external service to connect. Convenient — and, as Chapter 23 (Scaling, Maintenance, and Lock-In) will note, also the tightest coupling of the bunch, because that convenience is harder to pack up and take with you.

The honest takeaway across all of them: *your users' data is sitting on a real service run by a real company,* usually Supabase or something like it, and you have an account there even if the builder hid it from you. Knowing that account exists — knowing where your data lives — is not optional once real people are trusting you with their information. You cannot protect what you don't know you have.

There is a practical follow-on to that, which is to actually go and *find* the account, once, early. Even if Lovable created the Supabase project on your behalf and you never typed your name into Supabase's website, there is a way to reach it, and the day to learn how is not the day something has gone wrong. Logging in to the underlying service even once does three useful things. It makes the abstract concrete — you see the actual tables, the actual rows, the actual humans' data sitting there, and the responsibility stops being theoretical. It shows you where the bill will eventually come from, so the "second bill" Chapter 21 warns about is not a surprise. And it is the place you would go, or send a developer, if you ever needed to inspect, export, or move your data. The builder hiding the account is a convenience for building; knowing how to find the account anyway is a necessity for owning what you have built.

CRUD: The Four Things Every App Does to Data

Almost everything an app does with data comes down to four operations, and they have an unlovely but useful acronym: **CRUD**. Create, Read, Update, Delete. Once you can see these four verbs, you can see the skeleton of nearly any data-driven app.

Create is adding something new — a new book in my reading log, a new booking in the teacher's tutoring app from Chapter 1, a new row in a table. It is the form-and-save moment.

Read is retrieving and showing what's there — displaying the list, loading a single record, searching. It is the most common operation by far; most of what an app does is read data and put it on the screen.

Update is changing something that already exists — editing a rating, marking a booking as cancelled, correcting a typo. Same record, new contents.

Delete is removing it. Straightforward, and the one to be most careful with, because gone is usually gone.

You will not type these words at the tool, and you certainly won't write the code that performs them. But naming them changes how you describe what you want, and describing well is the entire skill, as Chapter 9 made the case. "Let users add a task, see their list of tasks, check one off as done, and remove ones they no longer want" is, underneath, the full CRUD set spoken in plain English — and an app builder will turn that one sentence into a working table with all four operations wired up. When something doesn't work — the list won't update, the delete button does nothing — knowing which of the four verbs is failing turns a vague "it's broken" into a precise request the AI can actually fix.

Seeing the four verbs also helps you notice the ones your first description quietly forgot, which is the most common gap in early apps. People reliably ask for Create and Read — "let me add a book and see my list" — and just as reliably forget Update and Delete, because in the excitement of a working list it does not occur to them that they will eventually want to fix a typo or remove a mistake. Then a wrong entry sits there forever, unfixable, because the app was never given a way to edit or delete. Running your idea through CRUD before you build is a thirty-second checklist that catches this: for each kind of thing my app stores, can the user create it, see it, change it, and remove it — and which of those do I actually want them to be able to do? Sometimes the answer is deliberately no (you may *not* want students able to delete their bookings), and that is a real decision worth making on purpose rather than discovering by accident. The verbs are a lens for thinking completely about your data, which is exactly what a clear description requires.

Two Kinds of "Delete," and Why It Matters

Delete deserves a second look, because it hides a distinction that has bitten plenty of people. When a user "deletes" something, there are two genuinely different things that can happen underneath, and which one your app does is a decision — even if you never realized you were making it.

A *hard delete* removes the row from the database entirely. It is gone, irrecoverable, as if it never existed. A *soft delete* leaves the row in place but marks it as deleted, so it disappears from the user's view while still existing in the data. To the user, both look identical — the thing vanishes from the screen. To you, the owner, they are worlds apart. With a soft delete, an accidental deletion can be recovered, a cancelled booking can still be counted in your records, and you have a history. With a hard delete, a mis-tap is permanent and a customer's "I didn't mean to cancel that" has no remedy.

You do not have to know the terms, but you do have to know the choice exists, because the builder will pick one for you if you don't, and it will usually pick the simpler hard delete. For anything you might regret losing — bookings, orders, anything involving real people or money — it is worth saying explicitly: "when something is deleted, keep a record of it rather than removing it permanently, and let the owner restore it." That one sentence converts an irreversible mistake into a recoverable one, and it is the kind of instruction you only think to give if you know there were two roads at the fork.

The Things That Bite You

A few honest warnings, because the smooth demo hides some sharp edges.

Data has shape, and changing the shape later is annoying. When you tell the builder to store books with a title and a rating, it creates a table with exactly those columns. If you decide three weeks later you also want to store the author, you are now changing the structure of a table that already has data in it — a "migration," in the jargon — and these can get fiddly. The lesson is not to plan everything perfectly up front; it is to expect that adding fields later is a real operation, not a free one, and to say so clearly when you ask for it.

There is a specific subtlety inside this that surprises people: what happens to the *existing* rows when you add a new column. If you add an "author" column to a table that already holds fifty books, those fifty books have no author — the field is empty for all of them, because they were created before the field existed. New books can have an author; old ones simply do not, until someone goes back and fills them in. This is not a bug; it is the unavoidable arithmetic of adding a field to data that already exists. But it means "add an author column" can leave you with a list where half the books proudly show their author and half show a blank, and the fix is to decide, deliberately, what the empty ones should show or whether they need backfilling. Knowing this in advance turns a confusing half-empty list into an expected, manageable consequence.

"It works" in the demo is not "it saves." My reading-log story is the canonical trap. Always test the thing that actually matters: add some data, fully close and reopen the app, and confirm it is still there. If it vanished, your data was never reaching the database — it was living in the page. This is a five-second test that catches a whole category of "looks done, isn't done" failures.

The strongest version of this test is to check persistence *across devices*, not just across a refresh, because the two failures look the same on your screen but mean different things. Add a book on your laptop, then open the app on your phone. If the book is there, the data genuinely lives on a shared server, which is the whole point — every user, every device, sees the same real data. If it is *not* there, you have a subtler problem than the empty-list one: the data is being saved, but only locally, in the one browser you used, rather than in a true shared backend. An app where each device sees its own private copy of the data is not a multi-user app at all, no matter how convincingly it persists on the single machine you tested. For anything more than one person will ever touch, the cross-device test is the one that tells the truth.

A database full of real people's information is a responsibility, not just a feature. The moment your `users` table or your `orders` table contains actual humans' actual data, you have crossed from playing to obligation. Where that data lives, who can read it, and whether you are even allowed to be collecting it are no longer technical curiosities — they are the subject of Chapter 22, and they are the part that can genuinely hurt your users if you get them wrong.

There is a quiet discipline that belongs to this responsibility and is easy to adopt early: collect only what you actually need. Every column of personal data you store is something you are now responsible for protecting, and the safest data is the data you never collected in the first place. The booking page needs a name and an email to function; it does not need a phone number, a home address, or a date of birth, however easy it would be to add those fields "just in case." Each extra field is a small extra liability — one more thing that hurts your users if your app is ever breached, one more thing a privacy regulation might ask you to justify. The habit of asking "do I genuinely need this to make the app work?" before adding a field is not just tidiness; it is the cheapest form of data protection there is, because you cannot leak what you chose not to hold.

The backend is the half of your app you cannot see, which is exactly why it is the half worth understanding. A user judges your app by the screen; reality judges it by what happens behind the screen when they trust it with something that matters. And the piece of the backend that decides *who* each user is and what they're allowed to touch is where the stakes climb fastest of all.

Chapter 16: Authentication and Users

There is a moment in building an app when it stops being yours alone and becomes other people's. For my reading log, that moment never came — it was a tool for me, on my screen, with my books. But the teacher's tutoring app from Chapter 1 crossed that line the instant a second person needed to use it. Students had to *log in*. Each student had to see their own bookings, not everyone's. The teacher had to see all of them, but the students could not. The app suddenly had a notion of *who you are* and *what you're allowed to do* — and the moment an app has that notion, it has authentication, and authentication is where the stakes stop being cosmetic and start being about real harm.

I want to be plain about the register of this chapter before we start. Most of this book is cheerful, because building this way genuinely is a delight. This chapter is quieter, because the thing it covers is the one where a careless app stops being merely disappointing and starts being dangerous to the people who trusted it. The good news is that the builders make adding login almost suspiciously easy. The catch is that "almost suspiciously easy" is exactly the feeling that should make you slow down, and this chapter is about why.

Two Words That Get Confused: Authentication and Authorization

They sound alike and they are constantly muddled, but the difference is the whole subject, so let's nail it down.

Authentication is *proving who you are.* It is the login screen — the email and password, the "sign in with Google" button, the code texted to your phone. When you authenticate, the app confirms that you are who you claim to be. It is the bouncer checking your ID at the door.

Authorization is *what you're allowed to do once you're in.* The teacher and the student both authenticate — both prove who they are — but they are authorized differently: the teacher can see every booking, the student can see only their own. Authorization is the bouncer's second job, the one that happens after the door: deciding which rooms you're allowed into.

Here is why this distinction is not pedantry. The most damaging failures in vibe-coded apps are usually *authorization* failures, not authentication ones. The login screen works fine — everyone proves who they are. What breaks is the part that's supposed to stop one logged-in user from reaching another user's data. The app checks your ID at the door and then lets you wander into anyone's room. We will see the worst version of this in Chapter 22 (Security and Your Users' Data); for now, hold the shape of it: getting people *in* is the easy half, and it is not the half that hurts you. Controlling what they reach once they're in is the hard half, and it is.

There is a reason the easy half gets all the attention and the hard half gets neglected, and naming it helps you resist it. Authentication is *visible* — the login screen is right there, you can see it work, a demo of "watch me log in" is satisfying and complete. Authorization is *invisible* — it is a set of checks happening out of sight on every request, and when it works, nothing happens, which is precisely the problem: there is nothing to demo, nothing to admire, no satisfying click. So the visible half gets built, tested, shown off, and declared done, while the invisible half quietly may or may not exist. Your instinct, having built a working login screen, will be to feel secure. That instinct is measuring the wrong half. The half you cannot see is the half that determines whether your users are safe, and you have to go looking for it on purpose because it will never announce itself.

How Login Actually Gets Added

When you ask one of these builders for user accounts, it leans on the same backend services from the last chapter. Supabase, in particular, has authentication built in — it can handle the entire login machinery, which is why the tools reach for it. You describe the feature in plain language ("let users sign up and log in with email and password," or "let people sign in with their Google account"), and the builder wires up a genuinely substantial amount of plumbing you never see.

It is worth appreciating just how much that "substantial amount of plumbing" actually is, because the speed of it disguises the difficulty. A real login system has to let people sign up, store their credentials safely, let them log back in later, keep them logged in as they move around the app without asking for the password on every click, let them log out, handle the person who forgot their password, and refuse the person who typed the wrong one. Each of those is a small project on its own, and getting any of them subtly wrong is how accounts get compromised. The reason these tools reach for a service like Supabase rather than building it fresh each time is that this is a solved problem best left to people who solve it for a living — and that is genuinely good news for you. Leaning on a mature, well-tested authentication service is *safer* than a hand-rolled login, not just faster. The risk is not in the parts the service handles; the risk, as we will see, is in the parts that are yours.

The common ways users log in, in rough order of how often you'll meet them:

Email and password. The classic. The user picks a password, the app remembers them. The critical, non-negotiable detail underneath: passwords must *never* be stored in a form anyone could read them back. A competent backend like Supabase handles this correctly by default — it stores a scrambled, one-way version (a "hash") that even the app's owner cannot reverse into the original password. You will not implement this; you rely on the backend to do it right. But you should know enough to *confirm* it's happening, because "the backend usually handles it" is not the same as "it definitely did," and this is precisely the kind of thing the security chapter tells you to check rather than assume.

The "one-way" part is worth a sentence more, because it is genuinely clever and explains a thing you have surely experienced. A hash is a scramble that only runs forwards: the same password always scrambles to the same result, but there is no way to run the scramble backwards to recover the password from the scrambled version. So when you log in, the app scrambles what you typed and checks whether it matches the stored scramble — never knowing your actual password, only whether yours produces the same scramble as the one on file. This is why a well-built service can *never* email you your old password when you forget it; it genuinely does not have it, only the irreversible scramble. It can only let you set a new one. The next time an app cheerfully emails you your existing password in plain text, you have learned something alarming about how it stores them — and it is the opposite of what yours should do.

Social login ("sign in with Google / Apple / GitHub"). The user clicks a button and proves who they are through an account they already have. This is often *safer* for you, because you never handle their password at all — the heavy lifting and the password storage live with Google or Apple, not with your afternoon-old app. For many projects this is the path of least regret.

The "path of least regret" framing is worth taking seriously as a default rather than a footnote. When you offer social login, the entire burden of storing passwords safely, handling the forgot-password flow, and resisting the constant attempts to break into accounts moves off your plate and onto Google's or Apple's, who are extraordinarily good at it. You are outsourcing the riskiest part of authentication to the most capable possible custodian, for free, with a button. The tradeoff is that your users need an account with that provider, and you are quietly depending on it — but for the overwhelming majority of apps a non-coder builds, "let people sign in with Google" is not just the easiest option, it is the one that removes the most ways for you to hurt your users by accident. When you are unsure which login method to choose, this is a sound default precisely because it minimizes what can go wrong on your side.

Magic links and one-time codes. No password at all — the app emails you a link or texts you a code, and clicking or typing it proves you control that address or phone. Increasingly common, and pleasant for users. They share social login's chief virtue: there is no password for you to store and therefore no password for you to leak. The thing you are trusting instead is the user's email or phone, which is a reasonable thing to trust for most apps.

Whichever you choose, the experience of adding it is the same: you describe it, the AI builds it, and within minutes you have a working sign-up and login flow. That speed is real and it is wonderful. It is also the moment to remember that *a working login screen tells you nothing about whether the authorization behind it is sound.* The visible part — the part that worked in thirty seconds — is the easy half.

Roles: Who Gets to Be the Teacher

Most apps that have users at all eventually have *kinds* of users, and this is where authorization gets concrete. The tutoring app has two kinds: students, who can book and see their own bookings, and the owner, who can see everything. An online store has customers and administrators. A team tool has members and managers. The general name for "what kind of user is this" is a *role*, and how your app decides and enforces roles is one of the most consequential things you will describe, even though it sounds mundane.

The dangerous question hiding inside roles is: *how does the app know you are the owner and not a student?* There is a tempting wrong answer and a necessary right one. The wrong answer is to let the front end decide — to have the page check something it can see and show the owner's view if it likes the look of it. The trouble, from the last chapter, is that the front end is public and the user controls it; anything the page decides, a determined user can re-decide in their own favor. The necessary right answer is that a user's role lives in the backend, attached to their account in the database, and every privileged action checks that role on the server, where the user cannot tamper with it. "Is this person the owner?" must be a question the server answers by looking at trustworthy data it controls, not a question the browser answers about itself.

You will rarely type the word "role," but you are defining one every time you say "only the owner can do this" or "students should not see that." The instruction to absorb, and to give the builder explicitly when stakes are real, is that these distinctions must be *enforced on the server for every request*, not merely reflected in what the screen chooses to show. Ask for it in those terms: "the owner role should be checked on the server, not just in the interface, before showing any bookings." Whether the builder did that correctly is something to verify rather than assume — which is the whole burden of the next section.

The Pitfalls, Named Plainly

This is the section to read twice. Each of these is a way that an app which *looks* fully secured is quietly wide open, and each points forward to the chapter where we deal with it properly.

The locked front door with an open back window. This is the big one. Your login screen works, so it *feels* secure — but security that lives only in the interface is an illusion, because a determined user does not go through your interface. They send requests to your backend directly, bypassing your pretty login screen entirely. If the backend itself does not independently check, on every single request, that this user is allowed to see this specific piece of data, then the lock on the front door is theater. The real check has to live on the server, on every request, for every record. This is the Broken Object-Level Authorization failure that Chapter 22 describes at scale, and it is the single most important thing to verify before real users arrive.

Trusting the screen instead of the server. A close cousin. It is easy for an app to *hide* a button — say, the admin controls — from a normal user, and for that to feel like security. It isn't. Hiding something on screen does not stop someone from reaching the underlying function directly. The question is never "is this button hidden?" but "if someone calls this function directly, does the server refuse them?" If only the screen enforces the rule, the rule is not enforced.

Letting users reach data by guessing. If your app shows a booking at an address ending in `/booking/41`, what happens when a logged-in user changes the `41` to `42`? In a sound app: nothing — the server checks that booking 42 belongs to them and refuses. In an unsound one: they're now reading a stranger's booking. This is a thirty-second test you can run yourself, and Chapter 22 walks you through doing exactly that.

It is worth understanding *why* this particular hole is so common in vibe-coded apps specifically, because it is not random. Those sequential numbers in the address — 41, 42, 43 — are the row IDs from the last chapter, and they are sequential because that is the simplest, most natural way for a database to number rows, which is exactly what the builder reaches for by default. So the easy, default path produces guessable addresses, and the default code often fetches "the booking with this ID" without the extra step of also checking "and does it belong to the person asking?" The result is that the *most likely* thing the builder produces, the path of least resistance, is the vulnerable one. This is not the tool being malicious; it is the tool being efficient in a way that happens to skip a check no one explicitly demanded. Which is precisely why you have to demand it, and then test that it took.

Assuming the defaults are safe because the demo worked. The builder's generated authentication is often quite good out of the box — and it is also capable of taking shortcuts when you ask for a feature in a hurry, shortcuts that loosen the very protections you assumed were airtight. Every time the AI substantially rebuilds part of your app, the access rules can quietly shift. Security here is not a one-time setup; it is something to re-confirm whenever the machinery underneath changes.

This last point deserves emphasis because it defeats the natural assumption that security, once checked, stays checked. It does not. Suppose you carefully verified, last week, that students cannot reach each other's bookings — you ran the guess-the-address test, it refused, you breathed easy. Then this week you ask for a new feature, an export button maybe, and the builder regenerates a swath of code to add it. The access check you confirmed last week was in that swath, and it may or may not have survived the rebuild intact. The unsettling truth is that a security property you verified can be silently undone by a later, unrelated change, with no warning and no error, because nothing visibly broke. The defense is to treat the guess-the-address test and its cousins not as a one-time graduation ceremony but as a thing you re-run after any significant change, especially changes near the data that matters. Security is a state you maintain, not a box you tick.

What This Means for How You Build

I am not telling you to avoid adding accounts. Accounts are what turn a personal tool into something other people can use, and that's often the entire point. I am telling you to treat the moment you add login as the moment your responsibilities change.

The practical posture is this. Add authentication freely — it is one of the genuine gifts of these tools that login, which used to take a developer real effort, is now a sentence. But the instant your app holds *one user's data that another user must not see*, slow down and treat authorization as a thing to deliberately verify, not assume. Ask the builder directly whether access is checked on the server for every record. Run the guess-the-address test. And if the data behind the login is genuinely sensitive — anything financial, medical, regulated, or seriously harmful if exposed — that is the threshold where Chapter 22 will tell you, without apology, to get a human who understands application security to look before you go live.

It helps to keep a short, concrete checklist for the moment you add accounts, because "be careful" is too vague to act on. Four questions, each answerable: Are passwords handled by a real authentication service rather than stored by my app directly? Is each user's role enforced on the server, not just reflected in the interface? When I change the ID in the address to a record that isn't mine, does the server refuse me? And have I re-checked these after the last big change the builder made? None of these requires you to read code. All of them require you to ask and to test. Running through them is the difference between an app that merely has a login and an app that keeps the promise a login implies.

A login screen is a promise. It says to the people who sign up: *what you give me, I will keep, and I will not let the next person have it.* The builders make the screen in seconds. Keeping the promise is the part that takes judgment, and it is the part that is genuinely yours.

Chapter 17: Connecting APIs and Services

Picture a small online shop built over a weekend — a single page selling one print, a button that says "Buy." You ask the builder for it, the builder produces it, and there it sits, looking entirely like a real store. Then you stare at the Buy button and realize you have no idea what is supposed to happen when someone presses it. Where does the money go? The app has no way to take a credit card, talk to a bank, or land dollars in your account. It can't — those things live *outside* the app, run by other companies, and a weekend project has no idea they exist. The button is a button. It connects to nothing.

That gap is what this chapter closes. Almost no real app is an island. The moment you want to take a payment, send an email, look up an address, generate something with AI, or pull in data from somewhere else, your app has to reach out and talk to a service it doesn't own — Stripe for money, a service like Resend or SendGrid for email, a maps provider for addresses, an AI provider for intelligence. The wiring that lets your app talk to those outside services is called an **API**, and learning to connect them is what turns a good-looking shell into an app that actually does something. It is also where one specific kind of carelessness can leak a secret that costs you real money — so we'll spend real time on handling that safely.

What an API Is, Without the Jargon

API stands for Application Programming Interface, which tells you nothing, so set the acronym aside. Here is the useful version: **an API is a service's official front desk.** It is the agreed-upon way that one piece of software asks another piece of software to do something or hand over some information.

Think of a restaurant. You don't walk into the kitchen and cook; you talk to the waiter, who takes your order in a known format, relays it, and brings back the result. The kitchen stays private; the waiter is the interface. An API is that waiter. When your app "calls the Stripe API," it is handing a request to Stripe's front desk — "charge this card twenty dollars" — and getting back an answer — "done, here's the confirmation." Your app never sees inside Stripe's kitchen, and it doesn't need to. It just needs to know how to talk to the front desk.

The reason the restaurant analogy holds up under pressure is that a real API enforces the same boundaries a waiter does. The waiter will take a valid order and refuse an invalid one. He won't let you walk behind the counter. He won't bring you someone else's meal. An API is the same: it accepts requests in a specific shape, rejects malformed ones, checks that you're allowed to ask before it answers, and never lets you reach past the front desk into the machinery. That discipline is what makes services safe to connect to — and it is also why, when something goes wrong, the error you get back is usually the API politely telling you that you asked for something it won't do.

The wonderful thing, for someone building this way, is that you do not learn the format of each service's front desk. The AI builder knows it. You say "let customers pay with a card using Stripe," and the builder writes the code that talks to Stripe's API correctly. What you supply is not the conversation — it's the *credentials* that prove you're allowed to have it. And those credentials are where the care comes in.

It's worth lingering on just how much this changes the job, because in the old world connecting to a service was itself a substantial undertaking. A developer would read pages of documentation, learn the exact names and shapes of each request, write code to format it, write more code to interpret the reply, and handle every way the call could fail. That work was real, and it was the reason "just add payments" was never a small ask. The builder collapses all of it. It has, in effect, already read the documentation for the major services and knows their front desks by heart. When you ask for Stripe, it doesn't look anything up; it reaches for a pattern it already holds. This is genuinely one of the places where building without code earns the most leverage — the integrations that used to cost a developer a day each are now a sentence. But the leverage has a sharp edge, and the edge is always the same one: the builder writes the conversation flawlessly and then trusts *you* to hand it the credential and to put that credential somewhere safe. The hard part didn't disappear. It moved, from the writing to the handling, which is exactly the move this whole book keeps describing.

What a Call Actually Looks Like

You will never type one of these by hand — the builder writes them for you — but seeing the anatomy of a single API call once makes everything afterward less mysterious, the way seeing the inside of a clock once makes the hands less magical.

A call has four parts. There is a **destination** — the address of the front desk, something like `api.stripe.com`. There is an **action** — what you want done, expressed as a verb the service understands: fetch something, create something, update something, delete something. There is the **payload** — the details of the request, such as the amount to charge and which card. And there is the **credential** — the key that proves the request is coming from your account, attached quietly to every call. The service receives all four, checks the credential first, performs the action if it's allowed, and sends back a **response**: either the thing you asked for, or an error explaining why not.

That round trip — request out, response back — is the whole of how software talks to software. Your app might make a dozen such calls to render a single page: one to fetch the user's data, one to load their saved items, one to check a payment status. Each is a small, quick conversation through a front desk. The builder orchestrates all of it. The only piece of the conversation you are personally responsible for is the credential, because the credential is the part that's tied to *you* and the part that, mishandled, costs you.

One more thing about the response is worth knowing, because it explains a lot of the "why isn't this working?" moments you'll eventually hit. The response is not always the thing you wanted. A service can hand back, instead of the result, a small message saying *no, and here's why* — your credential was wrong, the request was malformed, you've asked too many times in too short a window, the item you referenced doesn't exist, the service itself is temporarily down. These are not failures of your app exactly; they're the front desk doing its job and telling you something. When a feature mysteriously stops working, the cause is very often hiding in one of these returned messages, and a genuinely useful move is to ask the builder, "what is the actual response the service is sending back when this fails?" The answer usually points straight at the problem — an expired key, a missing setting, a limit you've crossed — rather than leaving you guessing at a silent breakage. The errors are not noise; they're the most direct diagnostic you have, written by the service that knows exactly what went wrong.

The API Key: A Password That Spends Your Money

To use most outside services, your app needs an **API key** — a long string of random-looking characters that the service hands you when you sign up. The key is how the service knows the request is coming from *your* account. When your app calls Stripe with your key, Stripe knows to route the money to you. When it calls an AI provider with your key, the provider knows whose account to bill for the usage.

Sit with that second one for a moment, because it is the whole reason this chapter has a stern streak. **An API key is not just an identifier — it is a credential that can spend money and access data on your account.** A leaked AI-provider key can let a stranger run thousands of dollars of usage on your bill before you notice. A leaked key to a service holding data can let them read that data. The key is, functionally, a password — and like a password, where it lives determines whether you're safe.

To make that concrete: there is a well-worn, ugly pattern where someone's API key ends up somewhere public, automated scanners find it within minutes — and they are scanning constantly, around the clock, because finding live keys is profitable — and the key gets used to run expensive workloads on the owner's account. People have woken up to four- and five-figure bills accumulated overnight against an AI key they thought was tucked away. The owner did nothing but leave the key reachable; the machinery of the internet did the rest, fast. This is not a horror story I'm inventing for effect. It is a routine enough event that the providers themselves have built automatic key-leak detection and revocation to limit the damage. The lesson is not "be afraid of keys." It is "a key is a live thing, and where you put it is a decision with money attached."

This connects directly to the front-end-versus-back-end boundary from Chapter 15 (Data and Backends), and it is the single most important idea in this chapter:

A secret key belongs on the back end. Never in the browser. Front-end code — anything running in the user's browser — is, by definition, handed to the user. They have all of it and can read every line by opening their browser's developer tools, which requires no skill at all. So if your API key sits in the front-end code, it is not secret. It is published. Every visitor to your app can read it, copy it, and use it as if they were you. The back end, running on a private server, is the only safe home for a key, because that code is never sent to the user.

The mental model worth fixing in place is this: anything in the browser is a postcard, and anything on the server is a sealed letter. A postcard is readable by everyone who handles it on the way — you would never write a password on one. The server is the sealed envelope. When your app needs to do something secret, the right design is that the browser asks the server to do it — "please charge this card" — and the server, holding the key privately, makes the actual call. The user's browser never touches the key; it only ever asks the server, politely, to use it on their behalf. The builders that handle this well are quietly setting up exactly that arrangement for you.

It's worth understanding *why* this is so easy to get wrong, because the danger isn't that builders are careless — it's that the unsafe version is sometimes the one that looks like it's working. Imagine you ask a builder to "add an AI feature that summarizes what the user types." The straightforward way to make that work *right now*, in the preview, is to have the browser call the AI provider directly with your key attached. It works immediately. The summaries appear. Everything looks finished. And it is, in the precise sense that matters most, broken — because your key is now sitting in code that every visitor can read. The trap is that the broken version and the safe version produce identical behavior in the demo; the difference only shows up when a stranger opens the developer tools, or when the bill arrives. This is why you cannot rely on "it works" as your test for this particular thing. Working and safe are not the same, and the gap between them is invisible from the outside. The only way to know which one you have is to check where the key lives, which is exactly the check the rest of this chapter is going to drill into you.

How to Add a Service Without Leaking the Key

The good news is that the safe path is also the standard one, and the builders mostly support it well. Here's what it looks like in practice.

Store keys as environment variables, not in the code. Every one of these tools has a dedicated, private place to put secrets — usually called "environment variables" or "secrets" or "environment settings." This is a vault, separate from your code, that the back end can read but that never gets sent to the browser and never gets exported into a public code repository. When you add a service, the right move is to put its key *there*, not to paste it into a prompt asking the AI to "use this key: sk-abc123..." in a way that ends up baked into the app's visible code.

It's worth knowing why this distinction is so sharp. Code is a thing that travels — it gets exported to GitHub, copied between environments, sent to the browser, shared with collaborators. An environment variable is a thing that stays put: it's injected into the running app at the moment it runs, on the server, and it is deliberately kept *out* of the code so that when the code travels, the secret doesn't go with it. A key written directly into code is a key that will eventually be somewhere you didn't intend, because code goes places. A key stored as an environment variable stays home. That's the entire reason the mechanism exists, and it's why every serious platform offers it.

Ask the builder directly where the key will live. You are allowed to interrogate the tool. A genuinely useful prompt is: "Add Stripe payments, and make sure the secret key is stored as a server-side environment variable and is never exposed in the client-side code." Naming the requirement out loud nudges the builder toward the safe pattern and, just as usefully, makes you check.

Verify it didn't end up in the browser. After connecting a service, this is the confirmation worth making: ask the builder plainly, "Are any API keys or secrets visible in the client-side code?" — and if your app is going anywhere near real users or real money, have someone who can read code confirm it. There is also a check you can run yourself with zero technical skill: open your live app, open the browser's developer tools (right-click, "Inspect," then look under the Sources or Network tab), and search the loaded files for the first few characters of your key. If you find it there, it's exposed, full stop — the browser would not have it if it were safe. This one check guards against the most common serious flaw in this entire category of software. It takes a minute. The failure it prevents can take a month's worth of someone else's AI bill out of your account.

Understand the difference between public and secret keys. Some services hand you two keys: a "publishable" or "public" key that is *designed* to be safe in the browser, and a "secret" key that absolutely is not. Stripe works this way, for instance. The public key is fine on the front end; the secret key must stay on the server. If a service gives you two keys and calls one of them secret, treat that word as literal and load-bearing. The reason the public key is safe is that it can only do harmless things — it can start a payment, but it cannot, on its own, move money or read your account; the secret key is the one with the real power. Confusing the two and putting the secret one where the public one belongs is one of the cleanest ways to turn a safe integration into a dangerous one, and it happens precisely because the two strings look almost identical.

There's a naming convention that helps you tell them apart at a glance, and it's worth committing to memory because it turns an abstract worry into a concrete look-for. Many services build the key's nature into its prefix. Stripe's publishable keys begin with `pk_` and its secret keys with `sk_` — `p` for publishable, `s` for secret — and several other providers follow a similar habit. So when you're about to paste a key, glance at the first few characters: a key that starts with the secret marker has no business anywhere near front-end code, and a key that starts with the publishable marker is the one allowed out in the open. Most services also distinguish *test* keys from *live* keys, often with a marker like `_test_` versus `_live_` somewhere in the string. While you're building and experimenting, you want the test keys, which talk to a sandbox where nothing real happens — test payments don't move test money and test charges hurt no one. Only when you're genuinely going live do you swap in the live keys. A surprising number of "why did this charge a real card during testing?" and "why is my test data showing up in production?" confusions trace back to mixing up test and live keys, so it's worth a deliberate pause every time you handle one: is this the test key or the live key, and is this the publishable one or the secret one? Two small questions, asked every time, prevent a whole category of expensive mistakes.

When a Key Leaks Anyway: Damage Control

Mistakes happen, and the honest thing is to tell you what to do when one does, because the difference between an inconvenience and a disaster is how fast you respond. If you have any reason to think a key has been exposed — you spotted it in the browser, you pasted it somewhere public, you committed it to a repository — the fix is the same and it is immediate: **revoke the key and issue a new one.** Every service's dashboard has a place to do this, often labeled "roll," "rotate," or "regenerate." Revoking instantly turns the old key into a dead string that does nothing; issuing a new one gives your app a fresh, uncompromised credential. Then you update the new key in your builder's secrets vault, and you're safe again.

The reason speed matters is the scanners from earlier: a leaked key is a race between you and them. Roll it the moment you suspect, not after you've confirmed beyond doubt — a needlessly rolled key costs you sixty seconds, a leaked one left live can cost you a great deal more. Many providers will also email you if they detect your key in a public place and may revoke it for you, but you should never rely on that as your safety net. Treat the key like a house key you've lost: you don't wait to see if anyone uses it before changing the lock.

One subtlety about rolling a key catches people mid-panic, so it's worth knowing in advance: rotating a key can briefly break your live app. The instant you revoke the old key, every part of your app still using it stops working, and it stays broken in that small window between revoking the old key and getting the new one into your secrets vault. For a low-stakes app this is a non-event — a few seconds of downtime while you paste the new value. But the implication is that you should do the rotation deliberately and have the new key ready to install, rather than revoking first and then wandering off to figure out where the new one goes. The right sequence is calm and quick: generate the new key, paste it into your builder's secrets vault, confirm the feature works, and only then, if the service requires it as a separate step, fully disable the old one. Done in that order, the gap is small and the panic is smaller. And to be clear, a brief outage is always the right trade against a live, leaked key — a feature being down for thirty seconds is recoverable; a stranger spending your money is the thing you're racing to stop.

It's also worth a sentence on how keys get leaked in the first place, because knowing the common routes helps you avoid them. The classic one is committing a key into your code and then syncing that code to a public GitHub repository — the key travels with the code, the repository is public, and the scanners do the rest. Another is pasting a key into a public forum or a chat while asking for help debugging, where it lingers in the message history. A third, specific to this kind of building, is pasting the key into a prompt in a way that bakes it into the app's visible front-end code, which we've already covered. Almost every real leak is one of these three: code going public with the key inside it, the key shared while asking for help, or the key written somewhere the browser can see. Avoid those three routes and store keys only in the secrets vault, and you've closed off the great majority of the ways this goes wrong.

The Services You'll Most Often Reach For

A quick orientation to the outside world your app will likely touch, so the landscape feels less foreign.

Payments. Stripe is the near-universal default for taking money, with others in the mix. The builders integrate it readily. The thing to internalize: real money raises real stakes, and a payment integration is exactly the kind of feature where the "verify where the secret key lives" check is not optional. A second subtlety worth knowing about payments specifically: do not trust the price the browser sends. If your checkout tells the server "the user is paying nine dollars," a malicious user can change that number to one cent before it leaves their machine, because the browser is theirs to tamper with. The correct pattern — and the one a careful builder will follow if you ask for it — is for the *server* to decide the price by looking up the item, never to take the amount on faith from the front end. When you connect payments, it's worth asking the builder directly: "Is the charge amount calculated on the server, or is it sent from the browser?" The right answer is the server.

Email. Apps constantly need to send mail — a confirmation, a password reset, a notification. Services like Resend, SendGrid, or Postmark exist solely to send email reliably on your app's behalf, and you connect them with a key like any other. (Names and offerings shift; check current options when you get there.) The non-obvious part of email is *deliverability* — getting your messages into inboxes rather than spam folders. These services help with the technical reputation work that makes that happen, which is a large part of why you use a dedicated service instead of trying to send mail directly from your app. If your app's emails start landing in spam, that's a deliverability problem, and it's usually solved by following the sending service's setup steps for verifying your domain, not by anything in the builder.

AI features. If you want your app *itself* to be intelligent — to summarize, generate, classify — it calls an AI provider's API, billed by usage against your key. This is the one where a leaked key burns money fastest, because usage scales without limit, so guard this key with particular care. It's also the one where you most want a *spending cap* set on the provider's side. Most AI providers let you set a hard monthly limit on your account, a ceiling past which calls simply stop working. Setting that cap is the seatbelt for this entire chapter: even if something goes wrong — a leaked key, a runaway loop in your app, a feature called far more than you expected — the cap turns a catastrophic bill into a merely annoying one. It is five minutes of setup against an open-ended downside, which is about the best trade in software.

File storage. Apps that let users upload things — profile photos, documents, images for a listing — need somewhere to put those files, and that somewhere is usually a dedicated storage service rather than your app's own database. Services exist whose only job is to hold uploaded files reliably and hand them back fast, and the builders connect to them the same way they connect to anything else. The thing to know is that storage, like everything else, meters: you pay for how much you store and often for how much gets downloaded, so an app where users upload large files at volume has a cost line you'll want to anticipate. The other thing to know is that uploaded files are a security surface of their own — letting strangers put files on your server is exactly the kind of thing that wants the careful, server-side handling the rest of this chapter preaches, because "let anyone upload anything" is a sentence with sharp edges.

Maps and addresses. If your app needs to show a map, validate an address, or turn a place name into coordinates, a maps provider's API does it. These are worth a specific mention because mapping APIs are notorious for two things: they almost always require a key, and that key, if left unrestricted, can be used by anyone who finds it to run up usage on your account. Most maps providers let you *restrict* a key so it only works when called from your own app's address, which is a good defense to set up and a question worth asking the builder about — "is the maps key restricted to my domain?" It's a case where even a key that's necessarily somewhat visible can be fenced in so a leak does less damage.

Everything else. Weather, SMS and text messages, calendars, data lookups, document generation — if a capability exists as a service, it almost certainly has an API your app can call, and the builder almost certainly knows how to call it. The pattern is always the same: sign up, get a key, store the key safely, describe the feature. Once you've connected two or three services, the fourth and fifth feel routine, because the shape never changes — and that sameness is the quiet gift of APIs. The whole sprawling outside world of capabilities reduces to one repeated motion you only have to learn once.

A Worked Example: Adding Email to a Booking App, Safely

Abstract advice slides off; a concrete walk-through sticks. So picture the teacher's booking page from Chapter 1, now working, and the feature she wants next: when a student books a slot, the app should email her so she isn't refreshing the page to check. Here is the whole arc of adding that, with the care threaded through, because the sequence is the same one you'll follow for any service.

First, she picks a service whose job is sending email and signs up for it — one of the dedicated providers exists precisely so apps don't have to send mail themselves. The sign-up hands her a key. Right here, at the very first step, the discipline begins: that key goes nowhere except, in a moment, the builder's secrets vault. She does not paste it into a prompt. She does not paste it into a note-taking app or a chat. She copies it and holds it for the one place it belongs.

Second, she tells the builder what she wants, naming the safety requirement out loud: "When someone books a slot, send me an email notifying me. Use [the email service]. Store the API key as a server-side environment variable, not in the front-end code." The builder writes the integration — the call to the email service's front desk, formatted correctly, fired whenever a booking happens — and prompts her for the key, which she pastes into the secrets vault it offers, not into the conversation.

Third, she verifies. She asks the builder plainly, "Is the email service's key visible anywhere in the client-side code?" and gets a no. Then, because this app is going to handle real people's bookings, she does the zero-skill check herself: she opens the live app, opens the browser's developer tools, and searches the loaded files for the first few characters of her key. It isn't there. Good — the key is living on the server, where it should, and the browser never sees it.

Fourth, she tests the real behavior, not just the appearance. She books a slot as a pretend student and waits for the email. It arrives — or it lands in spam, which is the deliverability issue from a moment ago and is solved by following the email service's domain-verification steps, not by anything in the builder. Either way, she's testing the thing actually working end to end, not assuming it works because the code looks done.

That's the entire pattern, and it generalizes with almost no changes to payments, AI features, maps, file storage, anything. Sign up and get a key. Tell the builder what you want and name the safety requirement. Verify the key didn't leak to the browser. Test the real behavior. Four steps, the same four every time, and the only one that's genuinely yours to get right is the third — keeping the key off the postcard and inside the sealed envelope.

Rate Limits and the Free-Tier Cliff

One more practical reality, because it surprises people who've done everything else right. Almost every API has a **rate limit** — a cap on how many requests you can make in a given window, there to protect the service from being overwhelmed. For a small app you may never touch it. But if your app calls a service on every page load and you suddenly get a burst of visitors, you can hit the ceiling, and when you do, the service starts refusing requests. To your users, this looks like the app breaking — features that worked yesterday now fail intermittently — even though nothing in your code changed and you did nothing wrong. The cause is just volume meeting a limit.

There's a graceful way to handle rate limits and an ugly way, and it's worth asking the builder for the graceful one when you connect a service you'll call often. The ugly way is for the app to fire its request, get refused, and simply break in front of the user. The graceful way is for the app to notice the refusal, wait a moment, and try again — most rate limits are about *bursts*, so a brief pause and a retry often slides right through. A second graceful move is *caching*: if your app keeps calling a service for the same answer — the same address, the same weather, the same lookup — it can remember the answer for a while instead of asking again every single time, which cuts both the cost and the chance of hitting the limit. You don't implement either of these yourself; you ask for them. "If the service is rate-limited, retry after a short delay rather than failing" and "cache results that don't change often so we're not calling the service repeatedly for the same thing" are requests a good builder will honor, and they turn a fragile integration into a sturdy one.

The related surprise is the **free-tier cliff.** Many services give you a generous free allowance to get started, which is exactly why your app worked perfectly while you were building and testing it. Then real usage arrives, you cross the free threshold, and either the service starts charging you or it stops working until you upgrade. Neither is a bug; it's the business model. The defense is to know, for each service you connect, roughly where its free tier ends and what happens when you cross it — does it bill you, or does it block you? Both are survivable if you've planned for them and a nasty shock if you haven't. There's a sharp asymmetry hiding in that question worth pulling out: a service that *bills* you when you cross the line keeps working and quietly costs more, which is a financial surprise; a service that *blocks* you keeps the bill flat and breaks the feature, which is a reliability surprise. Knowing which kind each of your services is tells you what failure to brace for — an unexpected charge or an unexpected outage — and they call for different preparation. For the billing kind, you want a spending cap or alert. For the blocking kind, you want to know your usage trend before you hit the wall, so the upgrade is a planned step rather than an emergency at the worst possible moment. This ties directly into the cost discussion in Chapter 21 (Cost, Credits, and Token Limits), where the "total cost of ownership" of a live app is the recurring theme.

The Shape Is Always the Same

The shape of every one of these is identical once you see it: an outside service does the hard specialized thing, your app talks to it through its API, and a key proves you're allowed to. The builder handles the conversation; you handle the key. Get the key's home right and connecting services is one of the most powerful, satisfying things you can do — the moment your weekend shop's Buy button finally connects to something and a real payment lands. Get it wrong and you've published a password that spends your money. Same feature, same afternoon; the only difference is where one string of characters ended up. That is a difference worth slowing down for, and Chapter 22 is where we make absolutely sure you have.

Chapter 18: Design and Polish

Picture two versions of the same app side by side. They do exactly the same thing — same data, same buttons, same features. One looks like a finished product: clean spacing, a coherent color scheme, text that lines up, a logo in the corner, buttons that respond when you hover over them. The other looks like what it is, a rough draft — cramped, mismatched, a little broken-feeling even though nothing is actually broken. The person using the first one trusts it. The person using the second one keeps asking, warily, "is this real?" Nothing under the hood differs. The only difference is polish, and polish is the difference between *people will use this* and *people won't*.

That is the uncomfortable, slightly unfair truth this chapter is about: how an app *looks and feels* is not decoration laid on top of the real work. It is part of whether the app works at all, in the only sense that matters — whether a human being can use it without friction and trusts it enough to put their information into it. The wonderful news for someone building without code is that these tools start you ahead. They generate genuinely good-looking interfaces by default, far better than most of us would produce by hand. The skill this chapter teaches is not how to design from nothing — it's how to *steer* a tool that already designs well, through the same plain-language conversation you've used for everything else.

You Are Starting From a High Floor

Worth saying plainly, because it changes the whole task: these builders produce attractive interfaces out of the box. v0 in particular (Chapter 4) is built around producing polished, modern React interfaces and leans on well-regarded, consistent design components, so its raw output already looks like something a competent team made. The others are not far behind. You are not facing a blank canvas and a box of crayons. You are facing a draft that is already 80 percent of the way to looking professional, and your job is the steering, not the painting.

This matters because it tells you where to spend your effort. Don't agonize over building a look from scratch — let the tool give you a strong starting point, then refine it toward *your* thing. The refinement is where design judgment lives, and judgment, as the whole book keeps insisting, is the part that's actually yours.

It also explains a trap that catches enthusiastic first-timers: rebuilding the look from zero when you didn't need to. Because the conversation makes it so easy to ask for sweeping changes — "make it look completely different" — people sometimes tear down a perfectly good default and end up worse off, because the default was the product of a great deal of accumulated design taste and their replacement is a series of off-the-cuff requests. The more productive move is almost always to keep the strong foundation and adjust it in specific, named ways. Think of it as editing rather than rewriting. You're not a worse designer than the tool; you just have a different job — knowing what *this particular app, for these particular people* should feel like, which is something the tool's generic good taste can't know on its own.

There's a sharper version of this trap worth naming, because it wastes both time and, in these tools, money: the sweeping vague request is also the *expensive* request. "Make it look completely different" sends the builder off to regenerate large swaths of the interface, which costs more units (Chapter 21's subject) and gives you back something you then have to react to in full, often discovering it threw away three things you liked to change the one thing you didn't. A specific, named request — "increase the spacing between the cards" — touches only what it names, costs less, and leaves everything you were happy with untouched. So the discipline of editing rather than rewriting isn't only about preserving good taste; it's about steering with a scalpel instead of a sledgehammer, which is cheaper, faster, and far more likely to land the change you actually pictured. When you catch yourself about to type "make it look better" or "redesign this," stop and ask what *specifically* feels wrong, then say that instead. The vaguer the request, the more the tool has to guess, and the more it guesses, the further the result drifts from what was in your head.

A Vocabulary of Small Steering Words

You don't need the language of a professional designer, but a handful of plain words make your requests land more precisely, and precision is what gets you the change you actually pictured instead of a near-miss you then have to correct.

Spacing is the air around and between things. The most common reason a draft feels cramped or amateurish is too little of it — text jammed against edges, buttons crowding each other. "Add more breathing room between the sections" or “this feels cramped, give the content more space” is a request that reliably lifts the felt quality of a page.

Hierarchy is the sense of what matters most. On a well-designed page, your eye knows instantly where to look first — the most important thing is biggest or boldest or set apart, and the secondary things recede. When a page feels like a flat wall of equally weighted stuff, it has no hierarchy, and “make the main action stand out more and the secondary options quieter” fixes it.

Alignment is whether things line up. Misalignment is one of those flaws you feel before you can name — a heading that’s a few pixels off from the text below it reads as sloppy even to someone who couldn’t tell you why. “Make sure these elements line up cleanly” is a useful catch-all.

Contrast is how clearly things stand apart — dark text on a light background, a bright button against a muted page. Low contrast looks elegant in a designer’s mockup and becomes unreadable for a real person in real sunlight on a real phone. We’ll return to contrast under accessibility, because it’s where good taste and genuine usability happen to point the same direction.

There are a couple more of these worth having in your pocket, because they cover the rest of the common complaints.

Consistency is whether the app looks like one thing rather than several things stapled together. The same kind of button should look the same everywhere; the same kind of heading should be the same size; the spacing between sections should follow one rhythm rather than varying at random. When an app feels subtly “off” in a way you can’t pin to any single element, inconsistency is usually the culprit — your eye is registering that the rules keep changing. “Make the styling consistent across all the pages” is the catch-all, and it’s one of the most reliably improving requests there is, because the tool is good at applying a single rule everywhere once you ask it to.

Density is how much you’ve packed into a given space. Too dense and the page feels overwhelming, a wall of information with no room to breathe; too sparse and it feels empty, like you have to scroll forever to find anything. The right density depends on the app — a dashboard for a power user can be dense, a sign-up page for a nervous newcomer should be airy — and naming which way you want it to move (“this page feels too busy, simplify it” or “there’s too much empty space, bring things closer together”) steers it.

You don't have to memorize any of these. But knowing that the cramped feeling is *spacing*, the flat feeling is *hierarchy*, the sloppy feeling is *alignment*, the stapled-together feeling is *consistency*, and the overwhelming feeling is *density* turns a vague "make it look better" — which gives the tool nothing to grab — into a specific instruction it can actually act on. The whole skill, really, is learning to translate the feeling into the word, because the word is what the tool can do something with.

Steering by Reference, Not Just Description

There's a second way to steer design that's often more precise than describing in words, and people underuse it: point at something that already looks the way you want. You don't have to invent a visual language from scratch when you can say "I want it to feel clean and minimal, like [a service known for that look]" or "more playful and colorful, the way [some app] is." The tool has seen enough of the design world to understand these references, and a reference carries information that's hard to put into adjectives — a whole coherent mood, a sense of restraint or energy, a relationship between color and space that would take a paragraph to specify and still come out vague.

This works best when the reference is for a *quality*, not a *copy*. "Make it look exactly like [a famous app]" is both legally and practically a bad idea — you don't want to clone someone's identity, and the tool can't perfectly reproduce it anyway. But "I admire how calm and uncluttered that app feels; aim for that quality" gives the tool a target it can move toward while still building *your* thing. Think of references as describing the weather you want, not the specific painting you want copied. A second useful form of reference is your own taste catalog: as you browse the web, notice which apps and sites feel good to use and try to articulate *why* — was it the generous spacing, the limited palette, the way the most important button was unmistakable? That noticing is design education by osmosis, and it makes your steering requests sharper over time, because you're building a vocabulary of what "good" looks like to you specifically.

Responsive: The Test People Forget

Here is the single most common polish failure I see, and it's invisible until it isn't. You build your app, it looks great — on your laptop, where you built it. Then someone opens it on their phone, and the layout falls apart: text running off the edge, buttons too small to tap, a menu that doesn't fit. The app was never tested anywhere but the screen it was born on.

Responsive is the word for a layout that rearranges itself sensibly to fit whatever screen it's on — phone, tablet, laptop — rather than assuming everyone has the same display you do. The builders generally produce responsive layouts by default, which is a gift, but "generally" is not "always," and the only way to know is to look. So make this a habit: every time you finish a meaningful change, view the app on a phone, or shrink your browser window down narrow and watch what happens. Most modern phones carry most modern web traffic; if your app breaks on a phone, it breaks for the majority of the people who'll ever see it.

There's a quick technique for testing this without owning a drawer of devices. In most browsers you can open the developer tools and switch on a "device" or "responsive" view that simulates a phone-sized screen, letting you flip between a narrow phone, a wider tablet, and a full laptop in seconds. It's not a perfect substitute for opening the app on your actual phone — touch, real screen size, and real network conditions all differ — but it catches the gross failures in a fraction of the time. The discipline is to look at the small screen *as part of the work*, not as a final check you do once before launch and never again. Layouts break on small screens silently, every time you add a feature, because each new thing is one more piece that has to fit somewhere narrow.

When something does break, you fix it the way you fix everything here — by describing it: "On mobile the navigation menu overflows; make it collapse into a menu button on small screens." "The buttons are too small to tap comfortably on a phone." "On a narrow screen the two columns should stack on top of each other instead of squeezing side by side." You don't need the vocabulary of a designer. You need to *notice the problem on a small screen* and say what's wrong. The most useful single habit here is the "thumb test": can you complete your app's main task one-handed, with a thumb, on a phone, without zooming or squinting? If yes, your responsive design is doing its job. If no, you've found exactly the thing to ask the builder to fix.

Branding: Making It Look Like Yours

A default-pretty app still looks like a default — pleasant and generic. Branding is what makes it feel like it belongs to you or your business rather than to a template, and it's mostly a few high-leverage moves you can request directly.

Color. The fastest way to make an app feel like yours is to set its colors to yours. "Use a deep navy as the primary color and a warm orange for buttons." "Match the palette to my brand: the main color is this shade of green." A coherent color scheme, consistently applied, does more for the felt quality of an app than almost anything else. A practical tip that saves a lot of back-and-forth: if you have an exact brand color, give the tool its precise code rather than a word. "Make the primary color #1A3D5C" lands the exact shade, where "use navy" lands *a* navy that may not be *your* navy. If you don't have a code, naming a feeling ("a calm, professional blue, not too bright") still steers well — just expect to refine it once you see it.

Typography. The fonts an app uses carry a surprising amount of its personality. A request as simple as "use a cleaner, more modern font for headings" can shift the whole tone. You don't need to know font names; describe the feeling — friendlier, more serious, more elegant — and let the tool choose. The one piece of typographic discipline worth keeping is restraint: two fonts is plenty for almost any app — often one for headings and one for body text, or even a single font used at different weights. The amateur instinct is to reach for several distinctive fonts; the result reads as chaotic rather than expressive. If your app feels visually noisy, "use fewer, more consistent fonts" is frequently the fix.

Logo and identity. Adding your logo, your name, a favicon (the little icon in the browser tab) — these small marks are what turn "an app" into "*my* app." They're easy to ask for and they matter more than their effort suggests, because they're the signals a user reads, half-consciously, as *this is a real, owned thing, not a throwaway*. The favicon especially is one people forget and then notice on everyone else's polished apps: it's the tiny icon next to the page title in a browser tab, and a generic placeholder there is a small but real "this is unfinished" signal. Most builders accept an image upload for it; it's a two-minute fix with a payoff out of proportion to the effort.

Dark mode and the small touches. A surprising number of users now expect apps to respect their device's dark-mode preference — to show light text on a dark background when their phone or laptop is set that way, especially at night. Many builders can add this with a single request ("support dark mode, following the user's system setting"), and it's a small touch that reads as thoughtful. It's not mandatory, and for a simple prototype it's wasted effort, but for an app people will use regularly it's the kind of detail that quietly signals care. The broader point is that polish is partly an accumulation of small respectful touches — dark mode, a proper favicon, hover states, smooth transitions — none of which matters alone, all of which together produce the felt sense that a competent person sweated the details.

Consistency over flourish. The mistake to avoid is reaching for flashy effects. The thing that actually reads as professional is *consistency* — the same spacing, the same button style, the same color logic everywhere. A plain app that is perfectly consistent looks more trustworthy than a fancy one that is slightly off in a dozen small ways. When in doubt, ask the tool to make things more consistent, not more elaborate. A concrete version of this: pick one style for your primary buttons and insist on it everywhere. When a user sees three different-looking buttons that all do roughly the same kind of thing, some part of their mind has to stop and re-learn the interface each time, and that friction reads as low quality even when they couldn't articulate why. "Make all the buttons use the same style" is one of the highest-return consistency requests there is. The same logic applies to anything that repeats: if your app shows a list of items, every item should be laid out the same way; if it has forms, every form should handle its labels and buttons the same way. Repetition done consistently is invisible in the good way — the user stops having to think about the interface and just uses it — which is exactly the goal.

UX: The Difference Between Pretty and Usable

Design is how it looks; **UX** — user experience — is how it *feels to use*, and the two are not the same. An app can be beautiful and still be confusing, and a user trips over confusing long before they admire beautiful. This is the deeper, harder half of polish, and it rewards thinking like the person who'll use the app rather than the person who built it.

A few things to refine, by describing what's missing:

Tell the user what's happening. When they press a button that takes a second to work, does anything acknowledge the press, or does it just sit there until they press it again, confused? "Show a loading indicator while the data loads." "Disable the submit button and show a spinner after it's clicked, so people don't submit twice." Feedback is the difference between an app that feels responsive and one that feels broken. The double-submit case is worth singling out because it's both common and consequential: a user clicks "Pay," nothing visibly changes for a second, so they click again, and now you've charged them twice. The fix — disable the button and show that something is happening the instant it's clicked — is one short request and it prevents a genuinely upsetting bug.

Handle the empty and the wrong. What does a brand-new user see when their list is empty — a blank void, or a friendly "No items yet. Add your first one"? What happens when someone types nonsense into a field — a clear "Please enter a valid email," or a baffling silence? These edge states are exactly what the cheerful demo skips and what real use hits immediately. The empty state in particular is the very first thing every new user sees — by definition they have no data yet — and a blank screen at that moment makes a worse first impression than almost anything else, because the user can't tell whether the app is empty-by-design or simply broken. A good empty state does double duty: it reassures ("nothing's wrong, you just haven't started") and it instructs ("here's the one thing to do first"). Asking for these — "show a helpful message and a clear next step when the list is empty," "validate the email field and explain what's wrong in plain language" — is some of the highest-value polish you can request.

Confirm before the irreversible. A delete button that deletes instantly, with no "are you sure?", is a trap waiting for a misclick. "Ask for confirmation before deleting." Small request, real protection. The principle generalizes to anything a user can't undo — deleting, sending, paying, publishing. A useful habit is to walk through your app asking, for each button, "what's the worst thing that happens if someone clicks this by accident?" Where the answer is "something they can't take back," put a confirmation in front of it. Where the answer is "nothing, they can just click again," leave it frictionless — confirmations on harmless actions are their own kind of bad UX, training people to click "yes" reflexively until the confirmation that mattered gets dismissed on autopilot too.

Reduce the number of decisions. Every choice you put in front of a user is a small tax on their attention, and a page crowded with options — six buttons, four links, three things competing to be clicked first — makes people freeze rather than act. The most usable apps are often the ones that ruthlessly narrow what you can do on any given screen down to the one or two things that matter there, tucking everything else away until it's needed. If a screen feels busy or people seem unsure where to start, the fix is frequently subtraction, not addition: "this page has too many options competing for attention; make the primary action obvious and move the rest somewhere secondary." The instinct when something isn't working is to add — another button, another explanation, another feature.

The more disciplined move is usually to take away, until the one thing the user should do is the one thing that's obvious.

Make the path obvious. The clearest sign of good UX is that a first-time user knows what to do without being told. If you have to explain how your app works, that's the app asking to be redesigned. Watch someone use it without your narration; where they hesitate is where the design needs work. This is genuinely the most valuable test in this chapter and the one people most resist doing, because watching someone fumble through something you built is uncomfortable. Do it anyway, and do it without helping — the instant you say "no, click the *other* button," you've contaminated the test, because real users won't have you sitting beside them. Their hesitations, the wrong turns, the place they give up — that is a free, unflinching design review, and it will tell you more than any amount of staring at the app yourself, because you can no longer see it with fresh eyes and they can.

A practical way to run this test, since "watch someone use it" is easy to say and awkward to do: give the person a *task*, not a tour. Don't say "here's my app, what do you think?" — that invites polite praise and tells you nothing. Say "you want to book a tutoring slot for Thursday afternoon; go," and then go quiet. Watch their hands and their face. The moment they pause and scan the screen looking for something is the moment your design failed to make that something obvious, and it's worth more than any compliment. Two or three people is enough; you don't need a research budget, you need a couple of honest friends and the discipline to sit on your hands while they fumble. Write down every place they hesitated, thank them, and then go fix the hesitations one at a time. This single habit, done a few times, will teach you more about your own app's UX than a whole shelf of design books, because it confronts you with the gap between how you *think* your app reads and how it actually reads to someone seeing it cold.

A Word on Accessibility

Polish has a dimension that's easy to skip and worth not skipping: whether people who don't see, move, or read the way you do can use your app at all. This isn't a niche concern. Plenty of your users will have less-than-perfect eyesight, will be on a phone in bright sun, will navigate by keyboard rather than mouse, or will rely on a screen reader that reads the page aloud. Designing so they're not locked out is partly a matter of decency, sometimes a matter of law, and almost always a matter of reaching more of the people you built the thing for.

The good news is that the highest-value accessibility moves overlap exactly with good design generally. **Sufficient contrast** between text and background — the same thing that keeps your app readable in sunlight — is the single biggest one; that fashionable light-gray-text-on-white look fails real readers, and "make sure the text has enough contrast against the background to be easily readable" fixes it. **Real text labels on buttons and form fields**, rather than relying on an icon alone or on color alone to convey meaning, helps both screen-reader users and anyone who finds a bare icon ambiguous. **Tap targets big enough to hit** helps people with imprecise motor control and also everyone using a thumb on a phone. You can ask the builder directly — "make this app more accessible: check color contrast, add proper labels to form fields and buttons, and ensure it works with keyboard navigation" — and a good one will make meaningful improvements. It won't be a substitute for a real accessibility audit on something high-stakes, but it clears the most common, most exclusionary failures, and most of those failures were quietly making the app worse for *everyone*, not only the people they locked out entirely.

Knowing When Polish Is Enough

A closing honesty, because this chapter could otherwise become a treadmill. Polish has no natural finish line — there is always one more refinement, one more shade to adjust, one more state to handle. So you need a stopping rule, and the rule depends on what the app is *for*. A prototype meant to test an idea with a few people (a use this whole book treats as legitimate — see Chapter 25) needs only enough polish that the idea comes through clearly; agonizing over its typography is wasted motion. An app you're putting in front of paying customers earns more, because for them the polish *is* part of whether they trust you with their money and their data.

Match the effort to the stakes. Make a throwaway look clear; make a real product look trustworthy; and don't confuse the two, in either direction. The builders make looking good easy enough that the temptation runs toward over-polishing the disposable and under-polishing the real — resist both. What you're aiming for, always, is the version of the app where a stranger opens it, isn't confused for a second, and quietly assumes a competent person made it. That assumption is the whole prize, and on a good day these tools will get you most of the way there before you've changed a thing.

Part V: Shipping

Audience: everyone.

"An app inside the builder is a rehearsal. Shipping is the moment it stops being yours alone and becomes something a stranger can break, judge, and rely on."

— A working principle

Chapter 19: Deployment and Hosting

Here is a moment that catches almost everyone exactly once. Your app sits on your screen, working perfectly — you click through it, fill in the form, watch the data appear — and then you want to show it to someone, and you realize you have no idea how. It lives inside the builder's editor, on a preview that exists only because you are logged in and looking at it. Nobody else has the address. The app works, and nobody but you can reach it.

That gap — between "it works on my screen" and "other people can use it" — is what this chapter is about. It is a smaller gap than it used to be, because every tool in this book handles the hard part for you. But it is a real gap, and the vocabulary around it (deploy, host, environment, production) is the kind of thing that gets explained either not at all or in a way that assumes you already know. So let me close it plainly.

What "Hosting" Actually Means

An app is a set of files and instructions sitting on a computer. When you build it in one of these tools, that computer is, in effect, the builder's preview environment — a temporary place that runs your app so you can see it, tied to your login. Nobody else has the address, and even if they did, that preview is not built to be the permanent home of a public app.

Hosting means putting your app on a computer that is always on, always connected to the internet, and reachable by anyone with the link. That computer is a *server* — not a special magical machine, just a computer whose job is to sit in a data center somewhere and answer requests from browsers all day. When someone types your app's address, their browser asks that server for the page, and the server sends it back. Hosting is renting space on that always-on computer so your app has a permanent home.

A small but clarifying distinction lives inside that word "app," because most modern apps actually have two halves that get hosted in subtly different ways. There is the *front end* — the pages, the buttons, the layout, everything the browser draws — and there is the *back end* — the database and the private logic from Chapter 15 (Data and Backends). The front end can be served from anywhere fast; it's just files. The back end is the part that runs your private code and holds your data, and it's the part that genuinely has to be a live, always-on, secured thing. When a builder "deploys your app," it is quietly arranging hosting for both halves and wiring them together. You don't have to manage that split yourself, but knowing it exists explains a lot — including why your backend service (Chapter 21) often shows up as a separate bill from your front-end hosting. They're two things being hosted, even though they feel like one app.

This is the part that trips people up. In the old world, you had to find a hosting company, pay them, configure a server, and copy your files onto it — a genuinely fiddly chore that scared a lot of non-technical people off entirely. The tools in this book fold all of that into a single button. You do not rent a server, configure anything, or copy files. You click *Deploy* (or *Publish*, or *Ship* — the word varies), and the tool puts your app on hosting it manages for you, and hands you back a live web address. The chore is gone. But understanding what the button *does* still helps, because the moment something goes wrong, the people who know what hosting is are the ones who can reason about it.

It's worth appreciating just how much that button is quietly doing, because the smoothness can make it feel like nothing is happening at all. When you click deploy, the tool finds a server (or, more accurately, a slice of an enormous fleet of servers it manages), packages your app into the form a server can run, copies it there, points an address at it, sets up the encryption that makes the address load securely, and arranges for the whole thing to stay running and to scale up if a crowd shows up. Each of those was, until very recently, a separate skilled task that a person did by hand, sometimes over hours. Now they happen in the time it takes to make coffee, invisibly, for free or nearly so. This is genuinely one of the marvels of the current moment, and it's easy to take for granted precisely because it works so well. The reason to notice it is not gratitude for its own sake — it's that knowing roughly what's under the button is what lets you reason calmly when one of those hidden steps is the thing that failed.

Deploy, Publish, Go Live — Same Idea

You will see these words used loosely and somewhat interchangeably. *Deploy* is the technical term — it means taking your app and installing it onto hosting where it can run for real. *Publish* and *go live* are the friendlier versions of the same act. All of them name the moment your app crosses from private preview to public reality.

The thing worth knowing is that this is a distinct step you take on purpose. Your app does not become public the instant you build it; it becomes public when you deploy it. Until then, you are working in private, and you can build, break, and rebuild without a single stranger ever seeing the mess. That privacy is a gift – it means you can get the thing right before anyone is watching.

There's a related step that usually happens invisibly inside that button, and it's worth a sentence because it explains a category of confusing errors. Before your app can run on a server, the builder has to *build* it – take the human-friendly project you've been editing and package it into the optimized form a server actually serves. Most of the time this is silent and instant and you never think about it. But occasionally a deploy fails at this stage with a "build error," and the surprise is that the very same app was working fine in the preview a moment ago. The reason is that the preview environment is forgiving in ways the real build is not; something that the live editor tolerated turns out to be a genuine problem when packaged for production. When you hit a build error, the move is not to panic that you've broken everything – it's to read the error (or paste it back to the builder and ask it to fix it), because the preview's version of your app is still safely intact. A failed build means nothing went live, which is exactly the safety the separation is there to provide.

The single most effective thing you can do with a build error is the least intuitive: copy the whole error message, paste it back into the builder, and say "the deploy failed with this build error; please fix it." The error text, which looks like intimidating gibberish, is in fact a precise description of what went wrong, written for exactly the kind of automated reader the builder is. It will often understand and fix the problem faster than a human could even finish reading the message. The mistake people make is to react to a build error the way they'd react to a kitchen fire – with alarm and frantic improvisation – when the right response is closer to handing a doctor a chart: here is the diagnostic information, please interpret it. The more of the error you give the builder, the better it can fix it, so resist the urge to summarize ("it said something about a missing thing") and just paste the whole thing. And remember, throughout, that the live app your users see (if you've deployed before) is unaffected by a failed build; you are working on the next version in private, and the failure has cost you nothing but a few minutes.

The Idea of Environments

Here is a concept that pays for itself the moment you grasp it: an app usually lives in more than one place at once.

There is the version you are actively building and breaking — call it *development*. And there is the version real people use — call it *production*. They are the same app, but they are not the same copy. Development is your workshop, where a half-finished feature or a typo that crashes the page does no harm because no real user is there. Production is the storefront, where everything is supposed to work because real people are depending on it.

Why this matters to you, specifically. When you deploy, you are copying the current state of your workshop into the storefront. That means two things. First, changes you make after deploying do not automatically appear in production — you have to deploy again to push them out. Second, and more importantly, anything broken in your workshop at the moment you deploy goes live broken. The discipline this asks of you is simple: get the app into a state you are actually happy with *before* you hit deploy, and after every significant change, deploy again to update what the public sees. Some tools blur this line and publish your changes continuously; others make deployment a deliberate, separate act. Knowing which behavior your tool has is worth a minute of checking, because the difference is "my users saw my half-finished experiment" versus "they didn't."

There's a second, sneakier way environments diverge, and it bites people who think they've done everything right. The workshop and the storefront often have *different settings* — most notably the secrets and API keys from Chapter 17. You may have pasted your live Stripe key into development to test it, but production is a separate copy and may not have that key set, so the feature that worked perfectly in your preview silently fails the moment it's live. "It works in development but breaks in production" is one of the most common and most baffling experiences in this whole craft, and a large share of the time the cause is exactly this: a setting or secret that exists in one environment and not the other. When a feature works in preview and dies in production, check first whether all the keys and settings it needs are actually present in the production environment, not just the development one. The builders try to carry these across for you, but "try" is not "always," and this is the first place to look.

A related habit worth forming early: real users mean real data, and real data is the one thing you can't casually rebuild. While you're developing, you can wipe and recreate your database a dozen times a day without a second thought — it's all test junk. Once you're in production, the database holds things that matter to actual people, and a careless "just rebuild it from scratch" instruction to the AI can take those things with it. The mental line to draw is that production data is sacred in a way development data never is. Before any instruction that might restructure or reset your live data, the question to ask is "what happens to the data that's already in there?" — and if you can't answer confidently, that's the moment to slow down or to ask the builder explicitly to preserve existing data.

The protection that makes this line safe to walk is *backups*, and it's worth a moment because most people don't think about backups until the day they desperately need one and discover they don't have it. A backup is just a saved copy of your data from a point in time, so that if something destroys or corrupts the live data, you can restore the copy and lose only what changed since. The good news is that the backend services these tools rely on often take automatic backups for you — but "often" is not "always," and the size of the safety net varies a great deal by service and by plan. So the question to settle *before* you have real users, not after, is concrete: does my backend back up my data automatically, how far back do those backups go, and how would I actually restore one if I needed to? Find the answer while you're calm. The day a bad instruction or a bug wipes something real is not the day you want to be discovering that no copy exists. If your backend doesn't back up automatically, or doesn't back up often enough for your comfort, that's a gap worth closing deliberately — even a manual export of your data once in a while is infinitely better than nothing. Data is the part of your app that can't be regenerated by describing it again; everything else, the AI can rebuild, but the data is the one irreplaceable thing, and it deserves a copy.

Each Builder's Path to Live

The four builders all get you to a public URL, but the road differs in ways that matter later — especially the question of whether you are tied to that builder forever or can walk away with your app. I will keep the specifics light, because deployment menus and plan details churn faster than any printed book can track; verify the current flow in each tool's own docs when you get there.

v0 (by Vercel) deploys into Vercel's world, and that is both its strength and its string attached. v0 is made by Vercel, a company whose entire business is hosting web apps, so deployment is about as smooth as it gets — a click sends your app onto Vercel's hosting, fast and polished. The trade is that the smoothness comes from tight coupling to the Vercel ecosystem. As of the major rebuild in early 2026, v0 also added real Git integration and the ability to export your code to GitHub, which loosens that string considerably — you *can* take the code elsewhere. But the default, frictionless path runs straight into Vercel hosting, and that is by design.

Bolt (by StackBlitz) gives you the most freedom about where to land. Bolt produces standard, portable code, and when you deploy you have genuine choices: ship to Bolt's own hosting, send it to Netlify (a popular hosting service Bolt integrates with), export the whole thing to GitHub and host it anywhere you like. If you care about not being locked to one company's platform, Bolt's deployment story is the friendliest in this book. The app you build is yours to take.

Lovable publishes with a click and syncs to GitHub both ways. Lovable is built for non-coders, and its publish step reflects that — one button puts your app live on a Lovable-hosted address. What sets it apart is bidirectional GitHub sync: your app's code lives in a GitHub repository you control, changes flow in both directions, and that means you are not trapped even though the default hosting is Lovable's. Good portability wrapped in a non-coder-friendly button.

Replit deploys inside the place you built it, which is the most seamless and the most sticky. Replit is a complete cloud development environment with hosting and a database built in, so deployment is less a hand-off to somewhere else than a flip of a switch in the place you already are. Its Agent can plan, build, run, fix, and deploy your app without you ever leaving Replit. That is the closest thing in this book to "describe it and get a deployed, running app." The catch, which Chapter 23 takes up in full, is that the same integration that makes it seamless also makes it the hardest to leave — your app is woven into Replit's database and Replit's hosting, and unweaving it later is real work.

If you noticed a pattern there, you read it right: the easier a tool makes deployment by handling everything itself, the more your app tends to depend on that tool. Bolt sits at one end (most portable, you do a touch more of the steering), Replit at the other (most seamless, most locked in), with Lovable and v0 in between. That is not a flaw in any of them. It is a genuine trade-off, and the right answer depends on whether this app is a quick experiment you will throw away or something you intend to live with for years. We come back to exactly that question in Part VI.

It's worth saying a word about what "lock-in" actually means in practice, because the term gets thrown around as a scare word and the reality is more textured. Lock-in isn't a lock on a door; it's a measure of how much *work* it would take to leave. A tool with low lock-in produces standard, portable code you could hand to any developer and host anywhere — leaving is a chore but a finite one. A tool with high lock-in weaves your app into its own proprietary services — its database, its hosting, its particular way of doing authentication — so that leaving means not just moving code but untangling it from machinery that only exists inside that tool, and possibly rebuilding parts from scratch. Neither is inherently wrong, and the high-lock-in tools are high-lock-in precisely *because* they integrate everything so seamlessly, which is the thing that made them pleasant to use in the first place. The point is to make the trade with your eyes open: a quick experiment you'll throw away should optimize for seamlessness and ignore lock-in entirely, while something you intend to build a business on should weigh portability seriously, because the cost of leaving is a cost you might really have to pay someday. Chapter 23 takes this up in full; for now, just know that the convenience and the lock-in are two faces of the same coin, and which face matters depends entirely on how long you mean to keep the app.

There is one practical move worth making regardless of which tool you choose, and it follows directly from that spectrum: **get your code into a GitHub repository early if your tool supports it.** Three of the four builders here can sync to GitHub, and doing so costs you almost nothing while buying you a great deal. It means there is a copy of your app's code that exists *outside* the builder — a copy you own, that you could hand to a developer, that survives even if you stop paying for the builder or the builder changes its terms or, in the worst case, shuts down. It's the difference between renting an apartment and renting one where you've also kept a copy of everything you own in a storage unit you control. You may never need it. The day you do, you'll be very glad it's there, and by then it's too late to set up.

Rolling Back When a Deploy Goes Wrong

A reassuring thing the deploy button doesn't advertise: going live is usually reversible. Most of these platforms keep a history of your past deployments, which means that when you ship a change and it turns out to be broken — and eventually you will — you can often roll back to the previous working version with a click, restoring the storefront to how it was before you broke it while you sort out the fix in your workshop. This is one of the genuine luxuries of managed hosting, and it changes the emotional stakes of deploying: a bad deploy is an inconvenience to undo, not a disaster to survive. It's worth finding out, before you launch anything that matters, where your particular tool keeps its deployment history and how rollback works there, so that you already know the answer in the moment you're staring at a broken live app and your pulse is up. The five minutes of looking when you're calm is worth an hour of flailing when you're not.

What Deploying Does Not Do

Two honest cautions, because the deploy button is so smooth that it can lull you.

Deploying does not make your app correct, and it does not make it safe. The button publishes whatever you have, flaws and all. If your app has a security hole — and Chapter 22 explains why vibe-coded apps are especially prone to a particular nasty one, secrets exposed in the browser — deploying does not fix it. It exposes it, to everyone, at a public address. The cheerful frictionlessness of going live is precisely why I have placed the security chapter before you would naturally launch anything that matters. A working app and a safe-to-ship app are not the same thing, and the deploy button cannot tell them apart. It's worth stating the asymmetry baldly: while it's private in your preview, a flaw is a flaw nobody can reach. The instant you deploy, that same flaw is a flaw at a public address that automated scanners will find on their own schedule, not yours. Deploying doesn't create the risk, but it's the moment the risk goes from theoretical to live, which is exactly why the deliberate pre-launch pass in the next chapter exists.

Deploying does not mean you are done paying attention. Once an app is live, it is live — running, costing something, holding people's data, occasionally breaking. Hosting is handled, but tended is not the same as forgotten. A live app has a small but real ongoing relationship with you: services it depends on can change, a dependency can need updating, a bill can creep, a user can hit a bug you never saw. “Set it and forget it” is a fine aspiration for a toaster and a poor one for software that holds other people’s information. We will get to the running costs in Chapter 21 and to the long-term maintenance reality in Chapter 23, but the seed to plant now is that the deploy button is the start of the app’s life, not the end of your involvement in it.

The Quiet Milestone

For all those cautions, do not let me talk you out of the moment. The first time you deploy an app you described into being, and you send the link to someone, and they open it on their own phone in their own house and it just *works* — that is a genuinely new thing in the world, and it was effectively impossible for a non-programmer to reach a few years ago. My booking-page teacher from Chapter 1 felt it. So did I, the first time I found the deploy button and texted someone a link instead of calling them into the room to look over my shoulder.

The address that comes back is usually a long, automatically generated one — something with the builder’s name buried in it, functional but not exactly yours. Making it *yours*, with a real name people can remember and type, is the next thing to handle, and it is more approachable than its reputation suggests.

Chapter 20: Custom Domains and Going Live

When my teacher friend deployed her tutoring booking page, the tool handed her an address that looked something like `tutoring-signup-7f3a.builder-name.app`. It worked. Students could reach it. But when she put it on a flyer in the staff room, she watched a colleague squint at it, try to type it, and get it wrong twice. The app was fine. The address was the problem — long, random, full of the builder's branding, and impossible to remember. What she wanted was `bookmytutor.com`, something a person could hold in their head and type without a typo.

Getting from the first to the second is the work of this chapter. It involves a piece of internet plumbing called DNS that has a reputation for being mystifying, and I am going to demystify it, because the actual idea is simple and the actual steps are short. Then I will give you a launch checklist, because "going live" is a moment worth doing deliberately rather than by accident.

What a Domain Is

A domain is the human-friendly name of your app — `google.com`, `bookmytutor.com`, the thing you type into the address bar. That is all it is: a name. The reason it feels like more is that names and the actual computers they point to are two separate systems, deliberately kept apart, and connecting them is the part that confuses people.

Here is the whole idea in one breath. Every computer on the internet — including the server hosting your app — has a numeric address, a string of digits called an IP address that browsers actually use under the hood. Nobody wants to type digits, so we invented a phone book: the Domain Name System, or DNS. DNS is the global directory that translates a friendly name like `bookmytutor.com` into the numeric address of the computer that should answer for it. When someone types your domain, their browser quietly asks DNS "where does this name point?", DNS answers with the address, and the browser goes there. That is the entire mechanism. A domain is a name; DNS is the phone book that says where the name points.

It's worth knowing the anatomy of a domain name itself, because the parts have names you'll see in the buying process and it saves confusion. In `bookmytutor.com`, the `.com` is the *extension* (the formal term is top-level domain) — the category the name lives in. The `bookmytutor` is the part you choose. And anything in front, like the `www` in `www.bookmytutor.com` or the `app` in `app.bookmytutor.com`, is a *subdomain* — a sub-section you can create under your main name without buying anything new. You buy `bookmytutor.com` once, and from then on you can point `www`, `app`, `shop`, or any other subdomain you like wherever you want, all under that single purchase. This is why a business can run its marketing site at the bare name and its actual application at `app.theirname.com` from one domain — the subdomain is free to create once you own the name.

A quick word on choosing the name, since it's the one creative decision in an otherwise mechanical chapter. Shorter is better, because people have to type it and remember it. Easy to spell beats clever, because a name that gets misheard or misspelled sends people to a dead address or, worse, a competitor's. A plain `.com` is still the default people assume and the one they'll type even if you tell them otherwise, so if your `.com` is available it's usually worth taking; the newer extensions are fine and often cheaper, but expect to spell the address out loud forever. And before you fall in love with a name, do a quick check that it isn't an existing trademark you'd be stepping on — a thirty-second search now is cheaper than a renaming later.

A few more naming traps are worth knowing because they're invisible until someone trips on them. The "radio test" is the sharpest one: imagine saying your domain out loud to someone who has to type it from memory, with no spelling. Does `bookmytutor.com` survive that? Mostly. Does a name with a number in it, or a deliberately misspelled word, or a hyphen? Rarely — "is that the number or the word?", "one word or two?", "where's the hyphen?" are exactly the questions that send people to the wrong address. Hyphens in particular look fine written down and become a nightmare spoken aloud, so avoid them if you can. Watch, too, for names that read differently when the words run together than you intended — squished-together domains have an infamous history of accidentally spelling something unfortunate, and the only defense is to look at the whole string with fresh eyes and ask what *else* it could be read as. Finally, think one step ahead about email: if you own `bookmytutor.com`, you can later have an address like `hello@bookmytutor.com`, which looks far more legitimate than a free webmail address when you start corresponding with users. You don't have to set that up now, but choosing a name you'd be happy to put after an `@` is worth a moment's thought, because the domain is going to be your identity in more places than just the address bar.

The Two Steps, in Plain Terms

To put your app at a custom domain, you do two things.

First, you buy the name. Domains are rented, not owned outright — you pay a yearly fee (often somewhere in the rough neighborhood of ten to twenty dollars a year for a common `.com`, though it varies by name and registrar, so check current prices) to a company called a *registrar*. Names like Namecheap, GoDaddy, Cloudflare, and Google's successor services are registrars; some of the builders will even sell you a domain directly from inside the tool, which is the simplest path if you do not want to manage a separate account. Buying the name reserves it for you. It does not yet connect it to anything.

A note on that "buy from inside the builder" option, because it's a real trade-off and not just a convenience. Buying through the builder is genuinely the path of least resistance — one fewer account, one fewer set of values to copy, and the connection often happens automatically. The cost is a little less independence: your domain and your hosting live with the same company, which is mildly more to disentangle if you ever move. For a first app or a small project, the convenience usually wins and the downside is small. For something you expect to grow or to outlive your relationship with any one tool, buying the domain at an independent registrar keeps the name — which is your identity, the thing on the flyers and in people's memories — under your own roof regardless of where the app itself is hosted. There's no wrong answer; just know that you're making a small choice about coupling, the same coupling theme that ran through the last chapter.

Second, you point the name at your app. This is the DNS step, and it is where the friendly name gets told which computer to send people to. In practice you log into wherever you bought the domain, find the DNS settings, and add a small entry that points the name at your builder's hosting. Your builder tells you exactly what entry to add — this is a standard, well-trodden path, and every tool in this book has a "connect a custom domain" screen that gives you the specific values to paste in. You are not configuring anything from scratch; you are copying two or three pieces of information from your builder into your registrar.

You'll see a couple of cryptic abbreviations in those DNS settings, and a one-line translation removes most of the fear. An **A record** points a name directly at a numeric IP address — "this name lives at that machine." A **CNAME record** points a name at *another name* rather than a number — "this name is an alias for that other address," which is handy because if the underlying machine ever moves, the alias keeps working. Your builder will tell you which kind to add and exactly what to put in it; you don't have to decide. The reason to know the words at all is so that when the screen asks you to choose "record type" from a menu, you're picking from a list you've at least heard of rather than guessing among acronyms. Paste in precisely what the builder gives you — the values are exact, and a single wrong character means it won't work — and you're done.

A few specific stumbles happen so reliably at this step that naming them in advance will save you the frustration. The first is the *bare name versus www* question. People expect both `bookmytutor.com` and `www.bookmytutor.com` to work, because both look right to a human, but to DNS they are two different names that each need their own pointing, and builders often want you to set up one to *redirect* to the other so they don't drift apart. If your domain works with the `www` in front but not without it, or the reverse, this is almost always the cause, and the fix is to make sure both names are configured the way your builder's instructions specify. The second stumble is a leftover entry: if the domain pointed somewhere before — at a parking page the registrar put up, or an old site — there may be an existing record fighting with the new one you're adding. Two records telling DNS different things about the same name produce confusing, intermittent results, so part of doing this cleanly is removing any old pointing for that name before adding the new one. The third is the copy-paste slip: a trailing space, a missing dot at the end of a value, a character that looks identical but isn't. Because the values are matched exactly, an invisible difference breaks everything while looking perfectly correct, which is maddening; the cure is to copy directly from the builder rather than retyping, and to compare the result character by character if it isn't working.

That is genuinely the whole job. Buy a name, paste a couple of values, wait. The waiting, it turns out, is the part that confuses people most, so it gets its own section.

Why You Have to Wait

After you add the DNS entry, the domain does not work instantly, and this catches almost everyone the first time, so let me name it before it scares you.

DNS is a worldwide phone book, copied across countless computers so that lookups are fast everywhere. When you change an entry, the update has to spread — *propagate* is the jargon — across all those copies, and that takes time. Usually it is minutes; occasionally it stretches to a few hours; the old worst-case warning was up to a day or two, though that is rare now. The practical upshot: if you set up your domain and it does not work right away, that is normal. Give it time before you assume you did something wrong. Most people, the first time, conclude they made a mistake and start frantically changing settings, which only makes it worse. The fix for "it's not working yet" is very often just waiting.

There's a particular trap inside this waiting period worth naming, because it sends people in circles. While propagation is partial, the domain can work *for some people and not others* — it resolves on your phone but not your laptop, or for a friend across town but not for you, purely because different copies of the phone book have updated and others haven't yet. This looks like a baffling intermittent bug and is in fact completely normal mid-propagation. It also explains a maddening loop: you change a setting, it doesn't work, you change it again, but now you're also waiting on the *second* change to propagate, so you can't tell whether your first change was right. The discipline that breaks the loop is patience — make the change once, carefully, matching the builder's values exactly, and then leave it alone for a few hours before touching anything. Changing settings repeatedly during propagation is the single most common way people turn a fifteen-minute wait into a day of confusion.

The Lock in the Address Bar

One thing your custom domain needs, and one thing you almost certainly get for free without thinking about it: HTTPS, the little padlock that tells visitors the connection is secure and encrypted. The `s` matters — it means data traveling between your user and your app is scrambled in transit rather than sent in the open.

The good news is that every builder in this book sets this up automatically when you connect a domain. You do not buy a certificate, install anything, or configure encryption. It is handled. I mention it only so that you know to *expect* the padlock — if you connect a domain and your app loads without it, or the browser warns visitors that the site is "not secure," something is wrong and worth pausing on, because users have rightly been trained to flee a site that throws that warning.

One detail fits the waiting theme: the padlock sometimes lags the domain by a little. The encryption certificate gets issued automatically once the domain is connected and propagating, and there can be a short window — usually minutes, occasionally an hour or two — where the domain resolves but the secure certificate hasn't finished provisioning yet, so the browser briefly shows a warning. Like propagation itself, this typically resolves on its own; the move is to wait a bit before assuming it's broken. If hours pass and the warning persists, *then* it's worth checking that your DNS entries exactly match what the builder asked for, because a certificate can't be issued for a domain that isn't pointing where it should.

A Launch Checklist

"Going live" is the moment you stop building for yourself and start being responsible to other people. It deserves a deliberate pass rather than a hopeful click. Here is the checklist I would run before sending the link to a single real user. Some of these point back to earlier chapters because launch is where everything you built gets tested at once.

Walk through the whole thing as a stranger would. Open your app in a fresh browser window where you are not logged in — a private or incognito window is the easiest way to guarantee a truly clean slate — and do the main task a real user will do: sign up, book the slot, submit the form, whatever the app is *for*. Things that work while you are logged in as the builder routinely break for a first-time visitor, because you have data, permissions, and a session they won't have, and this is the cheapest way to catch it. Pay special attention to the very first screen a brand-new account sees, the empty state from Chapter 18, because it's the one view you almost never look at once your own account is full of test data.

Try to break it gently. Submit the form empty. Type nonsense into the fields. Put letters where numbers go and a thousand characters where you expected ten. Click the buttons in the wrong order, or twice in a row. You are not trying to be cruel; you are finding the obvious cracks before a confused real user falls into them. Real users are inexhaustibly creative at doing things you never imagined, and the half-hour you spend deliberately misusing your own app surfaces a surprising share of what they'd hit by accident in the first week.

Check it on a phone. A large share of your visitors will arrive on a small screen, and an app that looks great on your laptop can be unusable on a phone. Open it on your actual phone, not just a resized window, and make sure the core task works with a thumb. The flyer in the staff room is the perfect example: people will scan a code or type the name on the device in their pocket, not the one on a desk, so the phone experience often *is* the experience for the audience you most want to reach.

Confirm the security basics before real data arrives. This is the one that cannot wait, and Chapter 22 is its full treatment: ask your builder, in plain words, whether any API keys or secrets are exposed in the browser-side code, and test whether one user can reach another user's data. That second test is concrete and you can do part of it yourself: make two accounts, put some data in the first, then log in as the second and try every way you can think of to see the first account's data. If account two can ever see account one's information, you have the most serious and most common flaw in this category of software, and you've found it before a stranger did. A launch checklist that skips this is not a launch checklist. If the app handles anything sensitive, this is the point to bring in a technical person, not after something leaks.

Know what happens when you change things post-launch. Recall from Chapter 19 that some tools push your changes to the public continuously and some require a deliberate re-deploy. Be certain which yours does, so you do not either leave a fix unshipped or accidentally publish a half-done experiment to live users. While you're at it, confirm you know where your tool's rollback lives, so that if a post-launch change breaks something, you can put the working version back fast instead of fixing under pressure.

Have a way to hear about problems. Even a simple "contact me" link or an email address gives your first users a way to tell you when something breaks — and something will. Going live without a feedback path means your users hit a wall silently and just leave, and you never learn why. The earliest users of anything are also your best source of the bugs you couldn't see yourself, but only if you give them a channel; a quiet user who hit a problem is indistinguishable from a user who never came back, and you want to be able to tell the two apart.

Confirm your costs won't surprise you under real load. Before strangers arrive, take a minute to make sure the services your app leans on won't either bankrupt you or break under success. The free-tier cliff from Chapter 17 and the metering from Chapter 21 both become real the moment usage stops being just you testing. The concrete pre-launch moves: set a spending cap on any AI provider your app calls, so a surge of usage — or a leaked key, or a bug — can't run an open-ended bill; glance at where each service's free tier ends, so you know roughly when the first charges arrive; and make sure you know which services *bill* you versus *block* you when you cross a line, because the first is a financial surprise and the second is an outage. None of this takes long, and it converts "I had no idea it could cost that" into a number you chose in advance.

Know your support story for when something breaks at 11pm. Related to the feedback path but distinct: decide, before you launch, what you'll actually do when a user reports a problem you can't immediately solve. Even a one-line plan helps — "I'll reply within a day," "I'll roll back if it's serious and investigate when I can." The point isn't to build a support department; it's to not be caught flat-footed and panicked the first time a real person tells you their booking didn't go through. Knowing in advance where your rollback is (from Chapter 19), how you'll hear about problems, and roughly how fast you intend to respond turns the inevitable first incident from a crisis into a procedure.

Decide who's actually allowed in, and when. A launch doesn't have to be a public detonation. For most first apps the wiser move is a *soft* launch — share the link with a handful of friendly people first, watch what happens, fix what surfaces, and only then put it on the flyer or post it widely. The cost of a quiet false start with five forgiving testers is nothing; the cost of a loud one in front of everyone you wanted to impress is real. Going live is a dial, not a switch, and turning it up gradually is almost always the calmer path. There's a second reason the gradual approach is wise that has nothing to do with bugs: a quiet launch lets you find out whether anyone actually *wants* the thing before you've spent your one big announcement on it. If five friendly testers use it once and never return, that's information worth having privately rather than discovering it in public after a splashy launch. The soft launch tests two things at once — whether the app works, and whether the idea lands — and both answers are cheaper to learn before the crowd arrives.

The Difference a Name Makes

There is a real psychological shift the moment your app lives at a name you chose. The random builder-generated URL says *experiment*. A clean domain says *this is a real thing I am standing behind*. My teacher friend felt it when `bookmytutor.com` resolved for the first time and the address on the staff-room flyer finally matched the app — the colleague who had fumbled the long URL typed the short one correctly on the first try and booked a slot to test it.

That shift is also a responsibility, which is why the launch checklist is not optional ceremony. A memorable name in front of an insecure or broken app just means more people reach the broken thing faster. Going live well means the name and the readiness arrive together: something worth typing, behind something worth using.

What you cannot see from the address bar, though, is what all of this costs to keep running — the domain is a yearly fee, but the app itself, the building and the hosting and the machinery underneath, meters in ways that surprise people. That is the next thing to understand clearly, before a bill does the explaining for you.

Chapter 21: Cost, Credits, and Token Limits

A founder I know built a prototype in one of these tools over a long weekend, loved it, and showed me the bill on Monday with the particular wide-eyed look of someone who has just learned how something works by being charged for it. He had signed up for a plan that cost, as he understood it, a fixed monthly figure. He had then spent two days asking the tool to build, rebuild, tweak, and rebuild again — and somewhere in there he had blown through the allowance the plan included and started consuming more, and the meter, which he had not realized was running per-action rather than flat, kept running. The app was good. The cost was not what the sticker on the plan had led him to expect.

He was not careless and he was not ripped off. He had simply not understood the *shape* of how these tools charge, which is genuinely different from the flat-monthly-fee model most of us are used to from streaming services and software subscriptions. This chapter is about that shape — how the metering works, why your costs grow with the size of your project rather than staying flat, and the costs that hide downstream of the sticker price. I am going to keep every specific number flagged and provisional, because pricing on these tools changes month to month and any figure I print will be stale before long. The *mechanisms*, which is what actually protects you, are durable.

Why the Meter Runs Per-Action, Not Per-Month

Most subscriptions you know are flat: pay a fixed amount, use the thing as much as you like. AI app builders mostly are not, and the reason is that every time you ask one to do something, it runs a large, expensive AI model on your behalf, and that costs the company real money each time. So instead of an all-you-can-eat fee, they charge for *usage* — and they wrap that usage in friendlier-sounding units called credits, tokens, messages, checkpoints, or effort, depending on the tool.

The names differ but the idea is the same: **you have a budget of these units, and actions spend them.** Asking the AI to build a feature spends units. Asking it to fix a bug spends units. A big, complicated request spends more than a small one. When the budget included in your plan runs out, you either wait for it to refresh on the next cycle or pay for more. A plan's monthly price is not the price of unlimited building; it is the price of a *bucket* of building, and the bucket has a bottom.

This is the single most important thing to internalize, because it inverts the instinct a flat subscription trains. With Netflix, watching more costs nothing extra, so you never think about it. With these tools, doing more costs more, every time, and the cheerful frictionlessness of "just ask it to rebuild that" is exactly what empties the bucket. My founder friend's mistake was bringing a flat-fee instinct to a per-action meter.

It helps to understand what the unit is actually measuring underneath the friendly name, because then the wide swings in cost stop feeling random. Most of these systems are, at bottom, counting **tokens** – the small chunks of text an AI model reads and writes, where a token is very roughly three-quarters of a word. Every request sends the model some text to read (your instruction, plus a chunk of your existing app so it has context) and gets back some text it generates (the new or changed code). You pay, in effect, for both halves: the reading and the writing. A "credit" or a "message" or a unit of "effort" is usually a packaged-up abstraction sitting on top of that token count, smoothed into something easier to reason about than raw numbers. The reason this matters is that it explains why two requests that feel equally simple to you can cost wildly different amounts: the one issued against a large app made the model *read* far more before it could *write* anything. The cost tracks the work, and the work is mostly the reading.

This reading-is-paid insight is the key that unlocks almost every cost-control habit later in the chapter, so it's worth pinning down with an everyday comparison. Imagine you're paying a brilliant but literal-minded assistant who, every single time you ask them to change one line of a document, insists on re-reading the entire document first to make sure they understand the context. For a one-page memo, that re-reading is trivial and the change is cheap. For a five-hundred-page manual, the same one-line change now requires re-reading five hundred pages, every time, and the cost of that change has quietly become enormous even though the change itself is identical. That's exactly what's happening with these tools. The model has no memory between requests; each time, it has to be re-shown the relevant state of your app to make a sensible change. So the cost of an edit isn't really about the edit – it's about how much the model had to re-read to make it, and that re-reading grows as your app grows. Once you see costs this way, the rest of the chapter's advice stops sounding like a list of rules and starts sounding like obvious consequences of one fact: you pay for reading, and a bigger app is more to read.

There's a second factor in the cost of any single request, separate from the size of your app, and it's worth naming because you have some control over it: how much *thinking* the request demands. A small, clearly specified change — "make this button blue" — is cheap to generate because the model writes a little and is done. A large, vague, or exploratory request — "redesign the whole dashboard to be more intuitive" — sends the model writing and rewriting a great deal, and on the effort-metered tools especially, exploration costs in proportion to how far the model wanders. So the cost of a request has two drivers: the reading (how big your app is, which grows over time) and the writing (how much you asked for, which you control each time). You can't shrink the first easily once your app is large, but you can absolutely shape the second by asking for less, more precisely, per message.

The Hidden Cost of a Failing Loop

There's one cost pattern worth flagging on its own because it's both common and avoidable, and it surprises people who think they're using the tool carefully. Sometimes you ask for a change, the AI makes it, the change has a bug, you ask it to fix the bug, the fix introduces a different bug, you ask again — and you're now in a loop where each round spends units and the app isn't getting better. The meter runs the whole time. A frustrating debugging spiral isn't just bad for your mood; it's one of the more expensive things you can do, because every lap is a fresh paid request against a project that, by definition, keeps growing more tangled.

The defense is to recognize the loop and break it rather than feed it. If two or three rounds haven't fixed something, more rounds of the same probably won't either — and each one costs. The cheaper moves at that point are to stop and describe the problem completely from scratch in one careful message, to roll back to the last good version and approach the change differently, or to step away and return with a clearer head. Throwing more increasingly frustrated one-line requests at a stuck problem is the exact behavior that turns a modest bill into a startling one, and it's entirely within your control to stop.

It helps to have a concrete signal for when you're *in* the loop rather than making progress, because in the moment the line is blurry — each fix feels like it might be the one that works. A reliable tell is that the bugs start *trading places* rather than shrinking: you fix A and B breaks, you fix B and A comes back, or a fix for one thing introduces a fresh, unrelated problem somewhere else. That pattern means the model is patching symptoms without grasping the underlying cause, and feeding it more one-line nudges just keeps it patching. The single most effective circuit-breaker is the rollback you learned about in Chapter 19: go back to the last version that genuinely worked, accept that the last several paid rounds were a sunk cost, and re-approach the change from that clean state with one carefully written request that describes the whole goal at once. This feels like losing ground — you're throwing away work you paid for — but it's almost always cheaper than the alternative, because the alternative is an unbounded number of further rounds against a state that's now tangled. Knowing where the rollback is *before* you're frustrated is what makes you able to reach for it when you are; few things are harder than calmly deciding to discard work while you're three failed fixes deep and the meter is spinning.

Why Bolt's Costs Scale With Project Size — and Why That's a Useful Lens

Bolt (by StackBlitz) makes one mechanism unusually visible, and it is worth understanding even if you use a different tool, because it illustrates the general principle.

Bolt is token-metered, and here is the honest catch its own community will tell you about: the cost of each message scales with the *size of your project*. The reason is structural. To work on your app, the AI has to be able to see your app — and Bolt syncs the relevant state of your project to the model with your requests so it has the context to make a good change. A small project is cheap to send; a large, sprawling project with many files is expensive to send, and you pay that cost on every message, not just once. So the same request — "change this button" — can cost noticeably more on a big mature app than on a small new one, purely because there is more app to ship to the model each time.

This connects straight back to the token picture: sending the project to the model means the model has to *read* the project, and reading is paid. The bigger the app, the more there is to read before a single line gets written, which is why the cost of trivial-feeling changes drifts upward as the project grows. It's not that the change got harder; it's that the reading got longer.

This is the part worth carrying to every tool, not just Bolt. As your app grows, your per-action costs tend to grow with it, because doing anything to a bigger, more complex app is more work for the model. The implication is practical and a little counterintuitive: these tools are cheapest exactly when you are starting and the project is small, and they get more expensive precisely as your app becomes the real, substantial thing you wanted. Budget for that curve. The weekend prototype is cheap; the same app six months and two hundred features later, still being edited the same way, is not.

There's a structural lesson buried in this curve that pays off if you act on it early. An app that's organized cleanly — focused, without piles of dead features and abandoned experiments cluttering it up — is smaller for the model to read and therefore cheaper to keep working on than a bloated one of the same apparent complexity. So the housekeeping habit of asking the tool to remove things you've abandoned, rather than letting them accumulate, isn't only tidiness; it's cost control. Every half-finished feature you left in is weight the model carries on every future request. Keeping the project lean keeps the meter slower.

A Quick, Flagged Map of the Four

Here is roughly how each tool meters, as of mid-2026, with every number to be treated as a starting point you verify on the current pricing page — these change constantly and sources frequently disagree, which is itself a sign of how fast they move.

v0 (by Vercel) meters on tokens and credits, with tiers along the lines of a free plan, a Team plan around thirty dollars per user, and a Business plan around a hundred dollars per user — verify, because these move. Its model branding (names like v0 Mini, Pro, Max) is a Vercel abstraction layered over an underlying frontier model, so think of the tiers as buckets of capability and usage rather than fixed quantities you can predict to the credit.

Bolt (by StackBlitz) is token-metered with a Pro tier reported somewhere in the rough twenty-to-twenty-five-dollars-a-month range — and I flag that range specifically because sources disagree on it, which tells you to go check rather than trust me. The size-scaling effect above is the thing to watch here more than the headline price.

Lovable uses credit-per-message metering, with a Pro tier around twenty-five dollars a month and a Business tier around fifty, last I checked — verify. Each message you send to build or change your app draws down credits, so a chatty, iterative building style spends faster than a planned one.

Replit (Agent 3) prices on effort and checkpoints — roughly, you pay in proportion to how much work the agent does to fulfill a request — with a Core tier around twenty to twenty-five dollars a month and a Pro tier near a hundred, subject to change. Because the agent can take on large multi-step tasks autonomously, a single ambitious instruction can represent a lot of metered effort. This is the model that most rewards thinking before you ask: a vague instruction that sends the agent off on a long, partly wrong expedition is metered for the whole expedition, including the wrong parts.

A note on the different unit names, because the variety is genuinely confusing and a little of it is by design. Tokens, credits, messages, checkpoints, effort — these are not five fundamentally different things so much as five different vantage points on the same underlying reality of "the model did some paid work for you." A token-based meter exposes the raw measure; a message-based one packages it per request; an effort-based one packages it per unit of agent work. The friendlier the unit sounds, the more abstraction sits between you and the actual token count, which makes the cost easier to talk about and harder to predict precisely. None of this is a scam — it's the same difficulty every metered service has in presenting usage humanely — but the practical consequence is that you generally can't forecast a bill to the dollar in advance. What you *can* do is watch the meter as you go, which the next-to-last section is about.

The Costs Hiding Downstream

Here is the trap that catches people who *did* read the pricing page carefully: the builder's subscription is not the whole cost of running your app. It is the cost of *building* your app. Running it for real often pulls in other bills the sticker price never mentioned.

The backend usually has its own meter. Several of these tools lean on a service called Supabase for the database and user accounts behind your app — Lovable bundles it natively as "Lovable Cloud," and others connect to it. Supabase has its own free tier and its own paid plans (a Pro tier in the rough neighborhood of twenty-five dollars a month, last I looked — verify), and once your app has real users and real data, you may well need the paid one. That is a recurring cost stacked on top of your builder subscription, for the same single app. This is the same front-end/back-end split from Chapter 19 showing up as two separate lines on your finances: you are, in effect, paying to build the app in one place and paying to run its data layer in another, and only one of those was on the sticker you read.

The domain is a yearly fee. From Chapter 20: a custom domain is its own modest recurring cost, often around ten to twenty dollars a year, paid to a registrar, separate from everything else.

Other services bill separately too. If your app sends email, takes payments, stores files, or calls an outside AI, each of those is typically its own account with its own pricing, scaling with your usage. The two from Chapter 17 to watch hardest are the AI provider, whose cost scales without any natural ceiling as your app gets used, and payments, which take a small cut of every transaction. Most of these have free tiers that mask the cost entirely while you're testing — which is precisely why the bill can arrive as a surprise the month real usage crosses the free threshold, the free-tier cliff from that chapter doing its quiet work.

The phrase worth knowing here is *total cost of ownership* — the real, all-in cost of having a live app, which is the builder subscription *plus* the backend *plus* the domain *plus* whatever services it depends on. The builder's advertised price is the first line of that bill, not the whole of it. A useful five-minute exercise before you commit to running something for real is to list every service your app touches and write down what each one costs at zero users, at a modest number of users, and at the number you actually hope for. The pattern that usually emerges is reassuring at the bottom and sobering at the top: a small app is genuinely cheap across the board, but the line items that scale with usage — AI calls, the backend, payment fees — are the ones that grow into the real money if the app succeeds. None of these costs are unreasonable, and for a small app they may all stay modest. But they are real, they recur, and the sticker price deliberately or incidentally hides them. Add them up before you build a business plan on the headline number.

There's a distinction inside that list worth making explicit, because it changes how you should worry about each line: some of these costs are *fixed* and some *scale with usage*, and they fail in opposite directions. The builder subscription and the domain are roughly fixed — you pay about the same whether ten people use your app or ten thousand, and they hold no surprises once you know the number. The dangerous lines are the ones that scale: the AI provider that costs more the more your app's intelligent features get used, the backend that costs more as data and traffic grow, the payment fees that take a slice of every transaction. The fixed costs are a known monthly floor you can plan around. The scaling costs are the ones that can quietly multiply if your app succeeds, which produces the slightly perverse situation where the better your app does, the more some of these bills grow. That's not a reason to fear success — most of the scaling costs grow roughly in step with the value or revenue the app is generating, so a payment fee that grows means money is flowing — but it is a reason to understand *which* of your costs are floors and which are slopes, so that the slopes don't catch you off guard. The exercise of writing down each service's cost at three usage levels is really an exercise in separating the floors from the slopes, and the slopes are where your attention belongs.

A worked version makes this concrete. Suppose the teacher's booking app grows from her one classroom to the whole school district. Her builder subscription doesn't move — it's a floor. Her domain renews once a year regardless — a floor. But now there are thousands of bookings a month: the backend holding all those records moves from the free tier to a paid plan; if the app sends a confirmation email per booking, the email service crosses its free threshold; if she added an AI feature that drafts a summary for each tutor, that AI cost scales straight up with the number of summaries. The app got more valuable and more expensive in the same motion, and the expensive parts are precisely the usage-scaling ones. Had she mapped the floors and slopes in advance, none of this would surprise her; she'd have watched the slopes approach their thresholds and planned the upgrades. Mapped or not, the costs are the same — the only question is whether she meets them as a plan or as a shock.

Spending Less Without Building Less

A few habits genuinely lower the meter, and they are worth forming early rather than after a startling bill.

Plan the request before you send it. A clear, complete instruction that gets you most of the way in one shot spends far less than ten vague ones that each nudge the app a little. The iterative conversational style is delightful and it is also the expensive style; tightening your prompts (Chapter 9's whole subject) is the cheapest cost control there is. The concrete version: before you send a request, ask whether you could fold the next two or three things you know you'll want into this one message. Bundling related changes into a single well-formed request is dramatically cheaper than dribbling them out one at a time, because each separate message re-reads the whole project before doing its small thing.

Do the big structural work while the project is small. Since costs scale with project size, the early, cheap phase is the right time to get the foundations right, not the late, expensive phase. Reworking the basic shape of an app is one of the more expensive operations there is, and it gets more expensive every week the app grows, so the instinct to "just get something working and fix the structure later" is, in cost terms, exactly backwards.

Watch the meter, not just the calendar. Most tools show you your remaining credits or usage somewhere. Glance at it. The founder who got surprised on Monday had never once looked at the number going down over the weekend, and a thirty-second habit of checking would have warned him in time to slow down. Better still, find out whether your tool and your downstream services let you set a spending cap or a usage alert, and set one. A hard cap on your AI provider (from Chapter 17) and a usage alert on your builder turn "I had no idea" into "I got a heads-up at seventy-five percent," which is the entire difference between my founder friend's Monday and a calmer one.

Know that idle is not free, but it is cheap. A deployed app sitting there with few users costs little to run; the expensive part is almost always the *building*, the AI doing work on your behalf. So the bill is largely under your control — it tracks how much you ask the tool to do, which is a lever you hold. The mental model that keeps this straight: *building* is the variable, often-large cost, driven by how much you ask the AI to do; *running* is the smaller, steadier cost of keeping the lights on once you stop asking. A finished app you've stopped editing is close to its cheapest. The meter spins fastest exactly when you're in the thick of creating, which is both the most fun and the most expensive part of the whole endeavor.

None of this should scare you off. These tools are, by any historical measure, astonishingly cheap for what they produce — a working app for the price of a couple of dinners is a deal that did not exist a few years ago. The point is only to go in understanding the *shape* of the cost, so that the bill confirms what you expected instead of teaching it to you the hard way. Cost, like security, is one of those realities of making real software that the no-code promise quietly waved away — and like security, it rewards the person who looks at it on purpose before it looks at them.

Part VI: The Honest Limits

Audience: anyone shipping to real users.

"The tool will happily build you something that looks finished and is not safe. Knowing the difference, and knowing when to call someone who builds this for a living, is the part no prompt can do for you."

— A working principle

Chapter 22: Security and Your Users' Data

This is the most important chapter in the book, and I have arranged everything so that you arrive at it before you put an app in front of real people. If you read nothing else in Part VI, read this. Because the central, uncomfortable fact about building apps without code is this: the tools make it just as easy to build something *insecure* as something secure, and they will not stop you, warn you clearly, or even necessarily let you see that anything is wrong. The app that leaks every user's data and the app that protects it can look identical on the screen. The difference is underneath, in exactly the place the no-code promise encouraged you not to look.

That is not a reason to avoid these tools. It is the reason this chapter exists. Security is the part of building software that does not announce itself — a missing lock does not throw an error, it just sits there, open, until someone walks through it. So you have to go looking, deliberately, for the things that will not surface on their own. This chapter is the map of where to look.

Why Vibe-Coded Apps Are Especially Exposed

Every application has security concerns. Vibe-coded apps carry an extra dose of risk for a specific, structural reason: the layer that normally catches security problems has been removed. In conventional software development, code is reviewed — by the developer who understands what it does, often by a second pair of eyes trained to spot the classic failures. That review is where someone notices the password stored in plain text, the database query open to injection, the secret key sitting somewhere the public can read it. Vibe coding skips that layer almost by definition: the person building does not read the code, and the AI that wrote it has no stake in the outcome and no reliable instinct for what must be protected. So the latent flaws that review normally catches sail straight through to production, unreviewed, because no one with the eyes to see them ever looked.

There is a second structural reason, subtler than the first. The AI builder is optimizing for one thing above all: making the feature you asked for *work*, visibly, right now, in front of you. Security is, almost by definition, the set of things that do not affect whether the feature works in the demo. A key hardcoded into the browser works perfectly in the demo. An access check that is missing does not break anything until a second user shows up with bad intentions. A password stored in plain text logs you in just fine. Every one of these flaws is invisible to the success criterion the AI is steering toward, which means the tool's own incentives quietly point away from the safe choice and toward the convenient one. You are not fighting a malicious tool; you are fighting an indifferent one, which is in some ways worse, because indifference does not warn you.

And there is a third reason, which is about you rather than the tool. The whole appeal of building this way is that you do not have to think about the plumbing. That is genuinely freeing — until the plumbing is the thing that leaks. The same mental posture that lets you build an app in an afternoon without learning React is the posture that lets a security flaw pass unexamined, because examining it would mean looking at exactly the layer you were promised you could ignore. The promise is true for getting it working. It is dangerously false for getting it safe.

This is not a hypothetical concern, and I want to be concrete rather than vague-and-scary about it, because the specifics are what make it real.

The Marquee Failure: Exposed Secrets

The single most common and most damaging security flaw in AI-built apps is exposed secrets — API keys, database credentials, and passwords ending up somewhere the public can read them. Security researchers at Wiz, investigating apps built with these tools, documented this pattern at scale: keys and credentials hardcoded directly into the browser-side code of the app, where anyone who knows how to open their browser's developer tools — which is to say, anyone — can simply read them. Among the exposed secrets they found were the kind of credentials that let an attacker run up charges on your AI provider account, or read and write your entire database directly, bypassing the app altogether.

To understand why this is so dangerous, you need one piece of how web apps work. Code that runs in the user's browser (the "front end") is, by definition, sent to the user — they have it, all of it, and can inspect every line. Code that runs on a server (the "back end") stays private. A secret key belongs only on the back end, never in the browser. But an AI builder, asked to make a feature work, will sometimes take the path of least resistance and put the key where it is convenient rather than where it is safe — in the browser code, where it works perfectly in the demo and is readable by every visitor forever. The app functions flawlessly. It is also wide open. Nothing on screen tells you the difference.

Here is what that actually looks like in practice, so the abstraction lands. Suppose you ask your builder to "summarize the user's notes using AI." The straightforward thing to do is call an AI provider's API, which requires your secret API key. The *safe* way is for your app's server to hold the key and make the call, so the key never leaves your server. The *convenient* way — the one a tool will sometimes reach for — is to have the browser call the AI provider directly, with the key written right into the page's JavaScript. Both versions produce identical behavior on screen: the user types notes, a summary appears. But in the second version, anyone who visits your app can open their browser's developer tools, find your key in a few seconds, copy it, and start running their own AI workloads on your account. You discover this when the bill arrives — and provider bills for leaked keys have reached thousands of dollars before the owner noticed, because automated bots scan the public web for exactly this kind of exposed credential and start spending within minutes of finding one.

A database credential leaked the same way is worse, because it does not just cost money. A database connection string in the browser lets anyone connect directly to your database — not through your app, which might at least check who they are, but *around* it, with full read and write access to every row. Every user's email, every order, every private note, exposed and editable by a stranger. The app still looks fine. The lock was simply never on the door.

This is the failure to fear most, because it is common, it is invisible from the interface, and its consequences are severe — a leaked database credential can mean every user's data exposed, and a leaked provider key can mean a bill that arrives like a punch.

The Quieter Failures That Are Just as Real

Exposed secrets are the headline, but they are not alone, and the others are worth knowing by name because they recur across every one of these platforms.

Missing access control. This is the failure that powers most large breaches, and it is deceptively simple: the app shows a user data without checking whether that user is allowed to see it. Imagine an app where each user has a profile at an address like `/profile/487`. If the app loads whatever profile number is in the address without checking that *you* are the owner of profile 487, then changing the number to 488 shows you someone else's profile. Multiply that by every piece of data the app stores — orders, messages, documents, payment records — and a single missing check exposes everyone's data to anyone curious enough to change a number. Security people call this Broken Object-Level Authorization, and it is one of the most common serious flaws in real-world apps precisely because the app works perfectly as long as everyone only looks at their own number. The flaw lives in the case nobody clicks through during testing: the case where someone deliberately tries someone else's.

Trusting the browser. A close cousin. Apps sometimes enforce rules only in the browser — hiding the "delete" button from regular users, for instance, but leaving the underlying delete operation reachable by anyone who knows how to ask for it directly. Because the browser is the part the user controls, anything enforced *only* there is a suggestion, not a rule. A real rule has to be enforced on the server, where the user cannot reach in and change it. An AI builder will often add the visible guard (hide the button) and skip the invisible one (check on the server), because the visible guard is what makes the demo look right.

Injection. When user input is mixed carelessly into a database query or a command, a malicious user can craft input that the app executes as instructions rather than data. The classic case is a login form where typing a cleverly malformed value into the username field tricks the database into returning everyone's records, or worse. Modern tools and frameworks defend against the common forms of this by default — but "by default" only holds if the AI used the framework's safe path, and it does not always, especially for anything slightly unusual.

Leaky error messages and logs. When something goes wrong, apps sometimes spill more than they should — showing a user the raw database error, complete with table names and query structure, or writing sensitive data into logs that the wrong people can read. None of this breaks anything visibly. It just quietly hands an attacker a map.

You do not need to become an expert in any of these. You need to know they exist, because knowing the names is what lets you ask the right questions — of the builder, and of a human reviewer — instead of assuming that "it works" means "it is safe."

When It Goes Wrong at Scale

The risk is not theoretical, and the public record now includes incidents that show what it looks like when it fails. In one documented case reported in 2025, a flaw of a type called Broken Object-Level Authorization — in plain terms, the app failed to check that the person *requesting* a piece of data was actually allowed to *see* it — reportedly ran through a large number of apps built on one of these platforms. The result, as reported, was that source code, database credentials, AI chat histories, and real customer data could be accessed across thousands of projects, and security researchers advised every affected builder to rotate their secrets immediately.

I am describing this carefully and with hedges because the details come from security reporting on a single platform and a specific window of time, and the platforms respond and patch — by the time you read this the particular hole will be closed. But the *lesson* is durable and platform-independent: a single systematic flaw in how these tools handle access control can compromise not one app but thousands at once, precisely because so many apps are generated the same way by the same tool. The vulnerability you did not know to look for is one a researcher — or an attacker — can find at scale.

There is a second lesson hiding inside the first, and it cuts against an instinct most people have. With hand-built software, a flaw in your app is a flaw in *your* app — an attacker has to find it specifically, in your code, among millions of other sites. With apps generated by a shared tool, the same flaw can appear in every app the tool produced during the window it had the bug, which means an attacker who discovers it once has a key that fits thousands of doors. Your app's security is no longer entirely a function of your own diligence; it is partly a function of the tool's, and of the moment in time you happened to build. This is an argument not for paranoia but for two specific habits: rotating your secrets whenever a platform discloses an incident, and never assuming that "the platform handles security" means you can stop paying attention. The platform handles *some* of it, imperfectly, and the part it gets wrong it gets wrong everywhere at once.

Who Secures What: Drawing the Line Honestly

A great deal of confusion — and a great deal of misplaced confidence — comes from a fuzzy picture of who is responsible for what. Your app is not one monolithic thing you alone secure; it is a stack of layers, some of which competent companies handle well on your behalf, and some of which are entirely yours no matter how big the names underneath you are. Seeing the line clearly is what lets you relax about the parts that are genuinely handled and worry, correctly, about the parts that are not.

The layers below your app are usually in good hands. The servers your app runs on, the network it travels over, the physical security of the data centers, the encryption of data as it moves across the internet — these belong to the hosting platform and the cloud providers beneath it, and they are very good at them, far better than you would be. When your app uses a managed database service or a hosted authentication service or a payment processor, those companies bring real security expertise to their slice. A reputable payment processor handles card data to a standard you could not meet yourself, which is precisely why the right move with payments is to let it hold the card numbers rather than touching them yourself. This is the kernel of truth inside "the platform handles security": the *infrastructure* layer largely is handled, and that is a real and valuable thing.

But the line stops there, and everything above it is yours. *Where your secrets ended up* is yours — no cloud provider can stop the AI from writing your key into the browser. *Whether your access checks exist* is yours — the database service will faithfully return whatever your app asks for, including another user's data, because enforcing who is allowed to ask is your app's job, not the database's. *What data you chose to collect, and whether you should have* is yours. *Whether your app trusts the browser when it should trust only the server* is yours. Every flaw catalogued in this chapter lives in this upper layer, the application layer, which is exactly the layer the no-code promise encouraged you to ignore and exactly the layer no platform secures for you. This division has a name in the industry — the *shared responsibility model* — and the single most expensive mistake people make with it is assuming the provider's half covers their half. It does not. The provider secures the building; you are still responsible for locking your own apartment.

There is a third party in this picture worth calling out on its own: the services you connect your app to. The moment your app sends data to an outside service — an email provider to send notifications, an analytics tool, an AI provider to summarize text, a spreadsheet your app writes to — that data has left your app and entered someone else's, under their terms and their security, not yours. This matters in two directions. First, you have now extended the circle of who holds your users' data, and a breach at any service in that circle is, from your user's point of view, your breach. Second, and easy to miss, sending personal data to certain services can itself be a problem — feeding a user's private information into a third-party tool that may use it for its own purposes is a privacy decision you are making on that user's behalf, often without realizing it. The discipline is to know, for every outside service your app talks to, what data you are sending it and whether you should be. Each connection is a convenience and a widening of your responsibility in the same stroke.

The Concrete Things to Check

Vague alarm is useless; here is what to actually do. Before any vibe-coded app touches a real user or real data, work through these.

Find out where your secrets live. Any key, token, or credential the app uses — for the AI itself, for a database, for an email or payment service — must live on the server side, never in the browser code. If you are not sure where yours are, this is the question to ask the builder directly ("are any API keys or secrets exposed in the client-side code?") and, if you can, to have a technical person confirm. This one check addresses the most common serious flaw. You can also do a rough check yourself: open your live app, open your browser's developer tools (usually F12, or right-click and choose "Inspect"), look at the Sources or Network panels, and search the loaded files for anything that looks like a long random string labeled "key," "secret," "token," or "password." Finding one there is a red flag; finding nothing is reassuring but not proof, because secrets can hide in less obvious places. The reliable check is still a human who reads the code.

Confirm that access is actually checked. For every piece of data the app stores, ask: can a user reach data that isn't theirs by changing a number in the address bar or crafting a request? Proper apps check, on the server, that you are allowed to see each thing you ask for. Test it: log in as one user, note the address of something you can see, and try to reach another user's equivalent. If you get it, the lock is missing. Do this deliberately and adversarially — create two test accounts, put distinct data in each, then log in as the first and try every way you can think of to reach the second's data: change the number in the URL, submit a form referencing the other account's records, use the browser back button after logging out. You are role-playing the curious or malicious user, and ten minutes of this finds the most common serious flaw there is.

Verify how passwords and personal data are handled. Passwords should never be stored in a form anyone could read them; personal data should be protected in transit and at rest. These are defaults a competent backend provides, but "should" is not "did" — confirm it rather than assume it. A useful proxy you can check yourself: if your app has a "forgot password" flow that emails you your *existing* password in plain text, that is a flashing red light, because it means the app stored the password in a readable form, which it never should. A safe app cannot tell you your old password; it can only let you set a new one. The same logic extends further: if any part of the app can show a user a stored secret back to them in its original form, ask hard questions about how it is stored.

Know what data you are collecting and whether you should be. Every piece of personal information you collect is a responsibility and, increasingly, a legal obligation. Collect the minimum you need, know where it is stored, and understand that "I built this in an afternoon" is not a defense recognized by privacy law. The discipline here is *data minimization*: for every field your app collects, ask whether you actually need it. A booking page does not need a date of birth. A feedback form does not need a phone number. Each piece of data you do not collect is a piece of data that cannot leak, cannot be subpoenaed, cannot become a liability. The most secure way to handle sensitive data is, wherever possible, not to hold it — let a specialized service handle payments rather than storing card numbers yourself, for instance, so that the riskiest data never lives in your app at all.

Understand which privacy rules actually reach you. This is not legal advice, and the specifics shift, so check the current state of the law for your situation — but the broad shape is worth carrying. If your app touches people in the European Union, the GDPR applies regardless of where you are; it expects a lawful basis for collecting personal data, honest disclosure of what you collect and why, and the ability to honor requests to access or delete that data. If your app touches residents of certain US states — California's CCPA/CPRA being the most prominent — comparable obligations attach. The EU AI Act adds another layer where AI is involved: its rules on certain prohibited and manipulative uses (Article 4 and the prohibited-practices provisions) became applicable on 2 February 2025, with broader obligations becoming enforceable on 2 August 2026, and the pending Digital Omnibus that would adjust some of this is, as of mid-2026, not yet law. The point is not that you must master any of this — it is that these obligations attach to what your app *does*, not to how it was built, and a tool that lets you collect data in an afternoon does nothing to lift the duties that come with holding it.

Rotate and re-check after every major change. Each time the AI substantially rebuilds part of your app, it may reintroduce a flaw you previously fixed. Security is not a one-time checkpoint; it is something to re-confirm whenever the code underneath changes significantly. This is one of the genuinely surprising hazards of building by conversation: a fix you applied last week can be silently undone by a rebuild this week, because the AI regenerated a section without knowledge of the careful adjustment you made to it before. Keep a short written list of the security fixes you have made — "moved the API key to the server," "added the ownership check on the profile route" — and after any big change, walk the list again and confirm each one still holds. Treat a disclosed platform incident the same way: when a builder announces a vulnerability, rotate every secret your app uses, on the assumption that it may have been exposed, rather than waiting to find out whether it was.

A Walkthrough You Can Do Yourself in Fifteen Minutes

The checks above are easier to do than they sound, and it is worth walking one all the way through so the abstraction becomes a thing your own hands can perform. None of this requires you to read code. It requires you to look in the places the polished interface does not show you.

Start with the secrets check, because it catches the most damaging flaw. Open your live app in a browser and open the developer tools — on most browsers that is the F12 key, or right-click anywhere on the page and choose "Inspect." A panel opens. Find the tab labeled "Network," then reload the page; you will see a list of every file and request the page made to build itself. Now find the tab labeled "Sources" (or "Debugger" in some browsers), which shows you the actual files the page loaded — the same code every visitor's browser received. Use the find function inside the developer tools (usually Ctrl+Shift+F, the search-across-all-files version, not the page search) and search, one at a time, for the words "key," "secret," "token," "password," and "apikey." You are looking for a long string of random-looking characters sitting next to one of those words. If you find one — say a thirty-character jumble after `apiKey:` — you have very likely found a secret that should not be there, and you have found it the same way an attacker's automated scanner would. If you find nothing, that is reassuring but not conclusive, because secrets can hide in references and bundled files the search does not obviously surface; it lowers your worry, it does not end it.

Now do the access check, which catches the other most-common serious flaw. Create two accounts in your own app — call them Alice and Bob — and put something distinct and identifiable in each, so you can tell them apart at a glance: a note in Alice's account that says "ALICE SECRET," one in Bob's that says "BOB SECRET." Log in as Alice and navigate to the thing only she should see. Look at the address bar. If the address ends in something like `/note/41`, that number is a handle to a specific piece of data, and the question is whether the app checks that *Alice* is allowed to see note 41. Test it directly: change the number — try `/note/42`, `/note/40`, a few others — and see what loads. If at any point you see "BOB SECRET," the lock is missing; the app handed you another user's data because you asked for it by number and nothing checked whether you were entitled to it. This is the single most valuable ten minutes of testing you can do, because broken access control of exactly this kind is among the most common serious flaws in real applications, and it is completely invisible to anyone who only ever looks at their own data.

Push the same adversarial spirit a little further while you are in there. Log out as Alice and, before logging in as anyone, try to reach `/note/41` directly by typing it into the address bar — does the app let an unauthenticated stranger see it, or does it send you to a login? Submit a form that references one of Bob's records while logged in as Alice. Use the browser's back button after logging out to see whether a previous page's data is still sitting there, reachable. You are not trying to be clever; you are trying to be the slightly malicious user the friendly demo never includes, and fifteen minutes of that mindset finds more real problems than hours of using the app the way it was designed to be used.

Write down what you find, fix what you can by asking the builder to fix it specifically ("any data the app returns must be checked, on the server, to confirm the logged-in user is allowed to see it"), and then — this is the part people skip — run the walkthrough *again* after the fix, because a fix you cannot read is a fix you have to verify by behavior. The flaw is gone only when changing the number no longer shows you another user's data, not when the AI tells you it handled it.

Common Mistakes That Feel Safe and Aren't

A handful of false comforts trip people up repeatedly, and naming them is the fastest way to immunize yourself.

"It's behind a login, so it's protected." A login screen protects only the things that actually check the login on the server. If the underlying data is reachable without that check — by hitting an address directly, or by trusting a guard that lives only in the browser — the login is a curtain, not a wall. Plenty of breached apps had login screens.

"No one knows my app exists, so no one will attack it." Obscurity is not security. Automated scanners crawl the public internet constantly, looking for exposed credentials and known flaws, and they do not care whether anyone has heard of your app. An app with a leaked key can be found and drained by a bot within hours of going live, with zero human interest in what your app actually does.

"The platform is a big company, so they handle security." The platform handles *the platform's* security, and some of the defaults, imperfectly. It does not handle the choices made inside *your* app — where your keys ended up, whether your access checks exist, what data you chose to collect. The most important security decisions live in your app, which is exactly the part the platform cannot make for you.

"I'll add security later, once it's working." Security added later is security added after a window during which the app was live and exposed. If real users and real data touched the app during that window, "later" may be after the damage. The honest version of "later" is "before the first real user," not "before the breach."

When to Bring in a Human

There is a threshold past which this stops being a checklist you can run alone, and recognizing it is itself part of doing this responsibly. If your app handles anything genuinely sensitive — financial information, health data, anything regulated, anything whose exposure would seriously harm your users — the honest answer is that it should be reviewed by someone who understands application security before it goes live. That is not an admission of failure; it is the same judgment a sensible person brings to any high-stakes task. You would not do your own electrical work on a commercial building. Some apps are the software equivalent, and the cost of a security review is trivial against the cost of a breach.

What does that review actually buy you, concretely? A person who reads code can do in an hour the things no amount of clicking can do from the outside: confirm where every secret lives, trace whether each data access is checked on the server, spot the injection-prone query, notice the error handler that leaks too much. You are not hiring them to take over your project — Chapter 24 is entirely about how to bring in a developer for a narrow, defined task without surrendering the work you did. You are hiring them for the one layer you were promised you could ignore and have now discovered you cannot, on the apps where the stakes make ignoring it unacceptable. Frame it tightly: "look at this app and tell me whether anyone's data is exposed and whether secrets are safe." That is a few hours of work for someone who knows what they are doing, and it is the cheapest insurance you will ever buy against the most expensive mistake you will never see coming.

The next chapter, on scaling and lock-in, deals with what happens to these apps over time and across more users. But security is the one that cannot wait for "over time" — it is the one that has to be right before the first real user arrives, because the whole point of a security flaw is that you do not find out about it until someone else already has. Build boldly; ship carefully; and treat the question "where are my secrets, and who can see my users' data" as the one you answer before you launch, not after.

Chapter 23: Scaling, Maintenance, and Lock-In

There is a message that arrives, in some form, from nearly everyone who builds something real this way and keeps it alive. It comes about three weeks in, after the app has worked, after people have signed up. It reads roughly like this: "It's slow, I'm getting weird errors when more than a few people use it at once, and I tried to add a feature and the AI broke two others. Also I just realized I have no idea how to get my stuff out of here. What do I do?"

That message is the subject of this chapter, and the thing to notice about it is the timing. None of those problems showed up on day one. The app that built cleanly and demoed beautifully developed every one of these troubles only after it had been alive in the world for a while and had picked up real users and real changes. Building an app is a moment. Living with one is a relationship, and the relationship has costs the moment never warned you about. This chapter is the honest accounting of what those costs are: what breaks as people show up, what it takes to keep an app running over time, and the quiet question underneath all of it — if you ever want to leave, can you?

What Actually Breaks as Users Arrive

"Scaling" sounds like a problem for companies with millions of users, and the version that makes the news is. But the version that will actually bite you happens much earlier and much smaller, and it has less to do with raw numbers than with the difference between a demo and a thing people are using.

The demo had one user: you. When you build and test an app, you are a single, polite, predictable user doing the things the app expects. Real users arrive several at once, do things in the wrong order, leave forms half-filled, hit the back button at the worst moment, and use the app on a phone with a bad connection. A lot of what "breaks under load" is not the server straining — it is the app meeting behavior it was never asked to handle, because when it was built, the only behavior in the room was yours.

The database is usually the first thing to groan. As of mid-2026, most of these builders sit on a managed database — frequently Supabase behind Lovable and v0, Replit's own bundled Postgres, whatever Bolt was pointed at. Those databases are perfectly capable, but the *queries the AI wrote* may be naive — fetching far more data than needed, or in a way that gets slower as the table grows. An app that is instant with twenty rows can crawl at twenty thousand, and the AI did not flag it because at build time there were twenty rows.

Free and starter tiers have ceilings you will hit without warning. The hosting and database under your app run on a plan, and that plan has limits — on storage, on simultaneous connections, on how much traffic is included. Cross the line and the app does not gently slow; it can start returning errors or simply stop. The fix is usually a paid upgrade, which is fine, but the surprise is the part that hurts. Know where those ceilings are before you find them by falling off one. Chapter 21, on cost and credits, maps the metering; this is the same story told from the other end, where the bill is for the running app rather than for building it.

The thing that worked is now intermittently the thing that doesn't. Bugs that appear only sometimes — only at busy moments, only for certain users, only on certain data — are the signature of an app that has outgrown its first build. They are also the hardest kind to fix by describing, because you cannot reliably reproduce them in front of the AI, and the AI cannot fix what it cannot see happen.

The Maintenance Burden Nobody Mentions in the Demo

The demos all end at "and now it's live." Real software does not end there; that is where the longest part begins. An app you ship is something you have signed up to keep alive, and keeping it alive is work even when you are doing nothing new.

The ground moves under you. The services your app depends on — the database, the login provider, the payment processor, the AI model you wired in, the framework the code is written in — all change. They release new versions, deprecate old ones, change their pricing, occasionally break things. A perfectly good app left untouched for a year is not frozen in amber; it is quietly drifting toward the day one of its dependencies changes out from under it and something stops working. Someone has to keep up with that, and on a vibe-coded app, that someone is you.

Every change risks the changes before it. This is the one behind that three-week message, and it is structural, not bad luck. When you ask the AI to add a feature, it works on a codebase it does not fully hold in its head, and it can quietly break something elsewhere that you had already gotten right. Regression — fixing or adding one thing and breaking another — is a normal hazard of all software, which is exactly why professional development wraps changes in automated tests that shout when something that used to work no longer does. A vibe-coded app usually has no such net. So the cost of every new feature is not just building it; it is re-checking the things you thought were already done.

The fix-it conversation can spiral. When something breaks and you describe the problem to the AI, sometimes it fixes it in one clean pass. Other times it "fixes" it by changing something that was not the cause, which creates a new problem, which you describe, which it addresses by changing something else. People have watched a small bug turn into an afternoon of the app getting steadily worse with each well-meaning round. Knowing when to stop, undo to the last good version, and try a different approach — or get a human — is part of the maintenance skill these tools demand and do not teach.

Maintenance is the cost that is invisible at purchase and unavoidable at ownership. It is the strongest argument in the book for the distinction Chapter 25 is built around: a prototype you can let rot; a production app is a standing commitment.

Lock-In: The Question to Ask Before You're Married to the Answer

Here is the question that message asked last, and it should have been first: if this tool stops working for me — too expensive, too limited, gone out of business, just not what I need anymore — can I take my app and leave? The answer varies enormously across the four builders, and it is the kind of thing that costs nothing to check at the start and a great deal to discover at the end.

Two things have to be able to leave: your *code* and your *data*. Code is the application itself. Data is everything your users have put into it — and your users' data leaving cleanly matters even more than the code, because you can rebuild an app and you cannot rebuild your customers' trust after you lose their information in a move.

Rather than a grid, here is the honest shape of each, as of mid-2026 — verify against each tool's current documentation, because portability is exactly the kind of thing that improves (or quietly worsens) release to release.

Bolt is the most portable. Its output is standard, ordinary code with no unusual dependence on Bolt itself, it exports cleanly to GitHub, and you can deploy it to Netlify or essentially anywhere that runs a normal web app. If leaving is a priority for you, this is the design that respects it most. The flip side, covered in Chapter 5, is that this same architecture makes large projects expensive to build, because the whole project gets re-read by the model on each turn.

Lovable is portable in good faith. It offers two-way GitHub sync, so your code lives somewhere you control, not only inside Lovable. The catch is the backend: because Lovable Cloud bundles Supabase for your database and login, leaving means accounting for that backend too, not just the front-end code. It is a real exit, but it is an exit you have to plan rather than one you can take in an afternoon.

v0 has the tightest coupling. It produces clean, standard React and Next.js code and does export to GitHub — that part is genuinely fine. But v0 is built to live in Vercel's world, and the deeper you lean into that ecosystem's conveniences, the more your app assumes them. The code can leave; how much of your setup comes with it depends on how much Vercel-specific machinery you built on. Go in with eyes open about which conveniences are also commitments.

Replit is the hardest to migrate. This is the trade for being the closest thing to "describe it and get a deployed, running app": the app is woven into Replit's own database and hosting, and untangling it to run somewhere else is the most work of the four. That is not a flaw so much as a different bet — you traded portability for the smoothest path from idea to live. Just make the trade knowingly, especially if there is any chance the app becomes something you need to own independently of the tool that made it.

Getting Your Code and Data Out

If you take one practical action from this chapter, make it this: do a test extraction early, while the app is small and the stakes are low, rather than in a panic when something has gone wrong.

Connect to GitHub on day one if the tool allows it. GitHub is a neutral place where your code lives under your account, not the builder's. Setting it up early means your work is never trapped in a single tool, and it costs you almost nothing to do. For the tools with good sync — Bolt, Lovable, v0 — this is the single highest-value portability move available to a non-coder.

Find your data's export before you need it. Your database almost certainly offers a way to export everything in it — Supabase, Replit's Postgres, and the others all do. Locate that button, run it once, and confirm you actually get a usable file. The day you need this is never a calm day, and "I assumed I could" is not the same as "I checked that I could."

Write down what your app depends on. Keep a plain list: which database, which login provider, which outside services, which plan each is on, and where the keys live. A developer handed this list can help you in an hour; a developer handed "it's all in Lovable somewhere" is starting from a cold read. This list is also, not coincidentally, the thing the next chapter says to bring when the moment comes that you need that developer.

The app that demoed in an afternoon can become something you depend on for years, and the gap between those two facts is everything in this chapter. None of it should scare you off building. It should change *how* you build — toward keeping your exits open, knowing where your ceilings are, and treating the running app as the commitment it quietly became the moment a real person started relying on it.

Chapter 24: When You Still Need a Developer

A founder who hit exactly the wall the last chapter described eventually hired a developer for two afternoons of work. Before she did, she was embarrassed about it — as if calling in a professional meant her whole no-code project had been a failure, a dress rehearsal for the "real" version someone else would now build properly. I want to push hard against that feeling, because it is wrong and it is expensive. She had built, in a weekend, something that would have cost thousands to commission cold and that proved the idea was worth pursuing. The developer did not replace her work. He looked at the one part that genuinely needed a trained eye — the way the app handled who could see whose data — found a real problem in twenty minutes, fixed it, and went home. That is not the no-code dream collapsing. That is the no-code dream working exactly as it should, with judgment supplied at the one point where it mattered most.

Knowing when you have reached that point is one of the most valuable skills this book can give you, and it is the opposite of an admission of defeat. A good builder of anything knows the edge of their own competence and hires across it without shame. So this chapter is not a list of your failures. It is a list of signals — honest, specific signs that the task in front of you has crossed from "describe it and steer" into "this needs someone who reads the code." Reading the signals correctly is itself the judgment the whole book is about.

The Signals, and Why Each One Matters

Not every wobble means call a professional. Plenty of problems are yours to solve by describing them better, undoing to a good version, and trying again — that is most of building, and you should not outsource it at the first frustration. But some signals are different in kind. When you see one of these, the smart move is not to push the AI harder. It is to bring in a human.

You are handling something that would genuinely hurt people if it leaked. This is the brightest line, and Chapter 22 drew it: if your app touches financial information, health data, anything regulated, or anything whose exposure would seriously harm your users, it should be reviewed by someone who understands application security before real people trust it with that information. The reason is structural, not a knock on you — vibe coding removes the code-review layer where security flaws are normally caught, and the flaws it lets through are exactly the invisible kind that work fine in the demo and leak quietly in production. You cannot eyeball what you cannot read. On anything sensitive, a security review is the cheapest insurance you will ever buy, and the absence of one is the most expensive gap you will never see coming.

The trap inside this signal is that "sensitive" creeps up on you. An app that started as a simple internal tracker quietly becomes sensitive the day you add a field for someone's home address, or accept your first payment, or start storing notes about clients. The threshold is not crossed by a decision; it is crossed by a feature. So the discipline is to re-ask the question — *would it hurt someone if this leaked?* — every time you add anything that holds more about a person than you held yesterday. The moment the honest answer becomes yes, you have hit the signal, whether or not you meant to.

The logic has gotten genuinely complicated. There is a kind of app whose rules are simple enough to hold in a sentence — a booking page, a directory, a form that stores answers. And there is a kind whose rules tangle: money moving between parties, permissions that depend on roles that depend on other conditions, calculations that must be exactly right because someone is paid or charged based on the result. When the *what* you are describing has become a knot you struggle to state clearly yourself, the AI will struggle to build it correctly, and — worse — it will produce something that looks right and is subtly wrong. Subtle wrongness in logic is hard to catch by clicking around, and it is precisely what a developer is trained to reason about.

Consider what "subtly wrong" actually looks like, because it is the most dangerous failure mode in this whole book. Imagine a marketplace app that takes a 10 percent commission and pays sellers the remainder. The AI builds it; you test a sale; the seller gets paid; it looks right. But the rounding is off by a cent in a way that only shows up on certain amounts, or the commission is calculated before a refund rather than after, or a discount code stacks with a promotion in a way that occasionally pays a seller more than the buyer paid. None of this throws an error. None of it is visible by clicking through a normal sale. It surfaces weeks later as a slow leak of money, or a furious seller, or a tax discrepancy — and by then it has happened hundreds of times. This is the category where "it works in the demo" and "it is correct" are most likely to be different things, and reasoning rigorously about which is exactly the trained skill you are reaching for when you hire.

Real scale is coming, and it's not a maybe. Chapter 23 covered the breakage that arrives with users. If you can see actual growth ahead — not "what if we go viral" but a real plan with real numbers — the architectural decisions that handle a thousand users are different from the ones that quietly built up under a demo, and they are hard to retrofit later. A developer brought in *before* the scramble can set things up to grow; a developer brought in *during* the scramble is doing emergency surgery. The cheaper visit is the early one. The asymmetry here is worth sitting with: the same change — choosing a data structure that holds up, putting the right indexes in place, separating the parts that need to scale from the parts that don't — costs a few hours when made deliberately ahead of time and can cost weeks when made under fire, with live users, with data already in the system that now has to be migrated without losing any of it. You are not paying for the change; you are paying for the calm in which it is made.

You are subject to rules, and "I didn't know" won't save you. Privacy law, accessibility requirements, industry regulation, payment-handling standards — these are not optional once they apply to you, and they do not care that you built the app in an afternoon. As covered in Chapter 22, the obligations attach to what your app does, not to how it was made. If your app operates anywhere these rules bite, someone who knows the rules needs to look. This is a place where confident ignorance is genuinely dangerous, because the penalty arrives long after the mistake. Worth naming specifically: anything that handles payment card data directly, anything that touches health records, anything that serves the public and therefore must be usable by people with disabilities, and anything that collects personal data from people in jurisdictions with real privacy regimes. The person you want here may not even be a developer in the usual sense — sometimes it is someone who knows the regulation and can tell you what the app must and must not do, which you then hand to whoever builds it.

The fix-it loop has stopped converging. Chapter 23 named the spiral: you describe a bug, the AI's fix creates a new problem, you describe that, and the app gets worse with each round instead of better. When you have undone to your last good version, tried a fresh approach, and *still* watch the problem outrun the AI's ability to fix it, that is a signal — not that you are bad at this, but that the problem has moved below the level where describing it works. Below that level lives reading the actual code, and reading the actual code is the job you are allowed to hire for. There is a recognizable rhythm to a loop that is not going to converge: the AI starts saying it has fixed the issue when it plainly has not, or it fixes the symptom you described while the real problem moves somewhere else, or each round trades one bug for another in a circle. A useful rule of thumb: if three honest rounds — describe, undo, fresh approach — have not moved you closer, stop. Further rounds usually burn credits and confidence without changing the outcome, because the obstacle is no longer in the description; it is in the code.

You need to do the things to the code that only make sense in the code. Some work simply lives at the level of the source: connecting your app to a system the builder does not natively support, writing a custom piece of logic precisely, optimizing a query that has gotten slow, untangling an app from the platform it was built on so it can move (the lock-in story from Chapter 23). These are not failures of your describing. They are tasks that were always going to require someone fluent in the code, and recognizing them quickly saves you the hours you would otherwise spend trying to talk your way around a wall. A clean tell for this signal: you find yourself describing the same connection or behavior five different ways and the AI keeps approximating it instead of nailing it, because what you want has no clean expression in plain language — it is a precise technical requirement that wants precise technical hands. The moment you notice you are translating an exact requirement into vague prose and hoping, you have found the wall.

Other people now depend on this for their work, and you are the only one who can touch it. This signal is about durability rather than any single technical problem, and it sneaks up on the apps that succeed. An internal tool you built for your team becomes the way the team works. People plan their day around it. And then you go on vacation, or change jobs, or simply get busy — and the app breaks, and nobody else can fix it because nobody else can read it and it lives inside a builder only you have access to. The risk here is not that the app is wrong; it is that it has become *load-bearing* while remaining a one-person dependency. When something real runs on your app and you are its single point of failure, the responsible move is to bring in someone who can share that burden — getting the code into a place others can reach, documenting how it works, and establishing that the app can outlive your attention. This is less a fix than an insurance policy, but the apps that earn it are exactly the ones whose failure would now genuinely disrupt people, which is the whole reason it matters.

How to Find the Right Person, and What to Pay For

The signals tell you *when*; this is the *who* and the *how much*, because "hire a developer" is uselessly vague advice on its own.

Match the person to the signal. A security review wants someone who does application security, not a generalist who builds front ends. Complicated financial logic wants a backend developer who is comfortable reasoning about correctness. A regulatory question may want a consultant who knows the regulation more than a coder. Scaling architecture wants someone who has run systems under load. You are not hiring "a developer" in the abstract; you are hiring for the specific gap, and naming the gap precisely is what gets you the right person rather than an expensive mismatch.

Buy a defined task, not an open-ended relationship. The most cost-effective engagement is a bounded one: "review this app for security issues and write up what you find," "fix the commission calculation and add tests so it stays fixed," "get this app off the builder and into a repository I control." Each of these is hours, has a clear definition of done, and produces something you can evaluate. Open-ended "help me with my app" engagements drift, cost more, and leave you unsure what you bought. The founder in this chapter's opening bought two afternoons with a clear task, not a co-founder.

Where to look. A reliable path is referral — a developer a friend has actually worked with beats a cold hire from a marketplace, because the hardest thing to assess from the outside is whether someone is good. Failing that, the freelance marketplaces work for bounded tasks if you write the task tightly and check that the person has done that specific kind of work before. For a one-time security review specifically, some firms offer exactly that as a packaged service, which sidesteps the hiring problem entirely.

How to tell, from the outside, whether someone is worth hiring. This is the genuinely hard part, because you are trying to assess a skill you do not have — which is the whole reason you are hiring. You cannot judge the code they would write. But you can judge how they talk about the work, and that turns out to be a surprisingly good proxy. Describe your situation and listen for two things. First, do they ask clarifying questions before quoting, or do they leap to a price and a promise? Someone good wants to understand the specific gap — what the app does, where the data lives, what exactly worries you — because they know the answer changes the work. Someone who quotes confidently before understanding the problem is either inexperienced or selling. Second, do they scope the work down or up? A trustworthy hire for a bounded task tends to *narrow* it — "let me just look at the access controls and the secrets first, and we'll see if there's more" — rather than talking you into a bigger engagement than the signal called for. And ask, plainly, for an example of similar work they have done: a security review for someone else, a payment integration they fixed, a system they scaled. You are not checking the technical details of the answer; you are checking that the answer exists and is specific, because the people who have actually done a thing describe it concretely and the people who have not stay vague.

Expect a range, and judge it against the downside. Prices move and vary wildly by region and seniority, so I will not quote figures that will be wrong by the time you read this. The framing that does not age: weigh the cost of the engagement against the cost of the thing it prevents. A few hours of review against a data breach that exposes every user. A day of correctness work against months of silently mispaid money. A scaling visit against the weekend your app falls over at the worst possible moment. In every case the math runs the same direction, which is why the embarrassment about hiring is not just wrong but expensive — it talks people out of cheap insurance against costly failure.

How to Bring In a Developer Without Throwing Away Your Work

The fear underneath the embarrassment is usually this: that handing the app to a professional means starting over, that they will look at the generated code, wince, and rebuild from scratch — making your weekend a waste. It does not have to go that way, and how you bring them in largely decides whether it does.

Bring the code, not just the problem. This is where the portability work from the last chapter pays off directly. If your app is synced to GitHub and your dependencies are written down, a developer can read what exists, understand it, and work *with* it. If everything is locked inside a builder they cannot access, you have handed them a sealed box and a description, and starting over starts to look like the path of least resistance to them too. Open access to real code is the difference between "I can fix this" and "let me just rebuild it." Before the engagement starts, get the code somewhere the developer can clone it, write down what services it connects to, and note any credentials they will need (and rotate those afterward). The smoother that handoff, the more of your weekend survives.

Hire for the specific gap, not the whole thing. You do not need a developer to take over your project. You need one for the part that triggered the signal — the security review, the tricky logic, the scaling setup, the one connection that won't connect. Framing it as a defined task ("look at how this app controls who can see what, and tell me what's wrong") gets you a focused engagement of hours, not a takeover of weeks. My founder friend bought two afternoons, not a co-founder.

Don't apologize for how it was built. A good developer in 2026 is not scandalized that an app was vibe-coded; plenty of them use these same tools to skip the tedious first stretch of their own work, as Chapter 1 noted. The generated code is, underneath, the same React and the same database queries they would have written. What they bring is the trained eye to read it, which is exactly the thing you were missing and exactly why you called. That is a clean trade, not a confession. If a developer reacts with contempt at the fact that the app was AI-built rather than engaging with whether it is *correct*, that tells you more about them than about your app — and it is a reason to find someone else, not a reason to feel ashamed.

Learn from the fix, don't just receive it. When the developer hands the work back, ask them to tell you in plain language what was wrong and why, not just that it is fixed. The point is not to become a developer yourself; it is to recognize the same signal faster next time. A founder who hears "your access checks were missing on the server, here is what that means" has bought not just a fix but a sharper eye — and the eye is what compounds across every future app you build.

What a Good Engagement Actually Looks Like

To make all of this concrete, here is a bounded engagement from start to finish, the kind you should aim to reproduce. Say you have built a scheduling app for a small clinic — appointments, patient names, a few notes — and you have hit the brightest signal of all: it holds health-adjacent information, so it should be reviewed before real patients touch it.

You start by writing the task down in two sentences, not ten. "Review this appointment app for security problems, focused on whether any patient information can be reached by someone it shouldn't be, and whether any keys or credentials are exposed. Write up what you find and what it would take to fix it." That is a defined task with a clear definition of done — a written finding — and it is hours, not weeks.

Then you prepare the handoff so the developer works *with* your app rather than around it. You sync the project to a repository they can clone, write a short note listing the services it connects to (the database, the email provider, whatever else), and create a throwaway test account they can log in with. You do *not* hand over your real credentials in a chat message; you arrange access cleanly and plan to rotate anything they touched once they are done. This preparation is itself the portability work from Chapter 23 paying off — the smoother the handoff, the less tempted anyone is to start over.

The developer spends an afternoon reading. They come back with three findings, ranked: a patient's appointment can be viewed by changing the number in the address bar (the access check exists in the browser but not on the server — Chapter 22's "trusting the browser"), the email-provider key is sitting in the client code, and the error page shows the raw database error when something fails. They tell you, in plain language, which of these is urgent (the first two, before launch) and which can wait (the third). You agree a small follow-on: "fix the two urgent ones and confirm." Another bounded task, another clear finish.

When the fix comes back, you do the thing most people skip — you ask them to explain what was wrong, not just confirm it is fixed. "The server now checks that you own an appointment before it returns it, and the email key moved to the server where the browser can't see it." You will not remember the mechanics, but you will remember the *shape*: appointments should be checked on the server, keys belong on the server. The next app you build, you will think to ask about both before a stranger does. That is the compounding eye, bought for the price of an afternoon and a follow-up.

The whole engagement was a few hours of someone else's time, scoped tightly, with your weekend of work fully intact and improved rather than replaced. Nobody rebuilt anything from scratch. Nobody was scandalized. You got a sound app and a sharper instinct, and the clinic got a scheduling tool that protects the patients who depend on it. That is the model: small, defined, handed off cleanly, learned from. Reach for it whenever a signal fires, and the embarrassment evaporates — because there is nothing embarrassing about an afternoon of expert help on the one part that needed it.

The Real Lesson Hiding in This Chapter

The whole book has been circling one idea, and this chapter is where it lands hardest: these tools democratized *making* software, and they did not democratize *judging* it. Building the app got easy. Knowing whether the app is secure, whether its logic is right, whether it will survive scale, whether it is breaking a law — that stayed hard, and it became the scarce, valuable part precisely because everything around it got cheap.

So needing a developer is not the tool failing. It is the tool succeeding all the way up to the edge of what it can do, and you being wise enough to see the edge. The person who builds a real app in a weekend and then pays for two hours of expert review at the one point that matters has not been beaten by the technology. They have used it better than the person who shipped the whole thing on vibes and found out about the missing lock from a stranger. The skill was never typing the code. It was always knowing what the code needed to be — and knowing, with clear eyes and no embarrassment, the moments when knowing that requires someone who can read it.

Part VII: Judgment

Audience: everyone.

"Making got easy; judgment did not. The one question the builder cannot answer is whether you built a prototype or a product — and you have to know which before anyone depends on it."

— A working principle

Chapter 25: Prototype vs. Production

There is one distinction that, if you internalize it, will do more to keep you out of trouble than everything else in this book combined. It is the difference between a prototype and a production app — and the reason it matters so much is that vibe-coded apps blur the line between them as no previous technology ever has. A prototype that *looks* like a finished product, that *runs* like a finished product, that you can put on a real URL and hand to a real person — and that is, underneath, still a prototype — is a genuinely new kind of object, and mistaking it for the real thing is the central way these tools get people hurt.

So this chapter is the one that asks you to be honest with yourself about which one you have actually built. Not which one it looks like. Which one it *is*.

Two Words That Mean Very Different Things

A **prototype** is something built to prove an idea, explore a possibility, or test a concept. Its job is to answer a question — does this work, do people want this, is this the right shape — quickly and cheaply. It is allowed to be rough underneath, because its purpose is learning, and the people using it are usually you, your team, or a handful of friendly testers who know what they are looking at.

A **production app** is something real people depend on, with their real data, their real money, their real trust. Its job is not to answer a question but to *work*, reliably, safely, day after day, for people who did not build it and have every right to expect it to be sound. The bar is entirely different, because the consequences are entirely different: when a prototype breaks, you learn something; when a production app breaks, you have failed someone who trusted you.

The same app — literally the same code on the same screen — can be a perfectly good prototype and a dangerously inadequate production app at the same time. The object did not change. What changed is who is depending on it and what they stand to lose.

A small story makes the point sharper than any definition. Imagine you build an expense tracker for yourself over a weekend — log a purchase, see your monthly total, a clean little chart. As a prototype it is excellent: it does its one job, you are the only user, and the worst thing that can happen is you mistype a number and fix it. Now a colleague sees it and asks to use it too, so you add a login. A second colleague joins. Word spreads on your team, and within a month forty people are logging real expenses, some of which feed into what they get reimbursed. Nothing about the *code* changed in any meaningful way across that month. But the object did. On the first weekend, a bug that lost your data cost you an evening of re-entry. By the end of the month, the same bug loses forty people's reimbursement records, and a missing access check means anyone can read what anyone else spent — including, perhaps, things people would rather their colleagues did not see. The app crossed from prototype to production without a single line being rewritten to mark the crossing. It crossed because the answer to "who depends on this and what do they stand to lose" changed underneath it while it sat there looking the same.

It helps to see the gap as a set of dimensions rather than a single switch, because that is what makes it honest. A prototype and a production app differ on *who uses it* (you and friendly testers versus strangers with no patience and sometimes bad intentions), on *what is at stake* (a lesson learned versus a person's data, money, or trust), on *how it behaves when things go wrong* (it is allowed to simply fall over versus it must fail safely and tell you), on *whether it is maintained* (abandon it the moment it answers its question versus tend it for as long as people rely on it), and on *whether anyone has checked underneath* (works in the demo versus has been examined where the demo cannot reach). An app can be production-grade on some of these and prototype-grade on others — and that mixed state is exactly the dangerous one, because the polished dimensions hide the unfinished ones.

Why These Tools Make the Confusion So Easy

Earlier ways of building software kept the two honestly separated, because a prototype *looked* like a prototype — rough, unfinished, obviously a sketch. The polish that signaled "this is real" took additional, visible work, and that work was a natural checkpoint: you could not accidentally ship a sketch, because a sketch looked like one.

AI builders erase that signal. They produce polish for free, instantly, from the very first version. Your prototype has rounded corners, smooth animations, a professional layout, and a real web address on day one. It *looks* every bit as finished as software that took a team months — and that visual finish is exactly what makes it so easy to forget that the finish is only skin deep. The interface is production-grade; the security, the reliability, the handling of edge cases and scale and failure may be nowhere close. The tools deliver the *appearance* of production while leaving the *substance* of it as your job — and because the appearance arrives first and free, it is dangerously easy to believe the substance came with it.

This is worth dwelling on because the danger is not just yours; it is everyone's who looks at the app. The polish fools *you* into thinking the substance is there. It also fools your testers, your early users, an investor, a boss — all of whom read the visual finish as a signal of underlying soundness, the way they always reasonably have, because for the entire history of software that signal was honest. A demo that looks this good has, in their experience, always *been* this good underneath. The tools quietly broke that correlation, and nobody updated their instincts. So a vibe-coded prototype does not just risk lulling its builder; it risks convincing a room full of people that something is ready when it is only dressed up to look ready. The mismatch between surface and substance is now the most reliable way to mislead, including yourself.

There is a related trap in how easy *changes* are. Because you can add a feature by describing it in a sentence, the cost of adding "just one more real thing" feels like nothing. In hand-built software, taking payments meant days of careful work, which gave you days to notice you were crossing into production. Here, "accept payments" is a sentence and an afternoon. The friction that used to mark the threshold is gone, which means you can walk across the line between prototype and production without ever feeling a bump.

It helps to name the specific features that quietly move an app across the line, because they tend to feel like small additions and are in fact thresholds. *Accepting a login* is one: the moment people have accounts, they have an expectation that their account is theirs and protected, and you have taken on the job of enforcing that. *Storing anything about a person* is another: a name, an email, an address, a note — each is data you are now responsible for keeping and, increasingly, legally obligated to handle properly. *Taking money* is the loudest of all: payments bring real financial stakes, real fraud surface, and a thicket of standards about how card data may be handled. *Sending messages to people on the app's behalf* — emails, notifications — is one most people miss, but the day your app emails a stranger is the day a bug in it can spam, mislead, or expose someone in your name. And *letting anyone sign up*, as opposed to a known list of testers, is the threshold where the friendly-tester assumption dies and you must now assume some users are careless and some are hostile. Each of these is a sentence to add and an afternoon to build. Each is also a step deeper into production, and the value of naming them is that you can feel the bump on purpose even though the tool removed it.

The Honest Checklist

So how do you tell which one you have? Ask these questions, and answer them truthfully rather than hopefully.

Who is going to use this, and what do they stand to lose? Just you, or your team, with nothing sensitive at stake — you likely have a prototype, and that is fine. Real outside users, with their personal data, their payments, their trust on the line — you are now talking about production, and the rest of these questions are not optional. Be specific about the worst case rather than the typical one. Production-grade thinking is about the user who does something you did not expect, the input you did not plan for, the person who is actively trying to break in — not the friendly tester who clicks exactly where you point. If the worst case among your real users is "mild annoyance," you have more prototype latitude than if it is "someone's private information is exposed."

Have you actually checked the security? Not "does it work" — have you worked through Chapter 22's checklist: where the secrets live, whether access is really enforced, how personal data is handled? A prototype can skip this because no one real is exposed. A production app cannot, ever. This is the single dimension on which the prototype/production line is least forgiving, because a security gap does not announce itself and does not wait for scale — one real user with one real piece of data is enough for it to matter.

Do you know what happens when it breaks? Production software fails — a service goes down, an input is malformed, a user does something unexpected. Do you know how your app behaves when it does, who finds out, and how it recovers? A prototype is allowed to simply fall over. A production app needs to fail safely and let you know. Press on this concretely: what does a user see if the database is briefly unreachable — a graceful message, or a raw error that exposes the app's internals? If a payment goes halfway through and then fails, does the user get charged without getting the thing they paid for? If two people act at the same moment, does the app handle it or does it corrupt something? These are the questions that never come up in a calm demo and always come up in real use.

Have you watched it fail on purpose? A close companion to the previous question, and one almost nobody does. A production-minded builder deliberately mistreats their own app before strangers do: submits the form with the required field empty, pastes a wall of text into a field meant for a name, double-clicks the submit button, loses the network connection mid-action, opens the same account in two tabs and acts in both. A prototype is excused from this; a production app is defined partly by having survived it. Twenty minutes of trying to break your own app teaches you more about whether it is production-ready than any amount of using it the way it was meant to be used.

Is there anything to recover with when it goes wrong? Production data needs backups, and someone needs to know how to restore them. If a bad change or a bug wipes out user data, a prototype shrugs — there was nothing real to lose. A production app without backups is one bad afternoon away from losing data it cannot get back, and "I didn't set up backups" is a sentence no one wants to say to the people who trusted them.

Can it handle more than a handful of users? Chapter 23, on scaling, matters here. A prototype that works for five people may buckle at five hundred. If real growth is possible, "works in the demo" is not "works in production." The honest version of this question is not "could it theoretically scale" but "do I have a real reason to expect more than a handful, and have I checked what happens then" — because most prototypes never need to scale and worrying about it prematurely is its own mistake.

Are you prepared to maintain it? A production app is an ongoing commitment — updates, fixes, security patches, support for the people relying on it. A prototype can be abandoned the moment it has answered its question. If you are not ready to own it over time, be honest that what you have is the former. Maintenance is the dimension people most reliably underestimate, because at launch the app feels finished and the work feels done. But software does not stay still while the world moves around it: dependencies need updating, a platform changes something underneath you, a security issue is disclosed, a user hits a case you never saw. Production is not a finish line; it is the start of a tending relationship, and choosing it means choosing the tending.

If you answered these in a way that says "prototype" — wonderful. Prototypes are enormously valuable, and these tools are arguably the best prototyping technology ever made. Use it as a prototype: to learn, to test, to show, to decide. Just do not quietly let it slide into production use without crossing the gap deliberately.

The Checklist on a Real App

Abstract questions are easy to nod along with and hard to apply, so walk the checklist with me against a single concrete app and watch where each question bites. Suppose you have built a tool for a community sports league: people sign up, register their kids for a season, pay a registration fee, and the organizers see a roster. It looks finished — it has a logo, a clean form, a confirmation screen — and the league wants to open registration next week.

Who uses it, and what do they stand to lose? Real outside families, with their children's names and birthdates, their own contact details, and their payment information. The worst case is not "mild annoyance"; it is a child's personal information exposed to a stranger, or a parent's card charged for a registration that did not go through. That answer alone settles it: this is production, and the remaining questions are not optional.

Have you checked the security? You open the live app's developer tools and search the loaded code for anything resembling a key — and because this app takes payments, you do not stop at your own check; you have the payment integration confirmed by someone who knows what to look for. You create two parent accounts, register a child under each, then log in as the first and try to reach the second family's registration by changing the number in the address bar. If you can see the other family's child, the lock is missing, and you have just found a problem that would otherwise have been found by a stranger.

Do you know what happens when it breaks? You ask the pointed version: if the payment provider is briefly unreachable mid-registration, does a parent get charged without their child being registered, or registered without being charged? Either is a real problem, and a calm demo will never surface it because in a demo the payment always succeeds.

Have you watched it fail on purpose? You submit the registration form with the child's name left blank, paste a paragraph into the field meant for a birthdate, double-click the pay button to see whether it charges twice, and open the form in two tabs to register the same child in both at once. Twenty minutes of this against a registration app tells you more than a week of it working the way you intended.

Is there anything to recover with? The roster is the league's season. If a bad change wipes it, you need a backup and a way to restore it, because "we lost everyone's registration" is not a sentence the organizers can say to two hundred families.

Can it handle more than a handful? Registration opens league-wide on one evening, which means most of your traffic arrives in a few hours on a single day — the textbook case where "works for the five people who tested it" and "works when two hundred families hit it at once" are different facts you need to have checked.

Are you prepared to maintain it? The league runs every season. This is not a build-and-abandon prototype; someone has to tend it, patch it, and answer the parent whose payment did not go through, for as long as the league uses it.

Notice what the walkthrough did: it took an app that *looked* completely finished and surfaced, question by question, a list of specific things that were almost certainly not done — the cross-family access check, the half-completed-payment case, the missing backup, the launch-night load. None of those were visible on the screen. All of them are the difference between a registration page that protects two hundred families and one that quietly endangers them. That is what the checklist is for: not to make you anxious, but to make the invisible work visible before someone else makes it visible the hard way.

The Legitimate Middle Ground

It would be dishonest to pretend everything is one or the other, because a great deal of useful software lives between the two poles, and pretending otherwise pushes people toward false choices. There is a real and respectable category of *internal tools* — the booking page for one teacher's class, the tracker for a small team, the dashboard you and three colleagues use — where real people depend on it but the stakes are bounded and the users are known and trusted. These are not prototypes (people genuinely rely on them) and they are not full production apps (no strangers, no sensitive data, low blast radius if it breaks). They have their own honest bar: it should work reliably enough for the people who use it, it should not leak anything that would matter, and someone should be willing to fix it when it breaks. That is a lighter standard than a public app handling payments, and applying the full production checklist to a five-person internal tool is its own kind of mistake — over-engineering a thing whose stakes never demanded it.

The way to place an app in this middle ground honestly is to be precise about the two things that set the bar: *who* uses it and *what they stand to lose.* As long as both stay small and known, the lighter standard holds. The danger is the same as everywhere else in this chapter — that the app drifts. The internal tool gets shared with a partner organization. The trusted-team tracker starts holding client data. The day either of those happens, the app has moved toward production whether or not you decided it should, and the bar moves with it.

Crossing the Gap on Purpose

The mistake is never building a prototype. The mistake is letting a prototype *become* a production app by accident — by adding one more real user, then another, then accepting one real payment, then storing one piece of sensitive data, until one day a sketch you built in an afternoon is quietly holding hundreds of people's trust and was never built to. Nobody decided to ship a production app; it happened a step at a time while no one was looking.

So make it a decision. When a prototype proves its idea and you want to take it into the world, treat that as a real threshold with real work attached: the security review, the reliability and failure handling, the scaling check, the maintenance commitment — and, for anything genuinely high-stakes, the involvement of someone who builds production software for a living. Sometimes crossing the gap means hardening what you have; sometimes, as Chapter 24 discussed, it means rebuilding the proven idea as real software. Either way, the work is the toll for the bridge, and the bridge is worth crossing deliberately rather than stumbling across in the dark.

A practical way to make the threshold a decision rather than a drift: write down, before you launch anything to real people, the conditions under which this stops being a prototype. "If I accept money, if I store anything I would not want public, if I get past twenty real users, I stop and do the production work." Naming the triggers in advance turns the invisible line into a visible one you have agreed to watch for — so that when you cross it, you notice, instead of finding out later from someone whose trust you broke without meaning to. The point of the line is not to slow you down before you need it; it is to make sure that when the stakes rise, your standard rises with them, on purpose.

Hold the two words apart in your mind, and you will get the best of these tools without the worst of them: the speed and joy of building a prototype in an afternoon, and the discipline to know that production is a place you arrive on purpose, with your eyes open, having done the work that the polish only pretended was already done.

Epilogue: From Idea to Shipped

This book opened with a teacher who needed a booking page and had no developer, no budget, and no time — and who, in a single afternoon, described the tool she wanted and watched it come to life, refined it by talking to it, and used it for the rest of the year. It is worth ending where we began, because that afternoon contains the whole of what these tools offer and the whole of what they ask in return.

What they offer is genuinely historic, and I do not want the cautions in this book to dim it. For the entire history of software until now, the ability to turn an idea into working software belonged to people who could write code, and everyone else stood on the other side of a wall, wishing. That wall is the oldest and most exclusionary boundary in technology, and these tools put a door in it. A teacher, a shop owner, a nurse, a student, anyone with an idea and an afternoon can now build a real, working application by describing what they want. That is not a small convenience. It is a redistribution of a power that was concentrated for decades, and the right response to it is something closer to wonder than to caution.

The specifics in these pages will age faster than anything else this series publishes. The four builders will rename their plans and reprice their credits; the AI models underneath them will be replaced by better ones; one of them rebuilt itself substantially in the time it took to write this book, and another will have done so by the time you read it. I have flagged the fast-moving details throughout so you can check them against the present. But the shape of the thing does not age, and the shape is what I want to leave you with.

Before the shape, though, it is worth pausing on how much ground we actually covered, because the distance from the first chapter to this one is the real measure of what these tools put within reach. We started by drawing the boundary of the category — what "building apps without code" means, how the AI underneath turns a description into genuine code, and the honest line between what these tools can build and what they cannot. We met the four builders and learned that they are not interchangeable: v0 for the polished interface, Bolt for the full-stack app in your browser, Lovable for the complete product a non-coder can ship, Replit for building inside a real development environment with hosting included. We learned to describe an app well — the *what* rather than the *how* —

and to steer by reacting, undoing to good versions instead of fighting a spiral. Then we made it real: data and backends, accounts and login, connections to the outside world, design and polish, a live URL with a domain on it. And then, in the back half, we got serious about the part the cheerful demos never mention — security, scale, lock-in, the moments you need a developer, and the single hardest question of all, whether the thing you built is a prototype or a production app. That arc — from "type a sentence" to "here is what you owe the people who will use it" — is the book, and it is also the journey of anyone who builds something real with these tools and is honest about what they made.

Here is the shape. These tools moved the bottleneck. For as long as anyone can remember, the hard part of making software was *producing the code* — and so that is what we trained people for years to do, and that is what separated those who could build from those who could not. The AI builders made producing the code easy. But they did not touch the other parts of making good software, and those other parts did not go away — they moved to the center. Knowing what to build and for whom. Judging whether what you built actually works. Recognizing when an app that looks finished is hiding a flaw that will hurt someone. Deciding when a prototype is ready to become something real, and doing the work to make it so. None of that automated away. All of it became *more* valuable, because it is now the scarce part — the part the tool cannot supply.

That is why this book runs the way it does, from the cheerful early chapters about building fast to the sober later ones about security and limits, and refuses to separate them. The enthusiasm and the caution are not in tension; they are the same honesty seen from two sides. A tool powerful enough to build you a real app in an hour is powerful enough to build you a real *liability* in an hour, and the difference between the two is not in the tool. It is in you — in whether you brought the judgment the tool cannot. The most important single idea in these pages is that *an app that looks finished is not the same as an app that is safe*, and the reason I repeated it until it annoyed you is that the gap between looking done and being done is exactly where the polish lulls people into shipping things they should not.

I want to make the difference between bringing that judgment and not bringing it concrete, because it is the whole argument standing on two legs. Picture two people who build the same app — say, a simple tool for a small business to take bookings and a deposit. The first describes it, watches it appear, sees that it works when she tests it, likes how it looks, and puts it live that evening with a link sent to her customers. It works for a week. Then a customer changes a number in the address bar out of idle curiosity and finds himself looking at another customer's booking and the last four digits of their card; or a bot finds the payment key sitting in the page's code and runs up a bill overnight; or the app simply falls over on the busiest morning because nothing about it was built to hold more than the handful of people who tested it. None of these announced themselves. All of them were invisible in the demo. She did nothing reckless that she could see — and that is precisely the trap, because the recklessness was in the part she was told she did not have to look at.

The second person builds the identical app, the same evening, with the same tool. But before she sends the link, she stops and asks the two questions this book keeps returning to. *Where do my secrets live?* — she opens the browser's developer tools, searches the loaded code for anything that looks like a key, asks the builder directly whether any credentials are exposed in the client, and when she is handling card data and real money, she pays someone who does application security for two hours to confirm it. *Is this a prototype or a production app?* — she answers honestly that the moment it takes a deposit it is production, creates two test accounts and spends twenty minutes trying to reach one's data from the other, deliberately mistreats her own forms, and sets up a way to recover the data if something wipes it. Same app, same tool, same evening — and one of them is a quiet disaster waiting for its first curious stranger while the other is sound. The tool did not make the difference. The half hour of judgment did. That half hour is the entire subject of the second half of this book, and it is the cheapest, highest-return work you will ever do as a builder.

If I could compress the practical half of the book into a path you could walk from memory, it would run like this, and it is worth saying plainly once at the end. Start by being honest about whether your idea is one these tools can build at all — a real app with an interface and data and users, not an automation between tools you already have, and not the kind of deeply specialized system that still wants a real engineering team. Describe it well, in plain language, the *what* rather than the *how*, and steer by reacting to what comes back. Iterate by undoing to good versions rather than fighting a spiral. When you make it real — data, accounts, connections to the outside world — remember that each of those is a responsibility as much as a feature. And before it touches another person, stop at the two questions that matter most: where do my secrets live and who can see my users' data, and is the thing I built a prototype or a production app. Answer those honestly and you will avoid nearly every way these tools hurt the people who use them carelessly. Everything else in the book is detail hung on that frame.

I want to be equally honest about what the tools will not become, so you are not surprised when the technology improves and the hard part stays hard. The models underneath these builders will get better — they will write cleaner code, catch more of their own mistakes, ask better questions before building. Some of the security failures this book warns about will get harder to commit because the defaults will improve; a builder that refuses, by default, to put a secret key in browser code closes off one of the most common disasters before you can stumble into it, and that kind of guardrail is exactly the sort of thing that arrives with each generation of these tools. That is real progress and you should welcome it. But the better the tools get at *making*, the more the remaining bottleneck is *judgment*, not the reverse. A tool that builds flawlessly still cannot tell you whether the app should exist, whether you are allowed to collect the data you are collecting, whether the thing that works for ten people is about to fail ten thousand, whether the convenient shortcut is the one that will cost someone their trust. Those questions do not get easier as the code gets easier; they get more central, because they become the whole of what is left for a human to supply. Betting on the tools to eventually supply the judgment too is the one bet this book asks you not to make.

There is a subtler reason not to make that bet, and it is worth naming because it cuts against the optimism that better tools will simply solve the problem. As the defaults improve and the obvious failures get rarer, the failures that remain will be the harder ones — the subtle wrongness in a calculation, the access check that is present but applies the wrong rule, the edge case the model genuinely could not anticipate because it lived in your specific business and not in any pattern the model had seen. Better tools do not just remove dangers; they raise the floor and leave the ceiling exactly where it was, which means the gap between "looks done" and "is done" migrates upward into territory that is harder, not easier, to spot from the outside. The day a tool stops making beginner mistakes is the day its remaining mistakes are the kind only a careful, knowing eye will catch. So the judgment does not become less necessary as the tools mature. It becomes necessary about more sophisticated things — which is another way of saying the scarce skill stays scarce, it just moves up the ladder.

A last word about what you do next, because a book like this is only worth anything if it changes what you make on Monday. The most common mistake after finishing a book like this is to wait for the perfect first project — the big idea, the thing worth doing properly. Do the opposite. Build something small and real this week, something with stakes low enough that getting it wrong teaches you instead of hurting anyone: a tool for yourself, a tracker for a hobby, a page for your own use. Build it, then run the two questions on it even though the stakes are low, precisely *because* the stakes are low — that is how you turn the checklist into a habit before the day it matters. Then build the next one a little more ambitiously, and run the questions again. The skill this book is really trying to give you is not "how to use v0" or "how to write a prompt"; it is the reflex of pausing, at the right moment, to ask what you actually built and what you owe for it. Reflexes come from repetition on low stakes, so that they are there for you on high ones. The teacher in chapter one did not read a book and then build the booking page; she built it, and the building taught her. Let your first few apps be your teacher, while the cost of the lesson is still small.

And do not build entirely alone. The fastest builders with these tools are not the ones with the most talent; they are the ones plugged into how other people are using them — the communities, the examples, the shared prompts, the running conversation about what works and what just broke. The tools change monthly, and no book can stay current with monthly change; the community can. When a builder ships a new model, when a security default changes, when a platform discloses an incident and tells everyone to rotate their keys, that news travels through people before it reaches any printed page. Treat the resources at the back of this book as a starting set of doors, not a finish line, and keep one ear on the conversation as you build. The judgment is yours to supply, but you do not have to develop it in isolation, and you will develop it faster if you do not.

So carry both halves out of this book. Build boldly — describe the tool you have always wanted and could never make, and feel the genuine thrill of watching it appear, because that thrill is real and you have earned the right to it. And ship responsibly — remember that the moment your app touches another person's data or trust, you have crossed from playing to building production software, and you owe them the discipline that comes with it: the security check, the honest prototype-or-production question, the willingness to bring in a real developer when the stakes demand one. The teacher with her booking page got it right not because she was a programmer — she wasn't — but because she built something whose stakes matched what she put into it. A booking page for her own class is allowed to be a prototype. Your users' financial data is not.

The wall has a door in it now, and you know how to walk through. You know how to describe an app, steer it, make it real, and put it in the world — and, just as importantly, you know how to tell what you have actually built, and what you owe the people who will use it. That second knowledge is the rarer and more valuable one, and it is the thing that will separate the builders who do good with these tools from the ones who do harm without ever meaning to.

Go build the thing you could never build before. Then look honestly at what you made, and ship it like it matters — because to the person on the other side of the screen, it does.

What follows is reference — a builder comparison for choosing, a project checklist to work through before you ship, a glossary, and resources for going further. The checklist in particular is worth keeping by your side for the first few real apps; it is this whole book compressed into the questions to ask before you launch. The argument behind it, by now, you have.

Appendix A: Builder Comparison

This is the appendix to flip back to when you have an idea and need to pick a starting point. Part II covered each builder in depth, and Chapter 8 walked through choosing between them; this is the compressed version, one card per tool, written so you can scan it in a minute.

Two warnings before you read it. First, everything below about prices, plan names, and model branding is the most perishable kind of fact in this book. These products change their pricing and their feature lists on a schedule measured in weeks, so treat every number here as "roughly true in mid-2026" and confirm it on the builder's own pricing page before you commit money or a project to it. Second, the right choice depends far more on what you are building and where it needs to live than on any single feature, so read the "how to choose" note at the end rather than just picking whichever card sounds nicest.

v0 by Vercel

Best for polished, professional-looking interfaces, and increasingly for full-stack apps that live in Vercel's world. After a major rebuild in early 2026 it grew from a UI generator into something closer to a full development environment — a code editor, Git integration, database connections, the ability to import an existing repository.

Backend is now genuinely part of the picture; it connects to hosted databases like Supabase and Neon rather than bundling its own. Earlier in its life v0 was front-end first, so older write-ups undersell this — check what it does today.

Portability is real but Vercel-flavored: you can export the code to GitHub, but the output is the tightest-coupled of the four to one company's ecosystem, and the path of least resistance always points back to deploying on Vercel.

Pricing shape is token- or credit-metered, with tiers along the lines of a free plan, a team plan around thirty dollars per user, and a business plan around a hundred per user as of mid-2026 (verify). The model branding (v0 Mini, Pro, Max, or whatever it is by the time you read this) is Vercel's own abstraction over a frontier model they do not pin down, so do not over-read it.

Watch-out: the interface quality can outrun the substance. v0 makes things that look shipped before they are, which is exactly the trap Chapter 25 (Prototype vs. Production) is about.

Bolt.new by StackBlitz

Best for full-stack apps when you care about being able to take the code and leave. Bolt runs a real Node.js development environment inside your browser (a technology called WebContainers), so you are working with standard, portable code from the first message.

Backend support is full-stack, built in the in-browser environment; you wire up your own database and services much as a developer would, with the AI doing the wiring.

Portability is Bolt's signature strength — its output is the most standard and the most portable of the four. Export to GitHub, deploy to Bolt's own hosting or to Netlify or essentially anywhere that runs a normal web app. If avoiding lock-in is your priority, this is the card to circle.

Pricing shape is token-metered, with a Pro tier somewhere in the low twenties of dollars per month (sources disagree on the exact figure — flag and verify). It uses Claude-family models, though the specific versions drift.

Watch-out: token burn scales with the size of your project, because the whole filesystem is sent to the model on each message. Small projects are cheap; large ones can get expensive fast, and the cost can surprise you. Chapter 21 (Cost, Credits, and Token Limits) covers how to keep this in check.

Lovable

Best for non-coders who want a complete product — frontend and backend together — without thinking about infrastructure. Lovable (a Stockholm company, rebranded from the earlier "GPT Engineer") is built around handing a non-technical person a working application, not a pile of parts.

Backend is its standout: "Lovable Cloud" bundles a Supabase backend (authentication, database) natively, so accounts and data storage work without you assembling them yourself. This is the strongest backend-included experience of the four.

Portability is good. There is bidirectional GitHub sync, so your code is genuinely accessible and you are not trapped — better on this front than v0 or Replit, if not quite as frictionless as Bolt.

Pricing shape is credit-per-message, with a Pro tier around twenty-five dollars a month and a Business tier around fifty as of mid-2026 (verify). The important catch is not the sticker price but the total cost of ownership: the subscription does not include the downstream infrastructure your app will eventually need, such as a paid Supabase tier and a domain.

Watch-out: because Lovable hides the infrastructure so well, it is easy to forget there is infrastructure, and to be surprised later by bills and decisions the smooth experience deferred.

Replit (Agent 3)

Best for getting from a description to a deployed, running app with the least fuss, all inside one place. Replit's agent plans, scaffolds, installs dependencies, runs and fixes the code, and deploys — inside a real cloud development environment with hosting and a database included.

Backend is the most batteries-included: hosting and a built-in PostgreSQL database come with the environment, so there is nothing external to set up to have a working app with stored data.

Portability is the weakest of the four. Because your app is coupled to Replit's own database and hosting, moving it elsewhere later carries the highest migration cost on this list. That convenience up front is a commitment.

Pricing shape is effort- and checkpoint-based, with a Core tier around twenty to twenty-five dollars a month and a Pro tier around ninety-five to a hundred as of mid-2026 (verify). You are roughly paying for how much work the agent does, which makes the cost less predictable than a flat seat fee.

Watch-out: the same all-in-one convenience that makes Replit the closest thing to "describe it, get a deployed app" is exactly what makes it the hardest to leave. Chapter 23 (Scaling, Maintenance, and Lock-In) is the chapter to read before you build something you might want to outgrow.

How to Choose

Do not start from the cards. Start from two questions about your project, and let the answers point you at a card.

The first question is **where does this need to live, and who has to maintain it?** If the honest answer is "I want it gone from any single company's grip, with the code in my hands," lean Bolt. If it is "I never want to think about a server and I just want the thing running," lean Replit. If it is "somewhere in between, and I'd like my code reachable on GitHub without managing servers myself," Lovable sits comfortably there. v0 makes most sense when you are already living in the Vercel ecosystem, or when the interface is the part you most need to nail.

The second question is **how much of a backend do you need on day one?** If your app is mostly a polished interface — a landing page, a dashboard over data you'll wire in later, something to show people — v0 is built for that surface. If you need real accounts and stored data working immediately and you are not a coder, Lovable's bundled backend or Replit's included database will save you the most struggle. Bolt gives you full-stack power but expects you to do more of the assembling.

A practical last word: the skill of describing and steering an app, which is the actual subject of this book, transfers across all four. Picking the "wrong" one rarely sinks a project, because what you learn moves with you. So do not agonize. Pick the card whose best-for line sounds most like your situation, build something small, and let the real experience — not a comparison appendix — tell you whether you chose well.

Appendix B: Project Checklist

Here is the whole book compressed into things you can actually do, in the order you do them. It is not a substitute for the chapters — the reasoning behind each item lives there — but it is the page to keep open while you build, so nothing important falls through.

Work through it top to bottom. The temptation, every time, is to skip from "it works" straight to "it's live," and the middle section — the security checks and the prototype-versus-production test — is precisely the part the skipping skips. That middle is where most vibe-coded apps quietly go wrong. Do not skip the middle.

Before You Build: Describe and Scope

- **Write down, in one or two plain sentences, what the app is and who it is for.** If you cannot say it simply, the builder will not build it cleanly. Chapter 9 (Describing What You Want) is the long version of this step.
- **Decide what it must do versus what would be nice.** Name the two or three things it absolutely has to do. Everything else is a later conversation, not a first prompt.
- **Decide honestly whether this is a prototype or a real product.** This single decision changes how careful you need to be downstream. Chapter 25 (Prototype vs. Production) is built around it; make the call now, not after you've shown it to people.
- **Pick a builder using Appendix A.** Match the tool to where the app needs to live and how much backend you need on day one — not to which one sounds best.

While You Build

- **Build in small steps and look at each one.** Describe a change, see what it made, react. Do not fire off ten requests and hope; iterate, the way Chapter 14 describes.
- **Keep notes on what you asked for.** When something breaks three changes later, you will want to know what changed. A running list of your requests is a cheap insurance policy.

- **Export or sync the code early, if the builder lets you.** Connecting to GitHub from the start means your work exists somewhere you control, not only inside one platform.
- **Test it as a real person would, not as its maker.** Click the wrong things. Leave fields blank. Try it on your phone. The demo path always works; the real paths are where the cracks are.

The Security Checks (Do Not Skip These)

These are the checks that separate an app you can responsibly let other people use from a liability. Chapter 22 (Security and Your Users' Data) is the full treatment; this is the minimum you confirm before anyone but you touches the thing.

- **Find your secrets and make sure they are hidden.** API keys and database credentials must live on the server side, never hardcoded into the code that runs in the user's browser. The single most common and most damaging failure in vibe-coded apps is a secret — especially a database's powerful "service-role" key — sitting in plain sight in the browser, readable by anyone who looks. Ask the builder directly where each key is stored, and verify it is not in client-side code.
- **Check that users can only see and change their own data.** Confirm that logging in as one person does not let them reach another person's records. Missing or broken access control is a documented, widespread class of flaw in AI-generated apps; do not assume the builder handled it because it was not asked to.
- **Confirm what data you are collecting and whether you need it.** Every piece of personal information you store is a responsibility and a risk. If you do not need it, do not collect it.
- **Look at how data is stored.** Passwords should never be stored as plain readable text. If your app handles anything sensitive, confirm it is protected in transit and at rest, and ask the builder to show you, plainly, how.
- **Remember the human review layer is missing.** Vibe coding ships code that no person reviewed, which is how latent flaws — injection, missing authorization, exposed secrets — get into live apps. You are the review layer now. Spend the half hour.

The Prototype-vs-Production Test

Before you treat this as a real product, answer each of these honestly. A "no" is not a failure — it may simply mean this is a prototype, which is fine, as long as you know it.

- **Would I be comfortable if a stranger used this with their real data?** If not, it is not ready for strangers' real data.
- **Do I know what happens when it breaks, and can I fix it?** Real products break. A prototype can break and wait; a product people depend on cannot.
- **Have the security checks above all passed?** This is non-negotiable for anything handling real users.
- **Do I know what this will cost to run as people use it?** Not the build cost — the ongoing infrastructure cost. Chapter 21 covers this; the sticker price of the builder is rarely the whole bill.
- **Can I maintain this, or get help, six months from now?** Chapter 23 (Scaling, Maintenance, and Lock-In) and Chapter 24 (When You Still Need a Developer) are the chapters to reread if this one is shaky.

Going Live

- **Set up the real infrastructure the app will actually need.** A paid database tier, email sending, whatever your app depends on — the smooth builder experience may have deferred these, and going live is when they come due.
- **Connect a custom domain if it is more than a throwaway.** Chapter 20 (Custom Domains and Going Live) walks through this.
- **Deploy, then test the live version, not just the preview.** Things that worked in the builder's preview can behave differently once deployed. Run your real-person tests again against the live URL.
- **Tell people what you collect, if you collect anything personal.** Even a one-line note about what data you hold and why is the honest minimum.
- **Watch it after launch.** Keep an eye on costs, on errors, and on whether it holds up as more than a handful of people use it. Shipping is the start of the app's life, not the end of your job.

Appendix C: Glossary

Plain definitions for the terms that come up across this book. Each entry is one sentence, written for someone building apps by describing them rather than coding them. Where a term has a fuller treatment in a chapter, that is where to go for the real explanation; this is the quick reference.

Access control – The rules that decide which users are allowed to see or change which data, and the thing most worth checking, because broken access control is a common way vibe-coded apps leak one person's data to another.

Agent (AI agent) – An AI that does not just answer but acts on its own across several steps – planning, writing code, running it, fixing errors, deploying – which is the mode Replit's builder and the newer versions of the others work in.

API (Application Programming Interface) – A defined way for one piece of software to ask another for data or actions, such as your app asking a maps service for directions or a payment service to charge a card.

API key – A secret password-like string that identifies your app to an outside service, which must be kept hidden on the server and never placed in code that runs in the user's browser.

Authentication (auth) – The part of an app that handles users proving who they are, typically by logging in, covered in Chapter 16.

Backend – The part of an app the user never sees: the server, the database, and the logic that stores data, enforces rules, and does the work behind the interface.

Client-side – Code that runs in the user's own browser, which is visible to anyone who looks and therefore the wrong place to ever put a secret.

Credit – A unit of usage that some builders meter you by, often spent per message or per amount of work, distinct from but similar in spirit to tokens.

Database – The organized store where an app keeps its data – users, records, bookings, whatever the app is about – so the information survives between visits.

Deploy – To put your app onto a live server on the internet so that other people can reach and use it, as opposed to it running only in your builder's preview.

Domain (custom domain) – The human-readable web address people type to reach your app, such as yourname.com, which you buy and point at your deployed app, covered in Chapter 20.

Frontend – The part of an app the user sees and touches: the pages, buttons, forms, and layout in the browser.

Full-stack – Describing an app or a tool that handles both the frontend and the backend together, rather than just the visible surface.

GitHub – A widely used service for storing and tracking code, which most of these builders can sync to, giving you a copy of your app's code that you control.

Hosting – The service that runs your deployed app on a server so it stays available on the internet, sometimes included by the builder and sometimes a separate arrangement.

Lock-in – The degree to which an app is tied to one platform's tools and is therefore hard to move elsewhere, lowest with Bolt and highest with Replit among the four in this book.

Portability – The flip side of lock-in: how easily you can take your app's code and run it somewhere other than where it was built.

Production – An app that real people depend on with real data, held to a far higher standard of security and reliability than a prototype, as Chapter 25 sets out.

Prototype – A working app built to test an idea or show people, where rough edges are acceptable because no one is yet depending on it.

React – A common framework for building app interfaces that several of these builders generate under the hood; you do not need to know it, but it is the kind of real code being written for you.

Server-side – Code that runs on the server rather than in the user's browser, which is the safe place to keep secrets and enforce rules users should not be able to bypass.

Service-role key – A particularly powerful database credential that grants broad access, and the single most dangerous secret to ever expose in client-side code, because it can hand an attacker the whole database.

Supabase — A popular hosted backend service providing a database and authentication, bundled natively by Lovable and connectable from the other builders.

Token — The unit of text that AI models read and write, and the thing many builders meter your cost by, which is why bigger projects sent to the model more often cost more, as Chapter 21 explains.

Token burn — The rate at which a project consumes tokens, which rises with project size in tools like Bolt that send the whole project to the model on each message.

Vibe coding — Building real software by describing what you want in plain language and steering the AI that writes the actual code, which is the central activity of this entire book.

WebContainers — The technology that lets Bolt run a real development environment inside your browser, which is part of why its output is standard, portable code.

Appendix D: Resources and Further Reading

A short, honest list of where to go next. I have deliberately not printed web addresses, for the same reason this book keeps flagging prices and model names: links rot, products rename their docs, and a URL I put here in mid-2026 may point at nothing by the time you read it. So these are descriptions of what to look for, not addresses to type. Searching for the builder's name plus the word "docs" or "community" will land you in the right place faster than any link I could freeze onto a page.

A word on how to use these. The best resource for any of these tools is the tool's own current documentation, because it is the only source guaranteed to describe what the product actually does today rather than what it did six months ago. Treat everything else — including this book — as orientation, and treat the official docs as the ground truth.

Each Builder's Own Documentation and Community

- **v0 (by Vercel).** Vercel maintains documentation for v0 and for the surrounding platform it deploys to; because v0 changed substantially in early 2026, lean on the current docs rather than older tutorials, which describe a narrower tool. Vercel's broader community and forums are active and worth a look when you hit something v0-specific.
- **Bolt.new (by StackBlitz).** StackBlitz documents Bolt and the WebContainers technology underneath it; the docs are the right place to understand token usage, since that is where Bolt's costs come from. There is an active community around it where people share prompts and patterns.
- **Lovable.** Lovable publishes documentation aimed squarely at non-coders, including guidance on its bundled "Lovable Cloud" backend, and it has a sizable community of people building products without a coding background — a good place to see what is realistically achievable.
- **Replit.** Replit has long, mature documentation covering its agent, its built-in database, and its hosting, plus one of the older and larger learning

communities in this space, including material aimed at complete beginners.

Each builder also tends to publish example projects or templates. Reading what the tool itself holds up as a good build teaches you the shape of a well-described app faster than starting from a blank prompt.

Learning the Basics of Apps, Safely

You do not need to learn to code to use this book. But a little vocabulary about how apps work makes you a far better describer and a far safer shipper, because you can ask the builder the right questions. Look for beginner-friendly, plain-language explanations of:

- **What a frontend, a backend, and a database are, and how they fit together.** Any reputable introduction-to-web-apps explainer will do; you want the concepts, not the code.
- **What authentication actually involves** — what it means for a user to "log in," and why password handling is something to get right rather than improvise.
- **What an API is and how apps talk to other services.** Once this clicks, a lot of what the builders do stops feeling like magic and starts feeling like plumbing you can direct.

Prefer sources that explain ideas over sources that make you write code. The free introductory material from well-established technology-education organizations is usually written by people who teach for a living, and it is calmer and clearer than most.

Security Resources

This is the section to take most seriously, because the security chapter (Chapter 22) names real failures that have hit real vibe-coded apps, and the resources here are how you stay on the right side of them.

- **Reputable web-security primers for beginners.** Look for introductions to common web application vulnerabilities written for a general audience — the recurring themes of injection, broken access control, and exposed secrets are exactly the ones that bite AI-generated apps. You do not need the deep technical version; you need to recognize the categories.

- **The well-known, regularly updated lists of top web application risks** maintained by established security organizations. These are written for professionals but the top-level summaries are readable, and they will tell you, in priority order, what tends to go wrong. Search for "top web application security risks" and trust the long-standing nonprofit sources over blog posts.
- **Reporting from security researchers on AI-generated code.** Researchers — including teams who have specifically examined apps built on these platforms — have documented patterns like hardcoded database credentials sitting in client-side code. Reading a few of these write-ups is sobering in the useful way: it turns the abstract warnings in Chapter 22 into concrete things you will actually check for.
- **Your builder's own security guidance.** Most of these platforms now publish notes on handling secrets and data safely, partly in response to the very incidents this book describes. Read them; they are specific to how that tool works.

A Closing Note on Sources

The honest truth about further reading in this field is that it ages quickly. The names of the models change, the prices change, the screenshots in every tutorial go stale within a season. What does not change is the shape of the thing: describe clearly, build in small steps, check the security, know whether you have a prototype or a product. If you hold onto that shape, you can read any new resource — official docs, a forum thread, a researcher's warning — and place it correctly. The specific facts in this appendix will drift. The way of reading them is meant to last.

www.ingramcontent.com/pod-product-compliance
Lightning Source LLC
LaVergne TN
LVHW060031210926
848481LV00013B/3834
* 9 7 9 8 9 5 0 5 3 3 2 6 6 *